Is It Okay To Call God *"Mother"*

Considering the Feminine Face of God

Table of Contents

Thanks

To my wife Karen who has traveled this journey with me for twenty-six years.

To the saints at Broadway Baptist Church in Kansas City, Missouri, who have had the courage to venture into corporate risk-taking and change as a Constantly Renewing Church for thirty years, and are still going strong. They are my true heroes in the faith.

To those enduring senior saints in our Women's Missionary Union with whom I have met for Bible study every month for more than a quarter of a century. I first tested the idea of reaffirming the feminine image of God with them, and with an average age now of over eighty, they were the first at Broadway to sing a hymn about God as Mother. These women warriors of the previous generation have had the courage to welcome the next generation, and in so doing have inspired me greatly.

To the writers of the one hundred twenty-eight books and eighty-four papers in my library on this and related subjects. I am either unbelievably well read, or so pathologically insecure that I need an inordinate amount of outside validation before I move forward with something. My apologies to any of those writers whose ideas and phrases nested in my mind and became such a part of me that I have failed to remember and credit them as the original source.

To the thirty-seven Broadway church members and friends who critiqued my writing at several stages. It was a dazzling array of insightful feedback.

To Rob Hatem and Tracy Icenogle for their pointed cartoons.

To Carol Dickson who meticulously edited my manuscript, making it better in every way.

To my editor at Hendrickson, Patrick Alexander, for his encouragement, expertise, and willingness to risk.

Introduction

I started my lover's quarrel with the church when I was eighteen. Sniffing around and realizing that my church didn't smell like the New Testament, I decided either it was possible to recover that aroma, or I needed to forget about church work and go make some money. The idea of spending my life as the bland leading the bland didn't appeal to me.

However, I kept finding pockets of renewal which energized me, and I eventually discovered a church that was willing to enter into an astounding degree of spiritual vitality and biblical faithfulness, exceeding all my expectations. The most recent of the nine major changes we have experienced over the thirty years of my pastorate there has been recognizing the feminine image of God.[1] In one sense I wrote this book so that our congregation could have a fuller explanation of why I believe it is important to call God "Mother" as well as "Father" in public worship.

---

[1] These nine changes are, with the year each became visible in some way: Small groups (1966), deepening work of Holy Spirit (1977), contemporary worship (1975), team leadership (1977), psychological resources (1978), hearing God today (1983), healing prayer (1985), women pastors (1987), and the feminine image of God (1988).

My larger audience are those evangelicals and charismatics who may be unfamiliar with the issues in the current debate over how we should speak about God. I have intended this to be a primer, keeping Hebrew and Greek references to a minimum and placing most references to other works in the footnotes, not to slight the many writers on whom I have greatly depended, but to maintain the flow of the book.

This is a controversial book, and I suppose there will be Christian bookstores that will refuse to carry it. I have no desire to be controversial, but I do see myself as a reformer, allied with those in past generations who challenged the divine right of kings and the legitimacy of slavery, using the same Bible that was claimed in support of such practices. However, I am not a very brave reformer. I particularly don't like being drawn into the minefield of "God language." Some Christians go through genuine anguish just thinking about calling God "Mother," and I hesitate to invite anyone on a journey that includes misery. When my fears are most intimidating, I think of God's audacity in revealing herself to us in the glorious scandal of pale, mortal flesh. God keeps refusing to show up in the "right way," or now, in the politically correct gender.[2]

I have been, and shall be, charged with treasonous tampering with the Scripture, departing from long-held beliefs and traditions. Those involved in reformation must see their work as a package deal—the excitement of following their joy, and the loneliness of isolation from those who do not see the point. So be it.

---

[2]The words "God herself" may seem a bit startling to some readers, especially before I have made my case for such language. I invite you to go ahead and savor whatever reaction is natural for you. Throughout this book I will seldom refer to God with masculine pronouns and images but will occasionally use feminine pronouns—and quite often female images, especially maternal ones. My reason for this is not because I advocate eliminating male images for God and only using female ones in worship and speech. I certainly do not! Rather, I desire a *balanced* use of gender metaphors for God in the over-all setting of worship and teaching. However, since you and I have had a lifetime of male symbols for God, for purposes of this book we probably don't need to see any more of them in order to know how they feel. What

To those who are sure this study is a sign of how far one can go down the path of weirdness, as well as to those who are sure this subject is The Most Important Thing, I remind us all that *God is incarnate neither in gender nor in language.* God is incarnate in Jesus Christ, born of our sister Mary, and now Risen and Transcendent, to whom be glory now and forever!

The Main Point

Why would Christians ever want to call God "Mother"? After all, the Bible never refers to God as a woman. Jesus said we should always call God "Father," definitely not "Mother," and if Jesus had wanted us to call God "Mother" today, he would have said so. Christians down through the ages have always called God "Father," never "Mother." We all know that God himself has chosen fatherhood, not motherhood, as the way we are to think of him. So why even bring up such a strange idea, unless we are going to listen to radical feminists instead of paying attention to the Bible.

Every statement in the preceding paragraph is false. There are valid biblical and theological reasons for calling God "Mother" today which many Christians have never considered.

My thesis is simple: Calling God "Father" and never "Mother" says something in our day that Jesus never intended, namely, that God is exclusively male or masculine. This in turn appears to make men more like God than women are. A simple and biblically-based solution to both problems is to call God "Mother" while continuing to call God "Father."

---

we have not had is a lifetime of female images of God. Therefore, in this book I will often use exclusively female imagery. My purpose is not to startle or upset, but rather to acclimate my readers to an expanded, biblically-based image of God so that any evaluation of female imagery for God may come from an orthodox theological basis, rather than simply because we are unaccustomed to such language.

Credo

I write out of a love relationship with Jesus Christ, who is my God, my Savior, and my Lord. Although a life-long Southern Baptist, I have also learned much from my charismatic friends. I am as much at home with charismatics as I am with evangelicals, to the degree that I am at home with anyone, since my incredibly strong reforming inclinations tend to make me critical of all groups, including my own. I am driven by my passionate belief that the church can be more—much more—than it is today.

God is love. The story of that incredible and stunning love is disclosed in Jesus Christ, who lived, loved, died, and rose again. Four statements summarize my theological position: I believe the Bible is true, God is Trinity, everybody needs Jesus, and we need each other. This not only puts me in the evangelical camp, but it keeps me out of close company with many Christian feminists. However, it is some of these feminists who have challenged me for the last fifteen years to ponder the issue of gender, first about the role of women in church leadership, and then how women are reflected in the image of God. Therefore another belief I have come to hold is that:

The most sexist hour in the American week is 11 o'clock on Sunday morning.

I am aware "sexist" can be a loaded word, conjuring up images of angry women and political agendas. If half a congregation were black, and they were systematically excluded from leadership and language, I would not hesitate to use the word "racist." So "sexist" may have the edge that conveys what I mean.

Sexism, like racism, is not just a problem or a topic; rather it is an unholy way of defining reality and living our lives which most of us learned along with learning how to tie our shoes and how to drink from a cup.[3]

---

[3]Sentence adapted from Paul Rothenberg, 1990 *Women's Review of Books*, quoted in *And Then She Said . . .* complied by J. D. Zahniser (St. Paul: Cailltech Press, 1990) 34.

Two Forms of Sexism

The sexism of our day, the dominance of male over female, comes in two inseparable forms, one directed towards persons, and the other towards God. Both social sexism and theological sexism developed from a common source, the fall of humankind described in Genesis 3. They both result in prejudice and discrimination against women, and they both distort our image of God. Neither problem was fully addressed or resolved in the life of the early church. To become aware of one form of sexism is inevitably to become aware of the other.

One result of a male-only God is a male-only church leadership. However, the idea of changing language about God makes no sense to many Christians until they first see women and men as equals and partners. "For anyone who does not love the masculine and feminine images of God in others whom they have seen, cannot love the masculine and feminine image in God whom they have not seen" (1 John 4:20, paraphrased—or massacred, depending on your viewpoint). The partnering of male and female in our leadership of the church and in our language about God is ultimately inseparable—a connection which those evangelicals and charismatics who advocate women in church leadership sometimes seem to avoid.

Focus on Language about God

Even though the male dominance in our human community and the male dominance in our image of God are closely connected to one another, I will primarily concentrate on our image of God, except for a brief overview of patriarchy in chapter four. There is a growing selection of fine books written from a scholarly and conservative viewpoint that make the biblical case for the partnership of women and men in church leadership. Evangelicals and charismatics are making some progress in affirming the teaching and leadership gifts of women, and we see at least a few women in leadership in government and in the workplace. So while most of us are somewhat familiar with the emergence of women into leadership positions, many Christians have never seriously thought about how their image of God, as reflected in their language, is exclusively masculine. Since both the church and our culture usually refer to God only in masculine terms, the idea of calling God Mother is typically new and infinitely more shocking than the idea of women in leadership.

I suspect many of us are like my friend Kevin to whom I had given a copy of this manuscript for his critique. As he began reading it, he scrawled in large letters after the title "Is It Okay To Call God Mother?" the exclamation "NO!!!" By the time he finished the manuscript he had changed his mind. I asked him why, and he said, "I was sure I knew what I believed, but I found that I hadn't *really* thought about it before." I'm not suggesting that all who read this book will change their minds, but at least some, perhaps for the first time, will have seriously considered the idea.

I was like Kevin until a few years ago: although I had a strongly negative opinion about the outlandish idea of calling God "Mother," I had never seriously studied the issue for myself.

Sunday Morning Is Key

I will narrow my focus even more from language about God in general, to Sunday morning worship service language specifically. The church at worship powerfully shapes our understanding of God, and every week at church services all over the world church leaders reinforce our male dominant image of God with religious fervor, pastoral authority, and incredible repetition. They talk as if God *is* male.

This in turn establishes the precedent and pattern for continuing such exclusively masculine language and images in our private worship and personal conversations. Calling God Mother in addition to Father will remain a novelty or merely humorous until the church embraces it in its liturgy.

My goal is not *to change how we address God in our own personal devotional life.* While I invite us to explore our own image of God and how we pray in private, it is not my purpose to ask us do to something that may not fit where we are in our personal spiritual journeys. For Christians there is no one right way to pray in private, just as there is no one right way to worship.

There are three things I do desire for us, as together we explore the feminine side of God.

(1) That our image of God will be expanded and that however we address God, it will become more meaningful.

(2) That we recognize that calling God Mother can be faithful to the Bible, beneficial to the church, and significant to others, whether we personally feel comfortable in doing so or not.

(3) That we understand the need for the church to recognize corporately both the masculine and feminine face of God when gathered for worship (symbolically referred to here as "Sunday morning at 11 o'clock"), even in the midst of diverse personal practices. There is a difference between our private prayer practices and the corporate worship of the church. Only we and God can determine what is meaningful for us when alone in worship and prayer, and that may be somewhat different at times than what strengthens the church gathered for corporate worship.

What about Monday Morning?

Since Monday morning obviously is also sexist, why do I claim that Sunday morning is more so? Certainly there are similarities between worship and work. The people in positions of authority are more often men than women—the result of meaningful advancement being more open to men. The written language involving persons often excludes women, and there are those not so subtle put-downs of women made in daily conversations. But in spite of the similarities there is a crucial difference that makes the church service more damning. The workplace does not pretend to represent God and spiritual values. The church does.

When secular values of masculine priority are brought into the church, it is much more serious than the bias that is evident in the workplace. Jesus' harsh words were never for the average sinner, but rather for the religious leaders whose distortions of spiritual things were truly dangerous because they used their authority to keep people from God. Sexism, like all ungodly things, keeps people from God—especially on Sunday morning at 11 o'clock.

What This Book Is Not about

This book is not about dismantling the Trinity. The idea of Trinity is central to orthodox Christian faith.

Nor is it about adding a fourth member to the Trinity. I do not wish to add Mother to Father, Son, and Holy Spirit. Rather, I want us to understand God, and especially "Father," in a fuller way.

I am not about lessening the authority of Scripture. My goal is to take the Bible even more seriously, perhaps in such a radical way that it means going against the stream of religious culture.

This book does not advocate a goddess religion. A female goddess would be just as unorthodox and deviant as a male god.

Nor is it about calling God Mother *instead of* Father. The Bible, church history, and most theologians affirm that God's image includes both male and female. I want to make that orthodox belief explicit, meaningful, and available for the average person by calling God *both* Father and Mother.

I do not seek to join a feminist bandwagon and adopt a secular agenda. While our goals may be similar in some areas, Christians have quite enough to keep us busy with the agenda assigned to us by Jesus.

This volume does not insist that we all change our personal prayer habits—unless God leads us personally to do so. I am writing about the *public* worship practices which dramatically shape our image of God.

Finally, I do not wish to promote controversy. We are not called to be contentious and dwell upon unimportant matters—we are called to be faithful to the Gospel of Jesus Christ. However, if being faithful results in being controversial, then we must be faithful, whatever the cost.

The Enigma of "Masculine" and "Feminine"

I reluctantly and with some ambiguity use the two words "masculine" and "feminine" throughout this book. It is not adequate or accurate to superficially define the masculine role with categories such as "supporting the family" and the feminine as "taking care of children." While all societies make some role distinctions between men and women, there seems to be no single distinction that holds for every society.

The Bible doesn't even have words for "masculine" and "feminine," even though women's and men's roles were rigidly defined in all Middle Eastern cultures. There are always those Christians who attempt to force everyone into these ancient and culturally defined roles by giving them divinely intended status. These attempts range from the humorous (women must have long hair and men short), to the disastrous (men are to be in charge of women).

The terms "feminine" and "masculine" have commonly been used in our culture to describe the division of human qualities into two rather distinct groupings. "Feminine" has traditionally been characterized as nurturing, receptive, gentle, and more oriented towards intuition and feeling than towards linear thinking. "Masculine" has traditionally been described as assertive, initiating, tough, and more oriented towards linear thinking than towards intuition and feeling. We use these definitions when talking about men "getting in touch with their feminine side," usually meaning they are beginning to get in touch with their own feelings, and starting to respond to the feelings of others. Or we use them when speaking about women who act in "masculine" ways, meaning they assert themselves and act confidently. But our language betrays us and pushes us into a false way of thinking. Who decided that knowing what you feel or nurturing others is feminine? And why is being potent and in charge considered to be masculine? In reality, these are human qualities and neither sex has a corner on them. Dividing up good and beautiful characteristics of humankind and assigning them to one sex or the other does injustice to us all. But since these common definitions hold some identifiable meanings which are used in the various debates over the significance of gender, I will sometimes use these traditional categories as a kind of "shorthand," often with quotation marks to remind readers of this qualification.

The other reason I use the words "feminine" and "masculine" is much more difficult to articulate. As the fire and smoke from the battle of the sexes begins to clear away, there is something emerging that may authentically be called differences between masculine and feminine. Of course there are developmental and psychological differences between women and men, and we are not served by dismissing the intuitive and demonstrable perception that these differences do indeed exist.[4] I delightedly affirm all these differences, whatever we discover they may be, because they make an even stronger case for the necessity of having both "male" and "female" viewpoints in leadership and decision making.

However, only as we get further away from the distortions of patriarchy will we be able to talk more meaningfully about differences between men and women without becoming en-

---

[4]See Carol Gilligan, *In a Different Voice* (Cambridge: Harvard, 1982) and Anne Moir and David Jessel, *Brain Sex* (New York: Dell, 1991) for an enlightened discussion of these differences.

tangled in the old stereotypes. We must avoid pushing people into what may be typical for a large number of persons but which does not hold true for everyone. The differences among men and among women are just are great as the differences between men and women. Women have been asking what it means to be a "woman" for several decades now. We men are just beginning to explore and affirm an authentic manhood which is not sexist or negatively defined as "not being a woman." When these journeys are further along I believe we will sense a new partnership between men and women, masculine and feminine.

So if you hear some ambiguity in my use of these words, it is because I am sensing something which is not yet clear enough for me to define. Perhaps masculine is simply feeling good about being a man, however that looks for any particular man. There are probably a large number of "masculinities" or "masculine" ways of acting, perhaps as many as there are men. The same may be true of feminine expression.

However, for my purpose in this book, whatever ways one defines masculine and feminine will not affect the thrust of my argument. It is only when one decides that God is more like one than the other that it becomes necessary to get into the tricky business of deciding which characteristics go with each word and which do not.

My prayer is that the Holy Spirit will use this book to help you come to know God, the Father of our Lord Jesus Christ, in ever deeper ways.

"No, Dolly, our father art
downstairs watching TV."

Prelude: A Visit to First Church

Dolly's little brother is not the only one confused by the limitations of human language for God. The challenge of using earthly metaphors for heavenly meanings invites all of us to explore the truthfulness, justice, and beauty in our worship practices. Many of us are so accustomed to our religious habits we do not perceive the male domination often present in our church leadership and religious language. I share the following story to give a fresh perspective of some of the forms sexism takes at 11 o'clock on Sunday morning. The story is a composite account based on actual experiences, using the very words which a number of persons have reported to me over the last few years or which I have personally experienced. Therefore, while all these events did not actually happen in the same church service, they did happen. I have been in some services that came very close to this inundating degree of sexism. I have added italics to call attention to the specific language used. Monitor your own thoughts and feelings while we listen to Doris and Sam as they attend a Sunday morning service.

Visiting—Only Once

Doris and Sam have been married for twenty-seven years now. She works in an advertising agency and he teaches in the local high school; both are aware of entering a new life stage as their children have moved away from home and are starting families of their own. Sam and Doris were raised in conservative churches, Southern Baptist and Lutheran, but they dropped out of church twenty years ago when it seemed to be increasingly irrelevant to their lives. Sensing a new spiritual hunger, they have decided to try church again, and for the first time in twenty years, they have arrived for the 11 o'clock service at First Church.

As they drive to the church building, the outside sign greets them with the church's name and the name of the male pastor. Each week a different slogan is put up on the sign to catch the attention of those passing by. The one for this week reads, "*He* who is born of God will resemble *his Father*." Sam appreciates the thought being presented, but he is very conscious that the language used is no longer appropriate in our culture. Since "he" and "his" no longer include "she" and "her," his wife as well as all other women have been linguistically excluded. The phrase "resemble his Father" gives the impression that women who become Christians will start to look like fathers!

They are pleasantly surprised at how friendly the church is. They are greeted by several members. One man asks Sam if he has ever sung in a choir, saying, "We've got plenty of *girls* in our choir but we need some more men." Moving on, Sam grins at Doris, asking her if it's fun being a girl among all these grown-up men. She grimaces and shakes her head.

Upon entering the auditorium, they are shown to their seats by one of the four male ushers. Sam overhears an animated conversation from two women seated behind him, sparked by a Sunday School class discussing the "inner man" from the Revised Standard Version of Ephesians 3:16. One woman, in a serious voice, asks the other, "How can I get the healing I need for my inner *man*?" Sam, familiar with the "inner child of the past" literature, feels a rush of sadness that this woman would so demean her sexual identity by referring to her deep inner self as a "man."

Meanwhile, as the service is ready to begin, the three men on the church staff are seated on the platform and the deacons, fourteen men, enter and sit in the front pew. Sam and Doris begin to think they have entered some patriarchal era from the past with this public display of male-only leadership.

They glance at the bulletin for the morning and see a pleasant woodland spring scene printed on the front in the latest beautiful four-color lithography. The technology is contemporary, in contrast to the archaic language of the verse from John 3:3 written across the bottom of the scene: "Except a *man* be born again, *he* cannot see the *Kingdom* of God." Doris knows the New Testament enough to know this includes her, but she has to consciously include herself because the language does not.

The traditional hymns this morning include these lines:

> *Father* love is reigning o'er us,
> *Brother* love binds *man* to *man.*

> Praise to the Lord, the Almighty,
>   the *King* of creation.
> O my soul praise *Him.*

> Rise up, O *men* of God!
> *His kingdom* tarries long.

Sam and Doris are aware that women have been edited out of history, conversations, jobs, salaries, professions, language, and now it seems, worship itself.

The congregation also sings two of the newer contemporary worship songs which seem to Sam even more masculine-oriented than the traditional hymns. They are filled with references to God as King, Father, he, him, and his, but contain no feminine imagery for God at all. As the congregation sings one particular line, "A *Father's* love is what you give to me," Sam wonders what his life would have been like without a mother's love also.

In singing another contemporary song the men and women are asked to sing different parts. The men always begin the phrase and the women echo what the men have sung. Doris wonders if the women always follow the men in singing, providing one more subtle reminder of this church's belief that the "woman's place" is to follow the man.

The male pastor baptizes several people at this point in the service. Our visiting couple recall the churches they grew up in where it was assumed that only pastors may baptize, and pastors must always be men. They realize things haven't changed much.

The Scripture reading for the morning includes: "If anyone would come after me, *he* must deny *himself* and take up *his* cross and follow me. . . . What good will it be for a *man* if *he* gains the whole world, yet forfeits *his* soul? Or what can a *man* give in exchange for *his* soul? For the Son of *Man* is going to come in his *Father's* glory with his angels, and then he will reward each person according to what *he* has done." (Matt 16:24–27, NIV)

Through the years Doris has maintained something of a relationship with God, and recently she has been sensing a real but fragile hunger to go deeper. Now Doris's inner voice whispers, "Why does it say 'man' when I think Jesus meant it for me, too?" Attempting to mentally edit these words, she asks herself, "Is God only a father and never a mother? Am I made in God's image, too?" The continuing onslaught of words that leave her out of both humanity and divinity finally seems too much. Doris begins to feel alienated.

The all-male group of deacons take the offering, and one of them leads the congregation in prayer. His prayer begins, "Heavenly *Father*, we know how much you have loved *man-kind*." He continues with, "*Father* we just pray for those not here today," using the word "Father" like punctuation to fill up the pauses. Several sentences of this ad lib prayer begin with the new word coined in the public prayers of evangelicals— "Fatherwejus." Sam muses to himself, "Besides offering a rather dull prayer, these people talk as if God is masculine." Sam, who years ago rejected the church he grew up in because of its racism, now begins to think there's another problem: sexism, which also needs to be dealt with.

The sermon from Matthew 14 is about the feeding of the five thousand and the text concludes with (v. 21, NIV): "The number of those who ate was about five thousand *men, besides women and children.*" Feeling a little sarcastic by now, Sam wonders if someone should start a real Bible-based denomination that counts only men in their statistics, as was the custom in the Gospels.

In the sermon, the pastor continually refers to God as Father, he, him, or his, communicating to Sam's and Doris's modern minds that God is male and masculine, and certainly that he has no feminine traits. The sermon abounds with quotes from male theologians and analogies about hunting and fixing cars, but none about activities like cleaning house or mending clothes such as Jesus used (Luke 15:8; Mark 2:21).

The pastor talks about the members as "*laymen*" and refers to "the church and its saintly *forefathers.*" Then he says, "We all have problems, every one of us, down to the last *man.*" Sam wonders how the laywomen, the saintly foremothers, and the last woman experience this exclusion.

Speaking about the homeless and lonely the pastor says, "What they need is a heavenly father like our God." Doris agrees they do need a heavenly father like our God but reflects that some of the lonely might also need a heavenly mother like our God.

At a supposedly humorous point in the sermon the pastor exclaims, "And if Satan doesn't remind you about it, your wife will!" The congregation chuckles. Sam doesn't find anything at all funny about the comparison between his wife and Satan.

The all-male deacons in the front pew serve communion. In their previous years of growing up in the church, Doris and Sam would not have had the negative thoughts and feelings flooding in at this moment. However, both are now acutely aware of sexual discrimination in the secular world, Doris because of her advertising business, Sam in keeping current with the teaching profession. As the men serve the Lord's Supper to the congregation, Sam remembers reading that the Pope recently said, "Only men may truly represent Christ here on earth."[1] It seems this Baptist church believes that, too.

The service concludes with the words of benediction, "And now, go in the name of the Father, the Son, and the Holy Spirit." Doris finds some humor as this biblical and hallowed phrase conjures up the image of an old man with a white beard, a rugged young man, and a religious phantom. Having been away from the Christian community long enough for these words not to simply slide by easily, she is once again jarred by their exclusivity. She reflects, "Is the Trinity, like the leaders in this church, an all-male club?"

As Sam and Doris drive home, they talk about how hard it was not to write off much of what was said as religious mumbo jumbo from another era, out of touch with their world. But even more seriously, they sadly resign themselves to believing that, in all probability, this is a congregation ruled by men who worship a masculine God. They will need to think again whether what they are searching for can be found in church.

Are Doris and Sam Deceived?

Many church-going Christians would not be aware of this church's overwhelming male dominance in leadership, images of God, and worship language. Until a dozen years ago I was oblivious to it, too. But as a Christian who believes the church desperately needs another reformation to stay faithful to biblical revelation, I began to ask myself some questions about this kind of church service.

Are Doris and Sam deceived in their reflections? Do they just need a big dose of the Bible so they can let go of their "radical" feminist ideas? Have they so departed from the faith

---

[1]In October of 1988, Pope John Paul II issued a major document on women that reaffirms the ban on female priests. His stated basis was that the difference between feminine and masculine means women should not be priests. "Christ," he said, "chose only men to be his apostles."

that they are now merely secular persons who have shut out the gospel? Are Doris and Sam overly sensitive or, more to the point, simply wrong about their desire for the recognition of the feminine side of humanity and God? Are their thoughts worldly and not the thoughts of God?

Or might they be closer to the intent of the gospel than we realize? Perhaps the questions we should ask of this church service are ones like:

- Do the words used in this service reflect the attitude of Jesus?

- Is this worship faithful to the biblical image of God?

- Is God really a masculine divine being?

- Does this gathering of Christians reflect the true intent of Scripture in the ways women and men are to relate?

- Would the apostle Paul approve of such a service in our culture?

- Does the language of this gathering of Christians reflect God's heart of justice in relationships between men and women?

- Is this service really evangelical? Does it invite today's person into a relationship with Jesus Christ, or is it so filled with cultural baggage from other centuries that it would be difficult for an increasing number of people today, both men and women, to hear the gospel?

Why Do Men Dominate the Leadership and Language of the Church?

The reason church leaders give for male-dominant practices is that they are "being faithful to the Bible." However, are they perhaps instead (often unintentionally) being faithful only to the male-dominant traditions of culture masquer-

ading in the disguise of biblical truth? Those who hold the
traditional position may be sincere and well-intentioned, but
I believe that they have unwittingly departed from the Scriptures and God's plan. A framework consisting of a number of
parts has been erected to form the traditional evangelical platform on the subordinate role of the feminine in humanity and
in God's image. When one piece is exposed as faulty, another
part is brought forth to repair the damage. Therefore, the
entire framework must be dismantled piece by piece and each
part reexamined in the light of Jesus and the totality of scrip-
tural teaching. When this is done, we will have built a quite
different but biblically based framework in which to understand the partnership of female and male in both humanity
and God's image.[2]

---

[2]The quote on the following page is from Dolly Patterson, ed.,
Questions of Faith (Philadelphia: Trinity Press International, 1990) 84.

As a theological student I always thought that God was a spirit and not an image. But I had an image of God as a Caucasian man with blue eyes, long hair, with a big nose and a white robe. My intellectual side said, "God has no image. God is spirit." But all my upbringing as a Christian in Korea in a Korean church that was founded by Western missionaries, all my Sunday school education, was based on this picture of God who looks like Moses in the movie The Ten Commandments.

Through a long personal struggle I realized one day that my image of God is like a middle-aged Korean woman looking like my mother—very warm, affirming, available, strong, and "down to earth." When I pray, this image comes to me. This is my image of God now. It's very liberating because before, when I prayed to God who was white, who was old, who was a man, it was difficult for me to feel connected with him.

—Hyung Kyung Chung,
Presbyterian, Professor of Theology
at Ewha Woman's University in Korea

How Do We Talk About God?

1

To whom then will you liken God,
 or what likeness compare with him? . . .
To whom then will you compare me,
 or who is my equal? says the Holy One. . . .
For I am God, and there is no other;
 I am God, and there is no one like me.

Isaiah 40:18, 25; 46:9

The most historic and orthodox way for Christians to talk about God is Trinity—Father, Son, and Holy Spirit. This way of naming God stands at the center of biblical faith and must not be abandoned, neglected or changed. Its intended meaning is not sexist or outmoded as some feminists would have us think. Jesus was not wrong to call God Father, though some claim that Jesus was the victim of a sinful patriarchal society. He chose precisely the right naming of God at the right time and in the right setting.

However, it is not enough as disciples of Jesus to merely repeat certain words, even Jesus' words, if we do not understand what these words were intended to mean. Languages lag and symbols slip.[1] That is, they eventually fail to represent faithfully the reality behind them as they once did. Since all languages lag and all symbols slip, including important ones like "Father, Son, and Holy Spirit," Christians who base their faith on the authority of biblical revelation have a true dilemma. The ever-changing and evolving meanings and nuances in language mean that the common, undefined, and unqualified use of this traditional trinitarian formula by almost all evangelicals and charismatics communicates something which was never intended by the New Testament writers. It communicates something which was also not intended by those who formulated the rather precise definition of the Trinity at the Council of Nicea in AD 325. This trusted naming of God as it is commonly used no longer defends our faith. It seriously distorts our faith in two ways:

(1) It increasingly implies today that God's image is male in some way that it is not also female, or that God is more "masculine" than "feminine" as we commonly understand those terms.

(2) Speaking of God in exclusively male terms implies that men are more like God than women are, a belief which buttresses the idea that only men should be in charge.

This distortion of our faith is illustrated by a letter I received:

> Dear Mr. Smith,
>
> Since God describes Himself as our Heavenly Father (male), why do we need to change His gender? Only an idiot could miss the fact that from Genesis to Revelation God is male because He is always referred to as "He."
>
> This also makes it clear why men should be in charge of the Holy Church of our Heavenly Father. How do I know God is male and men should be in charge? The Bible tells me so.

---

[1]The phrase "symbols slip" is from Marianne Micks, *The Future Present* (New York: Seabury, 1970) 159.

It seems to me that this gentleman is sincere but nonetheless misinformed. Pointing to the use of masculine pronouns and male metaphors for God in the Bible, he ends up with two inadequate conclusions—God is male and men should be in charge. Therefore to reclaim the original biblical partnership of male and female, both in the image of God and in humankind, we must first look at language and how we talk about God.

Language Is Limited

There is nothing else in our experience that is exactly like God. Therefore the only way the Bible can talk about God is by using various word pictures called metaphors, analogies, symbols, models, and similes. One scholar says that all of the language used by the Bible in referring to God is metaphor, with the one possible exception being the word "holy."[2] Whatever we call these figures of speech they all point to realities beyond themselves, while giving some authentic, though limited, knowledge of that reality. For simplicity I will group together these categories of words which are technically different forms of language and use them somewhat interchangeably. Three things are true about all metaphorical language.

(1) More than one word picture is needed to get a balanced understanding.

The less something is like anything else, the more analogies are needed to describe it. This is why the Bible uses so many word pictures for God.

In the Bible, God is referred to in human analogies such as shepherd, father, mother, redeemer, judge, deliverer, friend, lover, and helper, as well as in animal analogies such as mother bear, eagle, and mother hen. Sometimes God is depicted with impersonal word pictures like refuge, rock, shield,

---

[2]G. B. Caird, *The Language and Imagery of the Bible* (Philadelphia: Westminster, 1980) 18.

fortress. At other times there are abstract names like hope, glory, strength, and hiding place. Some scholars believe the closest the Scriptures come to actually naming God is in the Old Testament designation of God as "I Am" and Jesus' self identification as the "I Am" in John's Gospel.

Throughout church history God has been meaningfully referred to in other terms besides those found in the Bible. The early Christians invented the term Trinity, and today most Christians are comfortable with naming God "blessed Trinity" as the great hymn "Holy, Holy, Holy" puts it.

Poets and hymn writers have called God Ruler of History, Giver of Life, Infinite Other, Author of Justice, Source of All, Ruler of Time and Space, Judge of All Things,[3] and Light Eternal. These are all beautiful names for God, each reflecting some aspect of the biblical image of God. We need them all and more because no one name is enough.

(2) All analogies and metaphors, without exception, say something that is false, even as they say something true.

To say "Our God is a consuming fire" (Heb 12:29) is no more literally true than saying "God is our Father." Both analogies reveal some authentic truth about God, but both also say some things that are not true. For instance, it would obviously be false to conclude that since God is both fire and a father, God needs oxygen to survive. However, it may not seem as obviously false that although God is like a father, God cannot also be like a mother.

Another model or metaphor used in the Bible to describe our relationship to God is one of slavery. Psalm 123:2 in the New International Version says, "As the eyes of slaves look to the hand of their master, as the eyes of a maid look to the hand of her mistress, so our eyes look to the LORD our God, till he shows us his mercy." This analogy speaks of us as male and female slaves and God as a male master and a female mistress. Paul uses this same metaphor when he says we should be

---

[3] These names are ones used by Martin Bell in his book of inspiring praise and prayer, *Street Singing and Preaching, A Book of New Psalms* (Nashville: Abingdon, 1991).

slaves of Christ (Rom 6:22; Eph 6:6), and he often refers to himself as a slave of Christ. The truth of this model is that we are to obey God fully and completely, depending on God for all that we need to sustain our lives. What is not true about this comparison is that it automatically means God approves of slavery. The biblical writers used a metaphor that was meaningful to the society of their day in communicating truth about one aspect of our relationship with the Holy One of Israel. However, this slavery metaphor has presented a serious problem to many Christians because both the Old and New Testaments seem to approve of slavery, neither one containing any word of encouragement to abolish it. Rather than abolish slavery, the biblical picture appears to do just the opposite, as, for example, when the New Testament tells slaves to obey their masters. The biblical approval of slavery appeared so obvious in previous generations that certain Christians argued that slavery was God's idea and opposed abolition. That is a misuse of metaphorical language; they forgot that, while all good metaphors say something true, they also all say something false.[4]

The word Jesus used for father, *abba*, meant something like our word "daddy." It is a good analogy for God because it says something true: God is like a good daddy relating to his son, as the people of Jesus' day understood the father and son relationship. It describes Jesus' intimate, nurturing, personal relationship to God (Gal 3:23—4:7; Rom 8:12-30). It speaks of God's approachability, protection, care, and forgiveness. It emphasizes the ethical responsibility of the son as one who is to do the will of his father. We are to be faithful in carrying out the perfect will of our Father in heaven as we go about our lives on earth. *Abba* was not only a term of endearment for father used by young children, it was also used by grown children and carried a breadth of relationship from young to old.[5] It speaks of a caring, powerful God who is in charge of his own "family,"

---

[4]C. Keener, *Paul, Women, and Wives* (Peabody: Hendrickson, 1992).

[5]See Joachim Jeremias, *The Prayers of Jesus* (London: SCM, 1967) 59–62. Also James Barr, "Abba Isn't Daddy," *Journal of Theological Studies* 39 (April 1988) 35.

in a way that a mother was not in a patriarchal society, and who looks out for it in relationships and dealings outside the family in the larger world. Probably no other word in the patriarchal society of early Palestine comes as close to an ideal word to describe the relationship the earthly Jesus had with God.

However, like all word pictures, calling God Father also says something that is not true. Some obviously false comparisons include:

- God has a limited life span like earthly fathers.

- God is a young and foolish father of eighteen or an old and feeble one of ninety.

- God is a sexual being and has his children through a sexual relationship with a spouse.

- God might mistreat or abandon his children as earthly fathers sometimes do.

- God is a father like the Pharisees and Sadducees who were also called fathers.

- God is like Ba'al, a male god in the Old Testament, or the Greek gods who were male.

Another falsehood the father metaphor conveys is that God is male or primarily masculine. That Jesus called God "Father" was not meant to encase the patriarchy of one culture as God's ideal for all of creation. If we do not understand the limitations of analogical language, we will have a false understanding of God.

Much of our misuse of symbolic language would be corrected if we would simply see the little word "like" in front of every word describing God. We call God our "Rock," meaning God is *like* a rock, not that he actually *is* a rock. We have not as easily seen this in calling God our Father, meaning that God is like a father in some ways, but not in *every* way, or not like *all* fathers, or *only* like a father.

(3) We must understand what the word picture meant in the context it was originally given before we can understand what it means for us today.

Every word, phrase and idea in the Bible has a cultural context. The only word pictures available for use in communicating divine truth are the ones already present and meaningful in the particular culture. The father/son metaphor about our relationship with God teaches us a truth that can be seen in the special relationship of father and son in the Palestinian setting. This is especially difficult to grasp in the context of our industrialized society's frequently distant or absent father. The Talmud teaches that a father's responsibility toward a son consists of three things: "To circumcise him, to teach him the law, to teach him a trade." A son was taught the meaning of life and the secrets of the family trade by his father. These were passed down from father to son, generation after generation. Jesus understood this natural human relationship in spiritual terms when he said, "I must be about my Father's business" (Luke 2:49, KJV).

In Jesus' day only fathers had the social and legal authority that is shared by both fathers and mothers in our culture. In chapter three I will explore seven ways in which the word father communicated something different in first-century Palestine than it does in twentieth-century America. The point here is that we cannot directly appropriate metaphors from one culture to another, even those as seemingly familiar as father/son, without first discerning their meaning in the society in which they were originally used.

Language Has Changed

"DEVELOPMENT OF THE UTERUS IN RATS, GUINEA PIGS, AND MEN"[6]

Most of us find some humor in that title even as we Christians are being dragged kicking and screaming into the highly charged linguistic revolt of the last two decades, often referred to as the movement toward "politically correct" language.

---

[6]Research report quoted in Casey Miller and Kate Swift, *The Handbook of Nonsexist Writing*, 2d ed. (New York: Harper & Row, 1988) 11.

Some of this war over words is the eternal battle between the purists who want language to remain unchanged and those who understand language as a living thing, reflecting the constant evolution of thought patterns and communication. The debate includes such fine points as the academic battle over prepositions and dangling participles. As Churchill once wrote, "A preposition is a good word to end a sentence with."

However, words and their meanings are crucial to our faith, and theologians fill volumes attempting to define and understand certain words precisely, such as "justification," "Trinity," and "salvation." All serious disciplines of study do the same thing because communication within each discipline depends on a mutual understanding of words.

The constant change in words and word pictures from culture to culture and generation to generation presents enormous challenges, especially to translators and communicators of the Bible. Moving from the culture of ancient Palestine to contemporary America is a quantum leap.

For instance, Psalm 23:5, a text describing ancient practices of hospitality, says literally in Hebrew, "You have made my head fat with oil." Calling someone a "fathead" in our culture is not usually a good way to make the person feel welcome!

The New International Version changed the sentence's literal words and interpreted its meaning by translating it as, "You anoint my head with oil." The Today's English Version, which was under no mandate to sound like the King James Version, but only to be easily understood by people in our culture, translates it: "You welcome me as an honored guest."

Which translation is correct? That depends on whether you are after the correct *words*, "made my head fat with oil," or the correct *meaning*, "made me as an honored guest." The latter phrase is not the exact words of the original Hebrew, but it represents what the verse seeks to communicate!

I can see a worship leader in a Sunday morning service saying, "We're especially glad to have visitors with us this morning. May your heads be fat with oil." That's just being biblical. Or is it? Which is more biblical: to say the correct words and communicate the wrong meaning, or to update the words and thereby communicate the true meaning?

Words of Masculine Gender No Longer Include Women

The greatest furor in our changing English language has been over gender language, words which carry connotations of male and female. Never before in human history has a sense of feminine identity and a questioning of masculine and feminine connotations been the subject of such intense scrutiny. We have begun asking questions about gender words as never before. Why do we talk about Mother Earth and Father Time? Why is a ship called she, and the Grim Reaper called he? Why don't we say:

- Is it natural or womanmade?
- Workwomenship.
- The Businesswoman's lunch.
- Necessity is the father of invention.
- Checker team: Queen me!
- She who laughs last, laughs longest.
- A woman for all seasons.
- I now pronounce you woman and husband.
- Workwomen's compensation insurance.
- Woman the lifeboats! Men and children first!
- These are the times that try women's souls.
- What is your father tongue?
- Seniors, Juniors, Sophomores, Freshwomen.[7]

_____

[7]Jane Bartlett, *Ms. Bartlett's Familiar Quotations* (San Diego: Joseph Tabler, 1991) 45–51.

Someone who didn't appreciate the humor in this list angrily responded by saying to me, "What's wrong with the way we've always said things? It looks like a group of angry women came along and decided to steal our language to fit their political purposes. Who decided 'he' no longer includes 'she'?"

I replied, "Perhaps the real question is: Who decided 'he' should include 'she' to begin with?" The "theft of language"[8] occurred a long time ago. In the Fall it was stolen by Satan and it now toils in service of evil's oppressive work. The use of masculine generic language in English such as "he" and "man" for both male and female was proposed as a grammatical rule by John Kirby in 1746.[9] Building on centuries of patriarchy, the generic use of "he" and "man" in English became embedded in our legal system as the result of the politics of grammarians who finally convinced the English Parliament to put it into law in 1850—because men should "naturally" take precedence.[10]

It is estimated that the average person comes into contact with the generic "he" more than 10 million times during the course of a lifetime.[11] And each time, men are subtly reminded that women don't count, and women are told to find their identity in men.

But language belongs to women too, and they (along with many men) are simply taking back what was stolen from them for the political purposes of patriarchy throughout the centuries. As early as 1971 the Oxford English Dictionary declared the use of "man" as a generic term obsolete.

McGraw-Hill publishers, in their 1974 *Guidelines for Equal Treatment of the Sexes*, stated:

---

[8]Adrienne Rich, "Power and Danger: Works of A Common Woman," *On Lies, Secrets, and Silence: Selected Prose 1966–1978* (New York: W. W. Norton, 1979) 256.

[9] Sik Hung Ng, "Androcentric Coding of *Man* and *His* in Memory by Language Users," *Journal of Experimental Social Psychology* 26, 455.

[10]Letty M. Russell, *Household of Freedom, Authority in Feminist Theology* (Philadelphia: Westminster, 1987) 45.

[11]Sik Hung Ng, "Androcentric Coding," 456.

The word sexism was coined, by analogy to racism, to denote discrimination based on gender. In its original sense, sexism referred to prejudice against the female sex. In a broader sense, the term now indicates any arbitrary stereotyping of males and females on the basis of their gender.[12]

McGraw-Hill wished to "eliminate sexist assumptions . . . to make staff members and . . . authors aware of the ways in which males and females have been stereotyped in publications: to show the role language has played in reinforcing inequality . . ."[13]

In 1976 the National Council of Teachers of English published its book, *Guidelines for Nonsexist Use of Language* (Urbana). This group more likely reflects current usage rather than initiating change in language. They state that it is no longer acceptable to use masculine words to include the feminine. The meaning of "he" has changed so much that "he" now means a "male" person and no longer includes female.

The Joint Faculty of Fuller Seminary issued a statement in 1984 saying in part, "As members of the Joint Faculty of Fuller Theological Seminary, we are committed to the use of non-discriminatory language in all areas of the community's life. We recognize that many women and men no longer find 'man,' 'men,' and 'mankind' acceptable as generic terms. We understand that such exclusive language, though once normative in our speaking and writing, now tends increasingly to alienate a substantial group of people. We wish to challenge patterns of language that may be doing harm even when harm is inflicted unconsciously and without intention."

Even the venerable *Star Trek* television series has changed its original opening script lines from "where no man has gone before" to "where no one has gone before." It eventually became obvious to the writers that women were going too and from the beginning had been a part of the crew.

---

[12] *Guidelines for Equal Treatment of the Sexes in McGraw-Hill Book Company Publications* (New York: McGraw-Hill, n.d.) 1.
[13]Ibid.

We may or may not like this change, but the reality is that it has occurred. Christians must ask, in the light of this new usage, how do we best translate the Scriptures and preach the gospel?

Most of our translations and language about God do not reflect current usage. For instance (italics mine), 2 Corinthians 5:17 in the King James Version (1611) is, "If any *man* be in Christ, *he* is a new creature." The literal translation of the Greek it is, "So if anyone in Christ, new creation." The New International Version (1978) has, "If *anyone* is in Christ, *he* is a new creation." Since "he" no longer includes women, that passage communicates in an insensitive manner, giving the impression that the gospel excludes women. From a gender-inclusive perspective, the best translation, so far, is the New Revised Standard Version (1989), which is consistently sensitive to gender language, and has for 2 Cor 5:17: "So if anyone is in Christ, there is a new creation."

When patriarchy was the cultural norm, everyone understood that masculine pronouns like "he" and words like "mankind" and "brothers" included women. The situation is very different today, as patriarchy has theologically, morally, and intellectually crumbled, and our language is shifting to reflect this.

The Greek scholars on the translation team of the New Revised Standard Version (1989) have recognized this change by routinely translating the Greek word of address "brothers" as "brothers and sisters." This is a simple but vital recognition that adding "sisters" makes a translation that is more in keeping with the intent of the writers than a literal translation of only "brothers."

But how about pronouns for God? The NRSV translators recognized the necessity of adding the feminine to terms of address for humankind ("brothers and sisters"), but why did they stop short of doing the same thing with exclusively masculine pronouns for God? Does the word "he" as originally used for God in a strongly patriarchal society communicate the same meaning in our egalitarian one? Constantly using images with meanings rooted in a patriarchal context of two thousand years ago conveys to us today that God is only masculine and never feminine. Is this what the biblical writers intended?

The editor of the *Catholic World Report*, San Francisco Jesuit Joseph Fessio, says, "If you change the language of the liturgy and prayers and feminize it, you're ultimately changing the religion."[14] I believe just the opposite is true. Since language has changed, if we *fail* to update our religious language, it will become increasingly *masculinized*. It is *then* that we ultimately change our religion from worship of a God who both encompasses and transcends male and female to a God who is exclusively male.

Language Is Fallen

An extremely serious complication in communication is that language is "fallen." The fall of humanity is a key biblical understanding of our human condition and means that all things are in some way affected and distorted by the reality of sin. No system or part of creation was left out of the fall, including language. Fallen language is one of our Enemy's most powerful weapons in distorting our faith and keeping us from all that God has for us.

When sin entered the world Adam and Eve were affected in every way including linguistically. Language was now used to evade responsibility (Gen 3:12–13), to aid murder (4:9), and to challenge God's sovereignty (4:23–24).[15]

The story of the Tower of Babel (Gen 11:1–9) graphically portrays the effect of the limits of communication. Both the Old and New Testaments contain numerous admonitions about giving false witness (Ex 20:16), lying (Lev 19:11, 16), and the danger of false words (Prov 11:9; 12:18; 25:18). Paul quotes

---

[14] *Time*, November 23, 1992, 56.

[15] Moises Silva, *God, Language and Scripture* (Grand Rapids: Zondervan, 1990) 27.

three psalms which condemn speech that is not true: Ps 5:9; 140:3; 10:7 (cited in Rom 3:3–14).

In Ephesians 4:25—5:4 Paul gives a series of powerful commands about speaking the truth in love. The book of James often refers to our speech being tainted with sin, and the more we speak the more we are likely to sin. Throughout Scripture we see the power of language to bless and curse, to work for the purpose of redemption as well as to be an instrument for the Enemy and our rebelliousness against God.[16]

We can see this fallenness of language when women become linguistically invisible: language devalues the feminine by attempting to include women in words such as "man" when all of humankind is meant.

If you have two categories, A and B, and, when you refer to both categories, you call them A, you are linguistically eradicating B. You have made B disappear by including it in A, and you have made A all important. This is what happens when we use masculine words to include the feminine.

Language is our means of classifying and ordering the world. Therefore, if the rules which underlie our language system are invalid, then we are deceived daily.[17] Patriarchal language is based on the sinful concept that the standard or normal human being is male, and women are at best some kind of addition and at worst a deviation.

We see the degeneration of language when the masculine gender is used to connote value and honor while the feminine gender is often reduced to inferior or sometimes negative sexual implications. This can be seen in pairs of words which might seem to be equal in describing male and female but the female word has become diminished in startling ways. "Lord" and "Lady" both originally described titles of royalty and respect, but today lady does not carry the power that lord does. "King" and "Queen" describe equal titles but the latter does not convey the same authority as does the former. In recent

---

[16]I am indebted to Moises Silva for the biblical overview of fallen language in *God, Language, and Scripture*, 29–32.

[17]Dale Spender, *Man Made Language* (New York: Routledge and Kegan Paul, 1980) 2–3.

times in our culture "queen" has fallen even further when it is used in a homophobic or derogatory sense. "Madam" can mean the female leader of a house of prostitution, but "Sir" has no such possible connotation. "Master" carries great weight, but "mistress" has come to mean an illicit sexual partner. The female part of these pairs has become associated with sexual and illegitimate practices because our language is male-dominated and female-abusing. These examples show a profound devaluing of words associated with women.[18]

Yet Psalms uses the mistress image to refer to God (123:2), along with more than forty other metaphors such as guide, shepherd, shield, rock, tower, fortress, and hiding place.[19] We are comfortable with these word pictures, why not mistress? Why have we no hymns about God as our mistress similar to ones about God as our fortress and rock? Our language has fallen and needs saving by Christ, too.

We must not attempt to dodge the fact that the Bible itself is written in fallen languages and uses fallen cultures to communicate God's self-revelation. These were the only languages and cultures available for God to work through, and we must realistically face the challenge of understanding the message of God contained within the particular vehicle in which it is transmitted.

This acknowledgment of the human side of the Bible does not detract from its divine side in any way, but it does make it more complicated to understand. The Bible is the Spirit-inspired, true and trustworthy record of God's revelation to humanity and is the norm and authority for all Christian reflection, doctrine, and practice. But this authoritative revelation of God in scripture is contained in a vehicle that has been touched and shaped by its culture, namely language. The challenge is to learn to distinguish the content of revelation from the form of revelation. We must separate the message from the envelope.

---

[18]This paragraph is based on Marjorie Proctor-Smith, *In Her Own Rite* (Nashville: Abingdon, 1990) 59–84.

[19]Ps 48:14; 23:1; 3:3; 18:2; 61:3; 31:3; 32:7.

A Southern Baptist Resolution

My own denomination, in making an official statement about how we should talk about God, ignores the fact that language is limited, changed, and fallen. At the 1992 annual meeting of the Southern Baptist Convention, 15,000 "messengers" overwhelmingly adopted a resolution which said in part:

> WHEREAS, The Christian church is now confronted with challenges to its address of God as Father and is encouraged to accept alternatives which confuse the biblical witness or substitute impersonal language for God. . . .
>
> Be it RESOLVED that the messengers to the 135th session of the Southern Baptist Convention affirm biblical teaching concerning God the Father and call upon all Christians to remain faithful to biblical language concerning God, understanding that the revelation of God as Father is central and essential to trinitarian faith.
>
> it further RESOLVED, that we state clearly the scriptural witness that God is Spirit, beyond any human gender, and that He is transcendent, beyond the limitations of any human word; but confess that He has uniquely and explicitly revealed Himself to us as Father, by His sovereign and perfect will.[20]

I agree that we must "remain faithful to biblical language," "affirm the biblical teaching concerning God the Father," and that "God is Spirit, beyond any human gender." These are three of the primary concerns of this book. My objection is that the resolution itself does not seem to take these concerns seriously.

---

[20]SBC Executive Committee revision of Report of Committee on Resolutions, Second Day, *SBC Bulletin,* June 1992.

For instance, the constant capitalizing of masculine pronouns for God in this resolution puts an emphasis on masculine pronouns which is not present in the Bible. The Greek manuscripts, from which we translate into English, are written entirely in capital letters and there is no linguistic warrant for singling out or emphasizing pronouns. Many of the pronouns in our English Bible translations are added to the text because they are contained, unrelated to gender, in the verb form in the original languages. In biblical Greek, the subject, he, she, they, you, or it, is contained in the verb, and we are only reminded if the subject is plural or singular, and not if it is male or female. Special attention is not called to gender in the verb and it is not necessary to use gender-oriented nominative pronouns in Greek. If in English we choose to capitalize masculine pronouns referring to God, not only do we often use pronouns that were not actually present in the "biblical language," but we call extravagant attention to them. Therefore, in this respect the resolution itself is not "faithful to the biblical language for God."

The resolution affirms that ". . . God is Spirit, beyond any human gender, and that He is transcendent. . . ." To say God is beyond human gender and then to immediately assign gender as the (capitalized) masculine pronoun "he" does in our language today is not affirming the "biblical teaching concerning God the Father." Today "He" implies gender, namely male gender, and the biblical teaching that God is like a father was not intended to teach us that God is exclusively male. It would be more faithful to the biblical meaning to eliminate the "He" and say something like "God is Spirit, beyond any human gender because God is transcendent."

There is widespread agreement among Christian theologians that God transcends gender, but our pronouns speak louder than our theology and our qualifications. How will anyone believe us when we say that God both encompasses and transcends male and female if we talk as if God is only male?

Then there is the phrase in the resolution, "alternatives which confuse the biblical witness," presumably referring to the topic of this book. Calling God Mother as well as Father confuses the biblical witness only if God intends to be revealed as exclusively male, is never imaged as female in the Bible, and Mother does not communicate any of the truths about God contained therein.

The resolution assumes that the "biblical language" we use means the same thing today as it meant to those in the biblical time and culture. As we shall see, this is never a safe assumption, especially around words like father. We must remember that most Christians simply don't and can't use "biblical language" today. Our "biblical" language is always an American English interpretive translation of ancient Hebrew, Aramaic, and Koine (common) Greek.

Millions of Southern Baptists are now quite satisfied that a strong call has been sounded again for "biblical" Christianity and we need not bother about calling God anything but Father. I am disturbed by the confusing and unbiblical nature of this resolution. We have done it again—taken the Bible literally but not seriously. My denomination has refused to wrestle with how all language, even biblical language, is limited, changing, and fallen.

"It's a Boy!"

The first thing said about us when we were born was the joyful announcement "It's a girl!" or "It's a boy!" That word spread, repeated again and again, until everyone knew whether "it" was a girl or a boy. Our gender is a natural and important touchstone of identity for us as human beings.

However, is that the message we want to announce over and over again to the world about God: "It's a boy!"? This is what happens every time we refer to God only as "he" or "him" in our church services. Is this really what we want to proclaim to the world with incredible regularity, religious fervor and astonishing repetition?

The Enemy has seized our language and is using it to confuse and defeat us. We must boldly and radically reclaim our words in the name of Christ so language itself can enter fully into God's redemptive purposes of transmitting salvation, truth, beauty, and justice.

Understanding the Bible—Hermeneutics

Because the language of the Bible is limited, changed, and fallen, we must work to understand what words and images from other times and cultures originally meant to their readers. Theologians use the term "hermeneutic" to describe a system or way of interpreting the Scriptures so that we can comprehend their meaning for today.

The Bible is a dangerous book. When we read it we run the risk of having our lives disturbed and changed forever, for it is there many of us have found Jesus Christ, and we are being released into new life every day. However, some have read the same Bible and heaped abuse upon themselves and others. They have not found Jesus, but rather a weapon to promote, at various times in history, the divine right of kings, slavery, patriarchy, and legalism. And, like the Pharisees of Jesus' day, they put heavy burdens upon the faithful. Why do some read the Bible and find oppressive uses for it and some read it and find the very foundation and resources to oppose these same oppressions? Because different systems of interpretation can produce extremely different results.

A man claimed to have no "interpretive" system but just "took the Bible straight, doing what it says with no fancy interpretations." He was fond of repeating "It says what it means and it means what it says," implying any fool ought to know that. He was dismayed when a friend insisted they go down to the jail and find some way to help the prisoners escape because his friend said, "Jesus came to set the prisoners free." The man complained, "But that's not what he meant," and his friend's reply was, "But that's what it says and you're the one who keeps telling me to do just what it says."

This person was using a hermeneutic of literalism which assumes everything written in the Bible is to be taken literally, never symbolically or with an understanding of its cultural context. It often seems to those using this kind of system that others who disagree with them don't really believe in the truth or authority of the Bible. Yet there are times when to take the Bible literally means we do *not* take it seriously and we miss God's word to us.

There are many systems of interpretation. In the past we have seen the hermeneutic of spiritualizing, popular with Christians in the early centuries and occasionally today, where the historic meaning of the Bible is given second place to its hidden "spiritual" meaning. This has ranged from wild flights of fantasy, turning everything in the book of Revelation into obscure symbols, to making the Song of Solomon only an allegory about Christ rather than first of all an erotic love poem.

More recently there has been the hermeneutic of demythologizing, which attempts to make the Bible relevant for today by reinterpreting any supernatural elements, such as miracles, which do not appear to fit with today's world view. This robs the Bible of its historicity and authority.

Quite recently we have seen the feminist "hermeneutic of suspicion," which approaches a text with a basic assumption that it has been shaped and even distorted by male writers, editors, and interpreters.

A Hermeneutic of Renewal

I offer another approach to understanding the Scriptures. It is what has moved me to work in the church for almost forty years and how I came to change my mind about the language we use for God. The passion of my life has been to discern what God is saying to the church today and to translate that into practical reality within the local church. From my experience of wrestling with the Scriptures and God's call to renewal in the church today, I perceive what I call a "hermeneutic of renewal." It revolves around three key ideas: (1) the renewal of the church, (2) the dual focus of restoration and innovation, (3) the intent of God in the biblical writings.

The Renewal of the Church

A hermeneutic of renewal operates from a key frame of reference, namely the renewal of the church. It assumes the New Testament was written: (1) *by* the church, (2) *to* the church, and (3) *in order to* keep the church in a state of constant faithfulness.

Therefore, it postulates that the Scriptures can be best understood, perhaps *only* understood: (1) *by* the church (those with a passion for and deep experience in the church), whose task is directed (2) *to* the church, (3) *in order to* renew the church.

As much as we would like to think there are those, usually ourselves, who approach the Bible in a totally objective manner, this is not so. We all approach biblical interpretation with some frame of reference, and our inevitably subjective approaches are most dangerous when we are not aware of them. This bias is most powerfully shaped by our experience (or lack of experience) in the body of Christ, the church. A church renewal hermeneutic understands that we cannot read the Scripture from any other background than our own personal experience with the church.

As I look at the years of misleading interpretation of Paul's teaching about prophecy and praying in "tongues" (I prefer the marginal reading of the NIV which is "other languages," since we no longer commonly refer to language as a "tongue"—we don't sign up for The English Tongue 201), I realize most theologians and teachers had no experience with either one and had to make wild guesses about these phenomena. For instance, the New English Bible translates 1 Corinthians 14:6 as "*ecstatic* tongues," not because the word "ecstatic" was present in the Greek but because the translators' experience or assumption about speaking in other languages was that it was always highly emotional. Since the charismatic movement has demonstrated this is not necessarily the case, we must look again at our interpretations of passages about "other languages."

As I have experienced women coming into greater partnership with men in the church, I read the Bible in a different way. Never again can I read some passages without seeing the demeaning of women in a way that I missed before. In Judges 19 sexually abusing a man was a greater wrong than the gang rape of a woman. Solomon had 700 wives of royal birth and 300 concubines. I used to think the last of the Ten Commandments simply told all of us "Don't covet." But Exodus 20:17 makes it clear this is a commandment addressed to men, not women, and that a neighbor's wife is a part of the list of property along with his house, slaves, ox, and donkey, which men should not covet. Interpreters in previous generations could not see the sexism in these many passages because their own experience was so clouded by those same cultural attitudes. While the New Testament is remarkably free of "texts of terror"[21] such as gang rape, the system of patriarchy continues as the setting in which God's truth was communicated. Paul could say in Galatians 3:26 (NIV), "You are all sons of God through faith in Christ Jesus," because in a patriarchal society everyone knew sons had the greater value, and calling us daughters of God made little sense because it would mean we had no power, authority, inheritance, or rights. Because of my church experience with women as partners, I see that the Bible in these situations is giving a true record of a false idea— patriarchy.

A hermeneutic of renewal intimately connects biblical interpretation with the task of renewal. Studying the Bible must be directly connected to the renewal of the church, or it may become an exercise in intellectual curiosity pursued for scholarly interest or ideological agendas rather than dynamically connected to God's purpose for the church today. Our attempts at understanding the Bible must always focus on God's intention for the church, "so that through the church the wis-

---

[21]Phyllis Trible's term, in *Texts of Terror: Literary Feminist Readings of Biblical Narratives* (Philadelphia: Fortress, 1984).

dom of God in its rich variety might now be made known to the rulers and authorities in the heavenly places" (Eph 3:10). Some Christians attempt to understand and use the Bible only for purposes of personal spiritual renewal. This is inadequate because the Bible is about *corporate* renewal. While the personal dimensions of the spiritual life are crucial, they are always meant to find expression in the local church. God's goal is not merely redeemed individuals but a redeemed community!

A fascinating and often resisted observation is that the spiritual level of our own personal lives cannot rise much above the level of the corporate spirituality of the Christians with whom we associate. In spite of our frustrations with church life, the spiritual depth and breadth of our lives is intimately connected to the body of Christ and the particular expressions with which we are connected. We really do need each other.

It is my belief that all biblical scholars, interpreters, writers, and teachers should be intimately connected to dynamic church life while they pursue their studies. Preaching and teaching at different churches on Sunday mornings not only doesn't pass for an intimate church connection, it probably works against it! This may sound impractical or radical, but how could it be otherwise? Since the New Testament is written by, about, and to those who were passionately involved in the local church, how can it be understood except by those who are also thus involved? If all biblical scholars, interpreters, writers, and teachers were closely connected to dynamic churches wrestling with being faithful to Jesus Christ, we would be much further along in our understanding of Scripture.

Restoration and Innovation

A hermeneutic of renewal has a dual focus on *restoration* and *innovation*.[22] *Restoration* means returning again and again to the Bible and allowing God to show us what we have not previously seen. It is the uncovering of new levels of meaning

---

[22]I first found this idea, which he calls "renovation and innovation," in Hans Küng, *Reforming the Church Today* (New York: Crossroad, 1990) 42–51.

in the Bible and restoring the original depth of the biblical revelation. Since all biblical interpretation is shaped by our experience, as our experience changes, we are able to perceive what
we could not see before in Scripture. Restoration moves us closer
to our origins in the intent of Jesus and the New Testament.

Innovation is allowing the Holy Spirit to apply that which
we discover in the Scripture in fresh ways. Innovation allows
the Holy Spirit to make the gospel more and more relevant to
the culture in which we live. Application (innovation) has traditionally been left for someone other than the biblical interpreter
or separated from interpretation, but this is not adequate. Some
may focus on scholarship and some may focus on application,
but each must always have an eye on the other because the goal
is releasing the church to be all that it can be.

Separating interpretation (restoration) and application
(innovation) does injustice to the process of renewal. Scholarship becomes sterile and misses validation when it does not
live with its results in the Spirit-filled community of faith. A
hermeneutic of renewal is always asking how our interpretation of the Bible is dynamically tied to God's intention for the
church in the world today.

When application becomes disconnected from the scholarly norms of biblical research, it can become faddish, ridicu-
lous, or simply wrong. If *restoration* of the meaning of the
original texts is neglected, then renewal is loosened from its
biblical foundations and the church goes for the newest
fad—the Church of What's Happening Next. Because the Bible
was written in an ancient cultural setting, there is a tendency
for those who want the church to be relevant in today's world
to lessen the Bible's authority, but we cannot do this! Only as
we take scripture as our foundational and guiding authority
can we remain faithful to the original intent of God as revealed
in Jesus. Human error and our proclivity to drift from our original direction is so great that we must be anchored in the Incarnation and those documents that witness to it. Those
documents have been reliably collected in what we call the
Bible, and restoration means we constantly return to the Bible
to search out deeper understandings of God's intent there.

If *innovation* is neglected then the church becomes enmeshed in merely cultural practices, often two thousand years old—the Church of What Used to Happen. Renewal does not mean trying to duplicate something from the past, even the early church. The game of "New Testament Church" is always doomed to failure because replicating the structures and sometimes culture-bound practices of the early church results in the dead end of biblicism and legalism. It is a superficial attempt to come to grips with what the Spirit was attempting to produce in the early church, and it ignores what the Spirit is attempting to produce in the church today.

The New Testament Intent

The focus in restoration is to search for the *intent* of the New Testament, not merely its practice. Those who believe they should simply practice what the New Testament community practiced must wrestle with the fact that five times Paul tells slaves to obey their masters, and five times he instructs Christians to kiss when they greet one another.[23] One time he tells women not to teach or have authority over men and in the same passage he also tells women not to braid their hair, wear gold, pearls or expensive clothes, repeating the admonition about apparel again later.[24] I don't know of any church that adheres to every one of those clear commands and practices of the first-century churches. All churches, even the most conservative ones, have made some distinctions between that which was a culturally-limited practice and that which was intended for all time. Determining which, if any, of those practices we are to keep means we must rely upon an understanding of biblical languages and cultures, the most scholarly principles of interpretation we can muster, and the liberating work of the Holy Spirit in revealing written revelation to us. Transcending two thousand years of time and radically dif-

---

[23]Eph 6:5; Col 3:22; 1 Tim 6:1; 1 Pet 2:18; Titus 2:9; Rom 16:16; 1 Cor 16:20; 2 Cor 13:12; 1 Thess 5:26; 1 Pet 5:14.
[24]1 Tim 2:9; 2 Pet 3:3.

ferent cultural settings requires our most diligent work and the constant flow of the Spirit of Jesus.

Rather than merely duplicating first-century practices, renewal is a much more sophisticated, elegant, and profound process. While utilizing good scholarship and wise theological reflection, it is finally dependent on the Holy Spirit to reveal the intent behind the words and practices of the Bible and then to bridge the gap between the biblical cultures and those of today. Today's church often gets stuck somewhere in between its origins and contemporary society. Catholics get stuck in medieval centuries, mainline denominations forget their origins, charismatics can't break away from their sometimes fanatical beginnings, and evangelicals are always enamored with whatever was happening forty years ago!

The Bible for Today

All readers of the Bible understand it in terms of what is, and is not, intended as a practice for us today. John records in his gospel that Jesus fed the multitudes with five barley loaves and two fish, stating there were "about five thousand in all" (John 6:10). Yet in terms of our statistical practices today this is not an accurate account by any stretch of the imagination. The other three gospels remind us the number five thousand included only the men present, not the women and children (Matt 14:21; Mark 6:44; Luke 9:14). What a parable of both then and now—women were not counted! The practice of not including women (or children) in the estimate of crowd size reflects the blatant patriarchy of the day. I know of no denomination today that would settle for that biblical practice, even though they find other ways to not count women.

I mentioned earlier that five times in the New Testament we are given a clear, simple command which hardly anyone obeys. This repeated command is "Greet one another with a holy kiss" (Rom 16:16; 1 Cor 16:20; 2 Cor 13:12; 1 Thess 5:26; 1 Pet 5:14). Most would say that the intent of this command is that we are to warmly greet one another, but the form of that greeting is culturally shaped and our situation today is different from the ancient Middle East. Greeting with a holy kiss may not say the same thing today that it did then. The Living Bible translates this command as "Greet each other warmly in the Lord." J. B. Phillips gives it a proper British twist with, "a handshake all round, please!"

If we can recognize cultural influence in the early church practice of addressing one another with a holy kiss, why should we not also recognize cultural influence in the New Testament practice of addressing God with almost exclusively masculine imagery? One may be more important than the other, but is not the principle exactly the same? The challenge is to separate the message of God from the culturally determined linguistic systems and practices that have come to us in the Bible. Divine revelation comes to us in human packaging. We must separate the gift from the wrapping in order to understand what the Bible teaches as God's Word for us. In other words, while we must first discern what the biblical practices are, we cannot settle for that as our interpretive stance. We must immediately move on to discern the intent behind any particular practice and then to discerning what that intent means for us today.

In discussing this subject then, the question is not about the biblical practice of using primarily male metaphors for God, because that is self-evident. The question is: Was it God's intent that we should continue to do so today?

I should . . . comment on the special linguistic problem in addressing God. . . . I am the first to admit that our language is simply limited here. Clearly, God incorporates and transcends our categories of sexuality—that is, God is not a male deity as opposed to a female deity.

— Richard Foster[25]

---

[25]Richard Foster, *Prayer: Finding the Heart's True Home* (San Francisco: HarperSanFrancisco, 1992) xi.

Bible Verses You Never Memorized

2

Lucy is doing pumpkin theology again, delightfully pushing it into new realms of relevancy. And many of us are like Linus—the feminine side of God never even occurred to us, did it? Yet there are many implicit and explicit references to this neglected image of God both in the Bible and throughout church history. Here are some of these overlooked passages, each followed by a prayer or citation modeled after the biblical words. Naming God is done best not merely by the intellectual pursuit of biblical study but in the glorious worship of God.

God As Person: Male and Female

Genesis 1:27 (also Gen 5:1–2) provides our foundational attitude about God and gender:

> So God created humankind in his image, in the image of God he created them; male and female he created them.

The "first great surprise of the Bible" is that God's image includes both male and female![1] One Hebrew scholar says "Clearly, 'male and female' correspond structurally to 'the image of God,' and this formal parallelism indicates a semantic correspondence."[2] This passage saves us from "idolatry [imaging God as human] by witnessing to the transcendent Creator who is neither male nor female nor a combination of the two. Only in the context of this Otherness can we truly perceive the image of God male *and* female."[3]

God is not sexual. Therefore God is not male, female, bisexual, or androgynous. Yet, something of what it means to be male and female, masculine and feminine, is connected with the image of God. Because we do not usually conceive of a person as being both male and female, we may balk at the idea that God, who is also "person," encompasses and transcends both. This profound statement in Genesis about God's image can keep us from too easily making God into our human image.

The use of male pronouns in the text and even more extensively in our translations often hinders us from understanding the theological truth here (I will address the pronoun problem later). However, if we look past the masculine pronouns, we are confronted from the very first page of Scripture with the intriguing truth that the image of God as person is a "double image."[4]

> *Wonderful God, Intriguing Designer of the Cosmos, liberate us to encounter your image in both male and female. Then may we be impelled to glimpse both male and female in your image.*

---

[1] Paul Jewett, *Man as Male and Female* (Grand Rapids: Baker, 1977) 33.

[2] Phyllis Trible, *God and the Rhetoric of Sexuality* (Philadelphia: Fortress, 1978) 17.

[3] Ibid., 201.

[4] Aida B. Spencer, *Beyond the Curse: Women Called to Ministry* (Peabody: Hendrickson, 1985) 21.

God as Our Ezer

The account of creation in Genesis 2 has been misused to put women in a secondary role. However, it contains not one hint of anything but mutuality and full partnership between men and women. Here in Gen 2:18 is a key verse whose words are familiar but whose true meaning is not.

> It is not good that the man should be alone; I will make him a helper as his partner.

This verse has been used to discount the feminine because we have traditionally understood the word "helper" to mean someone who assists the main person in their tasks. It seemed to say Adam was the "boss" and Eve was his secondary or "helper." But the word "helper," *ezer* in Hebrew, carries different connotations. *Ezer* is used twenty-one times in the Old Testament. Twice it refers to Eve, three times it speaks of crucial help provided by other persons in a time of great need, and sixteen times it refers to God helping human beings. Typical of such passages where *ezer* refers to God is Psalm 70:5: "But I am poor and needy; hasten to me, O God! You are my help (*ezer*) and my deliverer."

In all of these passages *ezer* is seen as a strong helper who serves from an equal or divine position, never an inferior one. The only two times the Bible names the beings who are the *ezer* are with God and Eve. We must radically change our image of Eve as Adam's *ezer* from subordinate to equal partner if we are to use the word in its biblical understanding.

The word following *ezer, neged,* has been variously translated with implied subordination such as "suitable" for the man (NIV) or "fit" for the man (RSV). The NRSV has "as his partner" and is an excellent translation, coming close to the Hebrew meaning of *neged* as "a power equal to."[5]

---

[5]David N. Freedman, "Woman, A Power Equal to Man," *Biblical Archaeology Review* (Jan./Feb. 1983) 56–58.

God is the *ezer* to humanity and Eve is *ezer* to Adam. When we read of God being our helper (*ezer*) we can immediately think of Eve whom God created to be *ezer* to Adam.

> *O God, our Help in ages past, as you created Eve*
> *to be a help, a human ezer to Adam, so may you*
> *be our divine ezer. In Jesus' name, fill our lives*
> *with your heavenly Help.*

Elohim: An Unusual Name for God

The first name the Bible uses in Genesis for God, *Elohim*, is plural. Used throughout the Old Testament, its plural form is reflected in the occasional use of plural verbs such as in Genesis 1:26. We don't translate the Hebrew word, *Elohim*, as "Gods" for theological reasons but it is still, without dispute, plural.

While the writer probably did not have in mind a trinitarian understanding of God, as Christians we immediately see an analogy. Western theology has emphasized the oneness of God, while Eastern theology has emphasized the threeness of God. Both are true and we must keep them in tension. But since we Western Christians have overdone the oneness of God to the exclusion of God's threeness, I sometimes say "God is a small group." This is entirely correct as long as we are careful to also say that God is one and we do not have three gods. It properly emphasizes our Christian understanding of Trinity, God in three persons, which is a central tenet of orthodox faith. Trinity shows us within the Divine Community such perfect distinction and separateness that God can be spoken of as Three, and yet with such harmony, togetherness, and unity that God is One. This trinitarian understanding of God as a community of equals relating in mutual love with no trace of hierarchy has exciting implications for relationships of mutual partnership between men and women in human community. God's very self is the basis and model for human community.

Also of interest for our subject is that this Hebrew word, *Elohim*, probably comes from the combining of the names of an ancient Semitic female god, *Eloah*, a male god, *El*, and a court of female and male gods, *Elohim*. This is then underscored in the Genesis account by humanity's being created in the image of God, male and female (Gen 1:27). The intermixing of masculine and feminine forms for God by the biblical writers indicates both a combining of sexual images in God, and a transcending of all sexuality.[6] I am reminded of what Jann Clanton says about our Christian imaging of God: "If God can include three persons, can't God include two genders?"[7]

Sometimes I put it this way: "If God is who he says they are, then she is worthy of our worship!" While I don't recommend this as our usual way of speaking about God, it is theologically accurate in every way, and confronts our tiny, tidy, and trifling categories for the Divine.

> *Elohim, expand my vision of you. Smash the*
> *limiting containers into which I attempt to cram*
> *you. Entice me into your cosmic mystery, O*
> *Christ, until I find myself lost in wonder, love,*
> *and praise.*

God as a Seamstress

> And the LORD God made garments of skins for the
> man and for his wife, and clothed them.

In Genesis 3:21 God is depicted as performing a customarily female task in Hebrew society, serving as a seamstress for clothing her new human creatures. Job also refers to God's weaving of clothes and other activities that culture considered maternal.

> Did you not pour me out like milk and curdle me
> like cheese? You clothed me with skin and flesh,

---

[6]Leonard Swidler, *Biblical Affirmations of Woman* (Philadelphia: Westminster Press, 1979) 35.

[7]Jann Aldredge Clanton, *In Whose Image?* (New York: Crossroad, 1990) 55.

and knit me together with bones and sinews. You
have granted me life and steadfast love, and your
care has preserved my spirit
(Job 10:10–12).

Matthew 6 and Luke 12 tell us not to worry about what we shall
wear, for if God clothes the grass of the field, how much more
will God clothe us? God is like our Holy Seamstress who does
the maternal task of "clothing" us.

> *First Weaver and Patient Mender of the Universe,*
> *clothe me in your truth and righteousness,*
> *through Jesus my Lord.*

The Womb of God

Rechem in Hebrew means "womb," and the plural form,
rachamin, extends this to "compassion," "love," and "mercy."
The verb form, *rehm*, means "to show mercy," and the adjec-
tive, *rachum*, means "merciful." These words, translated in the
Old Testament as compassion and mercy, carry strong allu-
sions of God's mothering, womb-like love. This association is
lost to most English readers, but when we see them in their
original settings and nuances, their meaning is brought out.

One does not need a Hebrew lexicon or exotic reference
books to see this connection. I made this linguistic point to a
dubious pastor friend who, unfamiliar with biblical languages,
suspected I was pulling some Hebrew trickery on him. He later
called me up and excitedly told me he had found just such a
connection in his aging Strong's Concordance.[8] The number
of passages speaking of God's womb-like mercy and compassion are too numerous to begin to list, but an example can be
seen in Jeremiah. The passage becomes much more sensitive to Hebrew poetry and word meanings when we recognize

---

[8]James Strong, *Exhaustive Concordance of the Bible* (New York:
Abingdon Press, 1958) Hebrew and Chaldee Dictionary section under
racham, 108.

the Hebrew words related to *rachem* (womb) and translate
them accordingly. In the last line God speaks of herself with
the doubly uterine words *racham, arachamennu,* "motherly-
womb-love.[9]

> Is Ephraim my dear son?
>   Is he the child I delight in?
> As often as I speak against him,
>   I still remember him.
> Therefore, my womb trembles for him;
>   I will surely have motherly-compassion
>   upon him,
> says the LORD (Jer 31:20).

In Isaiah we again see images of the divine womb as God
declares:

> Listen to me, O house of Jacob,
>   all the remnant of the house of Israel,
> who have been borne by me from your birth
>   (lit. "belly," *beten*),
>   carried from the womb (*racham*);
> even to your old age I am he,
>   even when you turn gray I will carry you.
> I have made, and I will bear;
>   I will carry and will save (Isa 46:3–4).

While I have been writing this chapter and immersing myself in these Scriptures that so graphically depict the feminine
dimension of God, the Holy Spirit has made me aware in a new
way of God's loving presence. I have felt myself surrounded by
God's very being. The transcendent picture of the divine womb
that Paul uses in Acts 17:24–28 grew in meaning for me as in a
few sentences Paul gives a panoramic sweep of God as creator
who "made the world and everything in it." God does not live in
shrines made by human hands (nor in mental ones made by
human minds), nor does God need anything. Rather, it is the
Holy One of Israel who gives life and breath to all things and
whose hands have guided history. Now the days of searching
in the dark to find God are past. In Christ we can connect in a

---

[9]Swidler, *Biblical Affirmations,* 31.

radically new way with the One that is "not far from each of us." In fact it is in God "we live and move and have our being," (Acts 17:28) quoting, according to Clement of Alexandria, the sixth century BC Greek poet Epimenides. Although Paul does not use the word "womb" here, there is no other time in our lives where we "live and move and have our being" *within* another person. Paul immediately paraphrases another Greek poet saying, "We are all his offspring," referring again to the image of God as a birthing parent, an image of God as mother which would not be at all unfamiliar to Greeks.[10] Paul understands the entire human race as living, moving, and existing within the cosmic womb of the One God.[11]

With Paul's extensive Jewish education he would have been familiar with the Hebrew word *rachum* and its image of the womb, as well as with other Old Testament passages such as Job 38:8. Here God answers Job with a womb image, a wondrous picture of creation bursting out from God's womb. This is followed in 38:28–29 with balanced male and female images. God fathers the rain and gives birth to the ice from her womb.

> Or who shut in the sea with doors
>   when it burst out from the womb?—
> when I made the clouds its garment
>   and thick darkness its swaddling band.
> Has the rain a father,
>   or who has begotten the drops of dew?
> From whose womb did the ice come forth,
>   and who has given birth to the hoarfrost
>   of heaven? (Job 38:8–9, 28–29).

> *O Holy Mother of all creation, we have missed*
> *you. We have ached for you. Weep for us. We long*
> *to live and move and have our being, enfolded in*
> *your womb of relentless compassion.*

---

[10]Leonard Swidler, "God, Father and Mother," *Bible Today* (Sept. 1984).

[11]Virginia Mollenkott, *The Divine Feminine* (New York: Crossroad, 1983) 16. I am indebted to this elegant book for my understanding of many of these passages.

God as a Woman in Labor and Giving Birth

One of the most powerful depictions of the Holy One is that of a woman in labor, crying out and gasping for breath. God's anguish at our failure to do justice and love mercy describes One who suffers along with all those who are oppressed.

> For a long time I have held my peace, I have kept still and restrained myself; now I will cry out like a woman in labor, I will gasp and pant (Isa 42:14).

I wonder, why has the image of God being in labor not found its way into our public worship, hymnody and personal prayer as Christians? In the church of my youth we often sang about Jesus as the "Lily of the Valley" and the "Rose of Sharon." These beautiful metaphors are used only once in Scripture (Song Sol 2:1) and are only allegorically attributed to Christ. But once, and allegorically, was enough for us to use them quite easily. The virgin birth is mentioned only twice in the Gospels and not at all in the rest of the New Testament, but that's enough. But it has not been enough when it comes to the feminine face of God, in spite of numerous references in the Scripture to God as a maternal figure and a woman in labor.

Here in Deuteronomy is another example of the birthing image :

> You were unmindful of the Rock that bore you; you forgot the God who gave you birth (Deut 32:18).

Evangelical Christians are very much at home with the image of a "new birth" coming from Jesus' extended conversation with Nicodemus:

> Jesus answered him, "Very truly I tell you, no one can see the kingdom of God without being born from above." Nicodemus said to him, "How can anyone be born after having grown old? Can one enter a second time into the mother's womb and be born?" Jesus answered, "Very truly, I tell you, no one can enter the kingdom of God without

being born of water and Spirit. What is born of the flesh is flesh, and what is born of the Spirit is spirit. Do not be astonished that I said to you, 'You must be born from above'"(John 3:3–7).

But have we grasped how graphically feminine this imagery is? Sheila Kitzinger vividly describes her own experience of the birth process in her collection of childbirth case studies:

> I have felt gathered up on waves as contraction has followed contraction with relentless power, and the birth of the baby has come as if on a tide which streamed through me. . . .
>
> The waves come faster, and I must go towards each with measured pace, keeping above them with my breathing. If I try to turn and run away, they will engulf me. . . . My body is like an island fretted by waves, like a widening bay filled by the swollen tide. . . . The widening bay turns warm, prickles with heat, as the tide urges toward it. My body has become a vessel from which life is poured.
>
> The child's head, like the hard bud in the middle of the peony, pushes forward . . . [then] slides through and slips out, sweet and smooth . . . face puckered in displeasure at the world. Shoulders slither out, arms flailing, finger fronds uncurling, rib cage working, tough little thighs and heels thudding, knees churning—my child's body glowing pink—and her mouth opens in a roar as, with a tearless cry, she greets life with innocent rage.[12]

Jesus uses this image of giving birth to describe the pain of the disciples as they were being "birthed" into the life of the New Community. He comforts them with the assurance that after the travail of their "birth," there will be great joy.

---

[12]Sheila Kitzinger, *Giving Birth: How It Really Feels* (New York: Noonday, 1989) 45–46, quoted in Tom Sine, *Wild Hope* (Dallas: Word, 1991) 229–30.

When a woman is in labor, she has pain, because
her hour has come. But when her child is born,
she no longer remembers the anguish because of
the joy of having brought a human being into the
world. So you have pain now; but I will see you
again, and your hearts will rejoice, and no one
will take your joy from you (John 16:21–22).

Then, according to John's Gospel, Jesus began to pray, only
minutes later, the words, "Father, the hour has come" (17:1)
using the same words he used to describe a woman ready to
give birth. It was the hour of birth pangs.[13]

Later, Paul uses this analogy when he pictures the whole
creation going through birth pains as salvation is yearning to
be born.

We know that the whole creation has been groaning in labor pains until now; and not only the
creation, but we ourselves, who have the first
fruits of the Spirit, groan inwardly while we wait
for adoption, the redemption of our bodies (Rom
8:22–23).

Paul does not hesitate to use birth images for himself and the
Christian life as he identifies with the nurturing motherhood
of God. "My little children, for whom I am again in the pain of
childbirth until Christ is formed in you" (Gal 4:19).

In the magnificent words of medieval Christian mystic and
writer, Meister Eckhart: "What does God do all day long? God
gives birth. From all eternity God lies on a maternity bed giving birth."[14]

Mother God, birth in me your holy will. Christ,
be born in me today. Spirit, send me to minister
to all creation as it longs to be born anew.

---

[13]Mollenkott, *Divine Feminine*, 17.
[14]Quoted in Matthew Fox, *Original Blessing* (Santa Fe: Bear and
Company, 1983) 220.

God as a Nursing Mother

> Can a woman forget her nursing child, or show
> no compassion for the child of her womb? Even
> these may forget, yet I will not forget you (Isa
> 49:15).

God's love is like a woman's love for her nursing child.
Even though sometimes human mothers may neglect their
children, God will never neglect her little ones. Motherlove
is the sustaining foundation of our earthly life and God's
motherlove is even more consistent and reliable.

This image also occurs in Numbers when God is angry
with the complaining Israelites and Moses complains to God:

> Why have you treated your servant so badly? Why
> have I not found favor in your sight, that you lay
> the burden of all this people on me? Did I con-
> ceive all this people? Did I give birth to them,
> that you should say to me, "Carry them in your
> bosom, as a nurse carries a sucking child." . . .
> Where am I to get meat to give to all this people?
> For they come weeping to me and say, "Give us
> meat to eat!" I am not able to carry all this
> people alone, for they are too heavy for me (Num
> 11:11–14).

Moses is saying that God is not taking care of the people. They
are like babies crying out for their mother. Since God was the
mother who conceived and gave birth to the children of Israel,
then God should be the one to carry and nurse them. God
evidently agrees with Moses and immediately moves to help
in the situation.

These passages, along with many others such as "O taste
and see that the LORD is good" (Ps 34:8), are filled with images
of God as a mother who conceives, is pregnant, gives birth,
hugs the baby to her breast, and nurses the infant.

Teachers throughout church history have written about
the maternal side of God.

This is our nourishment, the milk flowing from the Father by which alone we little ones are fed. . . . Therefore, we fly trustfully to the 'care-banishing breast' of God the Father; the breast that is the Word, who is the only one who can truly bestow on us the milk of love. Only those who nurse at the breast are blessed. . . . little ones who seek the Word, the craved-for-milk is given from the Father's breasts of love for man (Clement of Alexandria, *Christ the Educator*, writing around AD 190).[15]

For from those divine breasts where it seems God is always sustaining the soul there flow streams of milk bringing comfort to all the people . . . (Teresa of Avila).[16]

It is striking how we have repressed these feminine images, even though they are entirely in line with the words of 1 Peter: "Like newborn infants, long for the pure, spiritual milk, so that by it you may grow into salvation—if indeed you have tasted that the Lord is good" (1 Pet 2:2–3).

Holy God, Life-giving Mother, nurse us with your spiritual milk so we may grow up strong in Christ.

El Shaddai: A Strong Maternal Name for God

Throughout the Bible God is often described in terms of human anatomy. Genesis 2:7 speaks of God breathing into the nostrils of the man the breath of life. This naturally brings to mind a picture of God having a "divine" mouth and nostrils. This picture is continued in such passages as Deuteronomy 8:3 , "one does not live by bread alone, but by every word that comes from the mouth of the LORD," and Psalm 18:8, speaking

---

[15]Clement of Alexandria, *Christ the Educator* (trans. by Simon Wood; New York: Fathers of the Church, Inc., 1954) 41, 43, devoting much of chapter 6 to the metaphor of God as a suckling, mothering figure.

[16]Teresa of Avila, *The Interior Castle* (trans. K. Kavanaugh and O. Rodriguez; New York: Paulist, 1979) 179–80.

of God, says, "Smoke went up from his nostrils, and devouring fire from his mouth."

The biblical writers have no difficulty in speaking of the hand of God (Exod 9:3; Mark 16:19), the finger of God (Deut 9:10; Luke 11:20), the arm of God (Exod 15:16; Isa 52:10), the bowels of God (Jer 31:20, KJV), the feet of God (Ps 18:9), the eyes of God (Ps 11:4), and the face of God (Gen 32:30; Ps 27:8-9).

These physical references to the "divine anatomy" are of course not meant in a literal sense, since all words and names for God are only word pictures reaching out to us in a frail attempt to give a glimpse of who and what God is like. But they do communicate something to our finite minds about a God who is beyond our understanding.

In a similar way, speaking of God as having a womb, giving birth, and nursing may bring to mind very physical human images of God, even a mental picture of God with "breasts." Therefore it should not be surprising that the idea of "divine breasts" may be suggested by the name *El Shaddai* for God. Before I elaborate on the evidence for this, I must make another comment to help with the reaction some of my readers may have to this image.

The idea of God having "breasts" may produce shock and distaste. While it may at first seem to be a reaction against an excessive anthropomorphizing of God (imaging God as human), I wonder if it is not more revealing of our prejudice against the female body in contrast to the male body. The images which come to our mind of God's mouth, nostrils, finger, hand, arm, feet, and bowels are very likely images of male anatomy although not directly specified in the Bible as such. Why should we not see a female nostril unless we assume God must always be imaged as male?

Michelangelo had no difficulty in conceiving of a very male God as he painted God reaching out his finger to touch the finger of Adam on the Sistine Chapel ceiling. The nude Adam is graphically pictured as a young man, and the clothed figure of God is just as clearly an older man. Those who disagree with the theme of this book by saying "You're trying to castrate God" evidently have no difficulty in metaphorically thinking of God having male sexual organs. I wonder if the image of God with breasts may seem unacceptable to some more because of our association of female sexual characteristics with evil, inferiority, or sexual seductiveness than because of biblical objections. (I will elaborate more on this idea in Chapter Seven.)

The Hebrews may not have had this degree of aversion to the female body or to the association of the name of God with a female image, as we can see in the use of *El Shaddai*, which is used as a name for God six times in Genesis (17:1; 28:3; 35:11; 43:14; 48:3; 49:25).

The archaeologist Albright argued that the original meaning of the name El Shaddai was derived from a word, *shadu*, meaning breast, which then came to mean mountain. From there it became common to translate it as "Almighty God." But some scholars believe its possibly more authentic meaning of "God with breasts" in Genesis can be seen most clearly in how it is used each of the six times there.[17] Five of these times it is connected to a fertility blessing such as "May God Almighty (*El Shaddai*) bless you and make you fruitful and numerous" (Gen 28:3), or "I am God Almighty (*El Shaddai*): be fruitful and multiply" (Gen 35:11). The sixth time it is connected to continuation of Rachel's line and also the word mercy with its connections to "womb." In the last of these passages in Genesis we see a striking intermingling of womb, breasts, fertility, and the name *Shaddai*.

> By the Almighty *Shaddai* who will bless you with blessings of heaven above, blessings of the deep that lies beneath, blessings of the breasts [*shadayim*] and of the womb [*racham*] (Gen 49:25).

My male experience is so limited in fathoming some of the Bible's feminine portrayals of God that I could not form a sat-

---

[17]David Biale, "The God with Breasts: El Shaddai in the Bible," *History of Religions* 21 (Feb. 1982). See also R. M. Gross, "Steps towards Feminine Imaging of Deity in Jewish Theology," in *On Being a Jewish Feminist: A Reader*, ed. Susannah Heschel (New York: Schocken Books, 1983) 245.

isfying prayer for this image. So I asked Sally Burgess, one of the co-pastors at Broadway Baptist, for help, and she offered this prayer:

> *O God who is El Shaddai, enter the wastelands*
> *of our lives. Make your living waters flow in the*
> *desolate, dry places and sow your seed in our*
> *barren landscapes that the fruit of your Spirit*
> *may be born in us and your blessings multiplied*
> *in all the earth.*

God as a Mother with Her Weaned Child

Eventually, the nursing child of God moves on to being weaned, moving from milk to meat, but still dependent on God as in Psalm 131:

> O LORD, my heart is not lifted up, my eyes are
> not raised too high; I do not occupy myself with
> things too great and too marvelous for me. But I
> have calmed and quieted my soul, like a weaned
> child with its mother; *my soul within me is like a*
> *weaned child* (Ps 131:1–2; italics NRSV margin).

This passage demonstrates several truths. First, God not only allows us to grow up, God insists that we grow up. While in a certain important sense we are always dependent on God, we are not to remain dependent the way a baby is with its mother. There is a time for weaning and moving on to solid food.

Second, this is an important healing passage for those of us who continually take on too much. The infant stage of life is characterized by a certain kind of grandiosity. All of life revolves around the infant. This infant grandiosity can carry over into adulthood if we don't grow up. Our serving and ministry can be especially pretentious. My vision for ministry is always greater than my capacity for ministry, and when I am grandiose, I take on too much. I begin thinking that there are so many who do not know Jesus and so many who need to be healed and discipled into a fuller life. There is the need for mercy and justice in a world of darkness, and I, alone, am responsible for all of this. I keep going after my Boss's job! It is difficult for me to be aware of these needs and not want to immediately rush out and do something about them. When I occupy myself with "things too great" and take on too much, I read this passage and know that I must release all of my messianic attempts to the Messiah.

And third, I am reminded to be like a child, calmed and quieted, resting in the lap of God my Mother. The grandiosity of my infant-like rush to save the whole world is tempered. God allows me to grow up and try reaching out by venturing into the great world of ministry. As I run out into the world's misery I am overwhelmed by the need. Then I rush back to God's mothering lap and am hugged and comforted and nurtured. When I am filled up I venture forth again. Ministry occurs when my filled up soul meets the great need of the world.

My prayer is Psalm 131, paraphrased:

> *O protecting and nurturing God, do not let my heart attempt to lift a burden too heavy for me. Do not let my eyes take in more vision than I can handle as I'm growing up. I will not occupy myself with marvelous things which are beyond my capacity. As an over-eager child, after attempting to do more than you have asked, I will calm and quiet my soul like a child weaned from its mother's milk and rest in your mothering arms.*

God as a Comforting Mother

For thus says the LORD: . . . As a mother comforts her child, so I will comfort you (Isa 66:12–13).

The first time I used the words of this passage in public prayer, "God you are like a mother who comforts her child," someone rushed up to me and told me I should stick with the way the Bible talks about God. When I pulled a Bible from the pew in front of us and turned to this verse, he was dumbfounded. I empathized with him because I too had been raised in a Southern Baptist tradition which loudly proclaimed to all that we really took the Bible—all of it—"seriously." Yet the warm, nurturing, maternal image of God was suppressed. I had read through and studied the entire Bible several times as a teenager, and I continued even more intensively through seminary and as a pastor and teacher in my adult life. But until I was fifty years old I had no appreciation of the maternal images in these passages. Since I hadn't heard about the feminine image of God, I didn't recognize it even when I read it. My experience in the church had radically influenced my interpretation of the Bible.

While the prophet Hosea sees God as the husband of a faithless Israel, he also sees God as a parent who teaches a child to walk, picks it up in healing arms, lifts it up, and bends down to feed it. These are all tasks that a mother, not a father, performed in the Hebrew society of that day. Finally, agonizing over the prodigal child, God rejects fierce male anger in favor of warm and tender female compassion, rejecting any identification with the male. The term *ish*, meaning male, is used.

> When Israel was a child, I loved him, and out of Egypt I called my son. The more I called them, the more they went from me. . . . Yet it was I who taught Ephraim to walk, I took them up in my arms; but they did not know that I healed them. I led them with cords of human kindness, with bands of love. I was to them like those who lift infants to their cheeks. I bent down to them and fed them. . . . My compassion grows warm and tender. I will not execute my fierce anger; I will not again destroy Ephraim; for I am God and no mortal [*ish*], the Holy One in your midst, and I will not come in wrath (Hos 11:1–4, 8–9).

Jesus freely identified with a mother animal image, likening himself to a mother hen who gathers her chicks under her wings.[18]

---

[18]Robert Bly, a leader in the contemporary men's movement, recognizes the psychological healthiness of a "male mother." Bly sees King Arthur as a model of male mothering, and I see Jesus, who represents the best of masculine and feminine strengths, however a culture may define them.

Jerusalem, Jerusalem, the city that kills the prophets and stones those who are sent to it! How often
have I desired to gather your children together as
a hen gathers her brood under her wings, and you
were not willing (Luke 13:34).

In John's picture of the new heaven and the new earth
described in Revelation, we see God's maternal presence doing
something that almost every society understands as a mother's delight.

And God himself will be with them; he will wipe
every tear from their eyes (Rev 21:3–4).

Many of the saints down through the ages have recognized
the motherhood of God,[19] and they are being joined by an
increasing number of the saints today who sing the praises of
the God who is both Mother and Father. My prayer is in the
form of one of these songs of praise by Miriam Therese Winter:

Mother and God, to You we sing.
Wide is Your womb, warm is Your wing.
In You we live, move, and are fed
  sweet, flowing milk, life giving bread.
Mother and God, to You we bring
  all broken hearts, all broken wings.[20]

---

[19]Mollenkott, *Divine Feminine*, 9–10, lists some of them: St. John
Chrysostom (AD 347–407) refers to the motherhood of God in his *Hom-
ilies on the Gospel of Saint Matthew*. Others in orthodox Christian
tradition who have followed these biblical images of God as maternal
included Gregory of Nyssa (d. about 395), The Venerable Bede (c.
673–735), Peter Lombard (1110–1164), Thomas Aquinas (1225–1274),
St. Bonaventure (1221–1274), Gregory Palamas (d. 1359), Blessed An-
gela of Foligno (1248–1309), Catherine of Siena (1247–1380, also recently granted official title of Doctor of the Church), Bridget of Sweden
(c. 1302–1373), Margery Kempe (d. after 1415), Bernard of Clairvaux (d.
1153), Ailred of Rievaulx (d. 1167), Guerric of Igny (d. 1153), Isaac of
Stella (d. about 1169), Adaom of Perseigne (d. 1221), Helinand of
Froidmont (d. about 1235), William of St. Thierry (d. about 1148), and
Benedictine Anselm of Canterbury (d. 1109).

[20]Words and music by Sister Miriam Therese Winter. Copyright:
Medical Mission Sisters, 1987. Reproduced with permission of copyright owner.

God as a Fierce Mother Bear

One of the dangers of life in biblical times was to encounter a mother bear whose cubs had been taken from her or killed. Perhaps this was a common enough experience that it found its way into everyday graphic speech, as in 2 Samuel 17:8, where Hushai describes David and his fighting men, saying: "You know that your father and his men are warriors, and that they are enraged, like a bear robbed of her cubs in the field."

Similarly, Proverbs 17:12 offers this tidbit of wisdom: "Better to meet a she-bear robbed of its cubs than to confront a fool immersed in folly." Not bad advice for those of us called to do some confronting from time to time. I think I have met a bear more than once!

With this setting in mind, we turn our attention to an intense passage from Hosea which describes God as an enraged mother bear in relentless judgment of Israel.

> When I fed them, they were satisfied; they were satisfied and their heart was proud; therefore they forgot me. So I will become like a lion to them, like a leopard I will lurk beside the way. *I will fall upon them like a bear robbed of her cubs, and will tear open the covering of their heart*; there I will devour them like a lion, as a wild animal would mangle them (Hos 13:6–8, emphasis mine).

Why is God so angry? The Israelites had made idols for themselves, silver calves, which they were kissing and worshipping (Hos 13:2)! They had forgotten the God who fed and cared for them in the wilderness. God is a jealous God, and with the powerful, instinctive affection of a mother bear for her cubs, she pounces upon those who would rob her of her little ones. It gets a little confusing since those who are robbing her are also her "cubs," but we must allow for some poetic license.

God as an angry mother bear has not rated very high on the list of all-time most popular pictures of God. Few pastors would offer a benediction with the words, "Now may God attack you like an infuriated bear if you get out of line," although sometimes they sound like that when they're preaching. What is the truth that God has for us here?

Perhaps we need to get over cringing at angry feminists. Just as blacks have a reason to be angry at the injustice done to them, so do mothers and fathers at the idea of their daughters and sons growing up in a sexist society. This anger has a righteous place as we learn to take the traditional ideas of "feminine" as soft, gentle, nurturing, and passive, and add to them images of strength, power, challenge, and action. We can learn to be comfortable with divinely intended images of the feminine in both humanity and God, images that are strongly protective, demanding justice, filled with compelling energy, and actively devoted to truth and mercy. To paraphrase C. S. Lewis's picture of God as the lion Aslan, the feminine of God is "good but not always safe." Let's release our mothering and fathering to be both nurturing and ferocious, gentle and relentless, just like God's!

The words to the fourth verse of Miriam Therese Winter's hymn, *Hear God's Word*, reflect such an image:

> Fierce as a storm, terrible as thunder,
> varied the form and force of Her rage
> Hear God's Word prepared to prune and plunder,
> as She shapes a new and holy age.[21]

God as Both Mother and Father

In a hymn of praise Isaiah describes God:

> The LORD goes forth like a soldier, like a warrior
> he stirs up his fury; he cries out, he shouts aloud,
> he shows himself mighty against his foes. For a
> long time I have held my peace, I have kept still
> and restrained myself; now I will cry out like a
> woman in labor, I will gasp and pant (Isa 42:13–14).

---

[21]Words and music by Sister Miriam Therese Winter. Copyright: Medical Mission Sisters, 1987. Reproduced with permission of copyright owner.

And again:

> Look down from heaven and see, from your holy
> and glorious habitation. Where are your zeal and
> your might? The trembling of your womb and
> your womb-tenderness? They are withheld from
> me. For . . . you are our father (Isa 63:15–16, literal
> translation).

The NRSV's "yearning (*hamon*-trembling) of your heart (*meah*-womb) and your compassion (*racham*-womb-tenderness)," like the words of Jeremiah 31:20, may be translated from Hebrew as above. One scholar says of this passage, "This shift in parental language approaches a balance that recalls our basic metaphor, the image of God male and female."[22]

A wonderful balance of metaphors occurs in Moses' speech to Israel, where he says to them:

> You deserted the Rock, who fathered you;
> you forgot the God who gave you birth
> (Deut 32:18, NIV).

Notice the mixed models—three different ones. We have a rock that fathers, a God that mothers by giving birth and, by implication, a mother who is a rock and a father. God is a motherly, fatherly rock!

"Wait," someone says, "We should not confuse mother and father. They are two different kinds of roles, and blurring the distinction between the sexes promotes androgyny." Yes, that might be true if we were speaking only at a human level. However, we should have no difficulty in using both words for God because no single image for God is totally adequate.

We must remember that the metaphors of mother and father are not describing sexual characteristics. The shock and clash of the two different metaphors provide some great advantages in using them together. The combination reminds us that God is not limited to masculine or feminine imagery. It also reminds us that God is a personal being, but not a human being. Finally, it reminds us of the metaphorical nature of lan-

---

[22]Trible, *God and the Rhetoric of Sexuality*, 53.

guage and its limitations in referring to God so we do not idolize our symbols.

The apostle Paul, so familiar with these passages, uses a balanced parental image for himself and his ministry in his first letter to the Thessalonians. In describing his relationship with them Paul writes: "But we were gentle among you, like a nurse tenderly caring for her own children. . . . As you know, we dealt with each one of you like a father with his children, urging and encouraging you and pleading" (1 Thess 2:7,11–12).

Some of the earliest orthodox Christian references to mother-father God occur in the second-century writings of Clement of Alexandria. In *Christ the Educator*, Clement understands Mother as the aspect of God's nature that has empathy with humankind. Clement says, "The Father became of woman's nature" and "The Word (Christ) is everything to His little ones, both father and mother."[23]

In the early fifth century the Bishop of Ptolemais in Lyby, Synesius, said of God, "You are Father, You are Mother, You are male, and You are female."[24] Of course, God is not literally male and female any more than God is literally a rock when we say, "You are my rock."

Mechtild of Magdeburg, 1210-1280, a nun and teacher of the church said, "God is not only fatherly. God is also mother who lifts her loved child from the ground to her knee. The Trinity is like a mother's cloak wherein the child finds a home and lays its head on the maternal breast."[25]

Of special interest is Julian of Norwich (about 1342–1423), a saintly and influential Christian writer. There were two kinds of women who dedicated themselves full-time to the work of the church, the nun who lived in community and the "anchoress" like Julian who lived a life of enclosed solitude, committed to living out the rest of their lives within the confines of a small cell. The church in Britain next to the cell where she lived still stands. She was a contemporary of Chaucer, who is

---

[23]Clement of Alexandria, *Christ the Educator*, 68.
[24]Mollenkott, *Divine Feminine*, 9.
[25]Quoted in Fox, *Original Blessing*, 221.

well-known as the first great English poet and writer in Middle English. But not as well-known is that Julian was "the first English woman of letters" and probably the first and only woman to write and be published in Middle English.[26] Her insistence on calling God Mother was not new but part of a long tradition. However, her original contribution was the theological precision with which she applied this symbolism to the Trinitarian relationships. She wrote often of God as both Father and Mother using such phrases as:

- As truly as God is our Father, so is truly God our Mother.

- God almighty is our loving Father, and God all wisdom is our loving Mother.

- The Father is "our Mother, brother and saviour." God is "our Mother in nature, our Mother in grace, because he wanted altogether to become our Mother in all things."

- God "wants us to act as a meek child, saying: 'My kind Mother, my gracious Mother, my beloved Mother, have mercy on me.' "[27]

> *Strong Mother God, Warm Father God, thank you for being there.*

God as a Midwife

In Psalm 22 God is seen in the intimate Hebrew characteristically female role of midwife.

> Yet it was you who took me from the womb; you kept me safe on my mother's breast (Ps 22:9).

God's role with us as midwife is a picture of God gently enabling us to emerge into all we are created to be. Midwife is

---

[26]Sandra M. Gilbert and Susan Gubar, eds., *The Norton Anthology of Literature by Women* (New York: W. W. Norton, 1985) 15, and lecture on Julian by Sally Burgess, Kansas City, Mo., 1988.

[27] *Julian of Norwich: Showings* (trans. Edmund Colledge and James Walsh; New York: Paulist, 1978) 293, 297, 301.

also a good metaphor for our helping and healing ministry as Christians. We are midwives of change and healing, assisting in the divine processes of birthing that are already at work. We do not conceive or cause ministry, we only assist what God is already doing and bringing forth in others. Understanding this keeps us from taking on too much, while at the same time it reminds us that we have a vital role.

I have sung many hymns that speak of God acting like a shepherd or a king, but never one that spoke of God acting like a midwife. As I reflected on this, I thought, "But I really don't know any midwives." Then I realized I don't know any shepherds or kings either! It seems like we could at least spread the imagery around to include not only male activities but also female ones.

> *Almighty Mother God of constant watchfulness,*
> *you were there as I was pushed from the womb,*
> *catching me and making me safe. Now help all*
> *those dreams which the Spirit has conceived*
> *deep inside of me to be born and bring life into a*
> *needy world.*

God as Master and Mistress

The power of a gender-balanced metaphor is seen in a beautiful passage from the Psalms that depicts us as God's servants and God as a man or a woman in charge of our lives and upon whom we can depend.

> As the eyes of servants look to the hand of their master, as the eyes of a maid to the hand of her mistress, so our eyes look to the LORD our God (Ps 123:2).

I am aware of a number of sermons and songs that image God as our Master but not a single one that sees God as our Mistress. As I pointed out in the previous chapter, this is due in part to the fallenness of language which has resulted in the devaluing of the feminine over the masculine. As stated earlier, "master" carries great weight, but "mistress" has come to mean an illicit sexual partner.

The Psalms use many pictures of God such as guide, shepherd, shield, rock, tower, fortress, hiding place and avenger. We are comfortable with these, so why not with mistress? This same devaluing which has produced the disparity between master and mistress has also influenced the choice of words for our hymns, theological discourses, and sermons about God. We simply avoid feminine words like "mistress" because of the effects of sin on our vocabulary. Will we let Jesus save and redeem our language, too?

Jesus may have had Psalm 123 in mind when he compared God to the woman who lost a coin, searched for it, and rejoiced with her friends and neighbors when she found it (Luke 15:8–10). On either side of this story are the much more familiar stories of the lost sheep and the prodigal son. How many sermons I have heard on how God is a shepherd searching for his one lost sheep or a father welcoming his prodigal son home, but precious few sermons on how God is a woman searching for her lost coin!

If someone offered a prayer in your worship service to God as our Master and Mistress, quoting the words of Psalm 123:2, but not identifying the source, how would it be received? I wonder if it would be like the town council which was given a resolution on freedom of speech that used the exact words of the First Amendment to the Constitution but without noting the source. After much debate, it failed to be approved because it would have "allowed too many bad things to go on." People did not recognize one of the key principles of our founding documents!

Is this a similar case? Even though a prayer might use the very words and images of Psalm 123, it might be viewed as subversively feminist or too radical. How far we have drifted from *our* founding documents!

> *Dear God, I joyfully receive you as the Master*
> *and the Mistress of my life. Direct my thoughts,*
> *words and actions. Teach me to depend upon*
> *you for all that I need.*

*In God there is a Father—"like as a Father pitieth His children";
and there is a Mother—"as one whom his mother comforteth."*
—G. Campbell Morgan[28]

God is a Father. More than that, God is a Mother.
—Pope John Paul I[29]

[28]Known as the "Prince of biblical expositors" in the early 1900s. G. Campbell Morgan, *The Gospel According to John* (Westwood, N.J.: Fleming Revell, n.d.) 47.

[29]From September 10, 1978 speech. Complete text may be found under the title "Praying for Peace" in Matthew O'Connell, ed., *The Pope Speaks* (Huntington, Ind.: Sunday Visitor, 23:4) 314.

FRANK & ERNEST reprinted by permission of NEA, Inc. ©

As human relationships are healed and matured, we become capable of true union with God who is both Mother and Father. It takes a lot of faith, waiting and darkness to speak such a full name for God. But what else would faith be?

—Richard Rohr, Franciscan
priest and founder of Center
for Action and Contemplation[1]

[1] Richard Rohr and Joseph Martos, *The Wild Man's Journey, Reflections on Male Spirituality* (Cincinnati: St. Anthony Messenger Press, 1992) 109.

But Jesus Called God Father, not Mother

3

When introduced to the idea of the feminine image of God, many Christians first respond with something like "But Jesus called God Father, not Mother. This seems to totally settle the question of what to call God without further discussion. Since we Christians must either take Jesus with the greatest seriousness or have little left about which to be Christian, any objection that lays claim to Jesus' practice and teaching must be thoroughly examined. I have heard this seemingly conclusive objection stated in different ways, all pointing to Jesus' practice and teaching:

- Jesus said we should call God Father and nothing else.

- If Father was good enough for Jesus, it's good enough for me.

- What makes you think you can improve on Jesus?

- Are you saying Jesus was wrong to leave out Mother?

- Jesus said Father, not Mother, because you can't have both.

- If Jesus had wanted us to call God something else he would have said so.

These reasons are based on four assumptions:

(1) By calling God Father, Jesus was implying we should not call God anything else.

(2) Calling God Father means you can't call God Mother.

(3) If Jesus had wanted us to call God Mother, he would have said so.

(4) We mean the same thing Jesus meant by Father.

Let's look at each of these and see how they hold up to the light of the Bible.

Assumption 1

By calling God Father, Jesus was implying we should not call God anything else.

The first time I heard someone tell me that I should only call God Father because that's what Jesus said to do, I couldn't believe the person meant it, and I challenged that belief. But he responded again, "If 'Father' was good enough for Jesus then it's good enough for me." So I decided to dig deeper into what Jesus meant about praying to "our Father in heaven," and especially what the people he said it to understood him to mean. I searched through the entire New Testament, noticing every time God was named and especially every time God was directly addressed in prayer. I made some intriguing discoveries.

How Did Jesus Address God?

When Jesus prayed, he not only called God Father, he didn't call God anything else! One possible exception might have been on the cross when Jesus cried out "My God, my God, why have you forsaken me?" Since these are the exact words of Psalm 22:1, we can perhaps understand them best not as

Jesus' own words but as Scripture coming to mind in a crucial time and serving as Jesus' prayer.

Calling God Father was central to Jesus' relationship with God, and we cannot understand Jesus without comprehending his unique naming of God as Father. One of my favorite seminary professors, Morris Ashcraft, was fond of saying, "God's work is done when men call God Father." Now, thirty years later, I would want to argue with him about his use of the word "men" and press him on what he meant by Father, but I agree with his point: we cannot grasp the significance of Jesus and his mission without coming to grips with what Jesus meant when he called God Father.

Jesus not only called God Father, but he taught us to do so. When his disciples asked him to teach them to pray, Jesus replied, "Pray then in this way: Our Father in heaven" (Matt 6:9).

Jesus referred to God as Father 170 times in the Gospels: 4 in Mark, 15 in Luke, 42 in Matthew, and 109 in John. He did this on three levels of intimacy: (1) "My Father" when he prayed personally and when he revealed his own identity to the disciples; (2) "Your Father" when he taught his disciples how to pray, summing up God's compassion, forgiveness, and care for them; and (3) "The Father" when defending his message against doubters and attackers.[2]

How Did Jesus' First Followers Address God?

I expected to find this strong argument for God as Father in the Gospels, but I was surprised with the rest of the New Testament. First I looked for any accounts of actual prayers offered by the early Christians, since here would be the strongest evidence for how the early believers understood Jesus' teaching on how to address God. I found eleven occasions where the actual words of a prayer or praise addressed to God were recorded. I have emphasized the term of address in each passage for ease of identification.

---

[2]Robert Hamerton-Kelly, *God the Father* (Philadelphia: Fortress Press, 1979) 81.

> Then they prayed and said, "*Lord*, you know everyone's heart" (Acts 1:24).

This is the first recorded prayer of the apostles after Jesus had ascended into heaven, leaving them on their own. They wanted to choose a replacement for Judas and asked for guidance, praying to Jesus.

> When they heard it, they raised their voices together to God and said, "*Sovereign Lord*, who made the heaven and the earth, the sea, and everything in them" (Acts 4:24).

This especially significant prayer is the only recorded corporate prayer of the early church in the New Testament.

> While they were stoning Stephen, he prayed, "*Lord Jesus*, receive my spirit." Then he knelt down and cried out in a loud voice, "*Lord*, do not hold this sin against them" (Acts 7:59–60).

This striking prayer to Jesus is particularly interesting because of its similarity to Jesus' prayer when he also was being killed. The major difference is that in Luke 23:34 Jesus addressed God as Father, and Stephen prayed to God as "Lord."[3]

> Then he heard a voice saying, "Get up, Peter; kill and eat." But Peter said, "By no means, *Lord*" (Acts 10:13–14).

> "Our *Lord*, come!" (*marana tha*) (1 Cor 16:22).

> "You are worthy, our *Lord and God*, to receive glory and honor and power" (Rev 4:11).

> Then the twenty-four elders who sit on their thrones before God fell on their faces and worshiped God, singing, "We give you thanks, *Lord God Almighty*" (Rev 11:16–17).

---

[3]Paul addresses Jesus as Lord in Acts 9:5, but we must consider that the term "Lord" here was the respectful address for someone with a big voice that could knock him off his feet. If he knew it was God he would not have asked.

And they sing the song of Moses, the servant of God, and the song of the Lamb: "Great and amazing are your deeds, *Lord God the Almighty!*" (Rev 15:3).

And I heard the angel of the waters say, "You are just, O *Holy One*" (Rev 16:5).

And I heard the altar respond, "Yes, O *Lord God, the Almighty*"(Rev 16:7).

Amen. Come, *Lord Jesus!* (Rev 22:20).

I was stunned! In all eleven prayers and the twelve namings, God was named four times as "Lord," three as "Lord God Almighty," twice as "Lord Jesus," once as "Lord and God," once as "Holy One," and once as "Sovereign Lord." And not at all as "Father."

It seemed these Christians closest to Jesus did not always follow Jesus' instructions to call God Father. To put it even more strongly, in terms of biblically recorded prayers, these earliest Christians *never* addressed God as Father. I was amazed by what I had discovered: *There are no accounts in the New Testament of anyone but Jesus addressing God as Father!*

How Did the First Christians Talk about God?

Eager to discover more, I decided to look past the four Gospels to the rest of the New Testament for even more clues about how God was named in connection with prayer and worship. The prophets and teachers in Antioch were reported as "worshiping the Lord and fasting" (Acts 13:2). In another account, "about midnight Paul and Silas were praying and singing hymns to God" (Acts 16:25). During the storm at sea Paul took bread and gave "thanks to God in the presence of all" (Acts 27:35). I found eighteen passages with nineteen namings which talked about addressing God, although they are not actual prayers. The terms of address were: "God" eleven times, "Father" three times, "Lord" two times, "*Abba*" once, "God the Father of our Lord Jesus Christ" once, and "God through Jesus

Christ" once. The name "Father" did a little better here with five out of nineteen times.

I wondered how the overall pattern looked for the New Testament writers, so I explored how often God was referred to (not just addressed in prayer) in the New Testament, outside of the four Gospels. I was amazed again as I found that deity is most referred to as God (1055 times), next as Lord, including references to Jesus (476 times), and then, a distant third, as Father (78 times).[4] The New Testament writers did not even prefer Father as their most used term in talking about God. Indeed, besides never addressing God as Father, they named God as Father only about one time out of every twenty times God is named.

How Do We Address God Today?

Christians down through the ages have addressed God with a variety of names, following the biblical model that no one name for God can suffice and a variety of symbols is necessary.

Some of these names, such as Eternal Healer, Holy Friend, Light Invisible, and Blessed Trinity, are not even found in the Bible. Since these are not names of address used of God in the Bible, we must wonder why it is acceptable to call God some nonbiblical names but not others?

However, in many evangelical and charismatic churches today God is constantly addressed and spoken about as Father. Furthermore, I often get the impression in some of these groups that God is addressed in prayer *only* as Father. Public prayers begin with "Heavenly Father," and thereafter are filled with Father thrown into every gap between sentences like an irritating "and uh" while the speaker is trying to think of what to say next. While monitoring over two dozen televised, evangelical, mostly Baptist church services, I found that

---

[4]The word Father is only found three times in all of Acts, twice when Jesus refers to God (1:4 and 1:7) and once by Peter in his address to the crowd after the coming of the Spirit where he says that Jesus had "received from the Father the promise of the Holy Spirit" (2:33).

every prayer but one began with Father! Over a period of a year I listened carefully to the spoken prayers in a number of small group meetings in several churches and observed the vast majority of the prayers were addressed to Father.

Unlike the Christians of the New Testament and down through history, some today evidently believe they must always or primarily use the word Father in order to be faithful to Jesus. What may we conclude from our study of New Testament prayers?

Our conclusions must be very carefully made because we do not want to imply that we may not or should not address God as Father. Calling God Father as Jesus understood the word father is an important part of our Christian foundation, history, and contemporary practice. However, we must take seriously the biblical account of the early church's understanding of Jesus' teaching about calling God Father. These first Christians, including Paul and the other writers of the New Testament, as well as most Christians down through history until recent times, clearly have not understand Jesus to have said, "Don't call God anything else but Father." Why not?

Jesus used a name that was meaningful for him and strikingly relevant for the cultural situation. He invited us to use that name also. But nowhere did Jesus indicate that it would not be acceptable to address God in other ways, and so the Bible uses other names for God, both before and after Jesus. We Christians today, like those in the New Testament, should be free to address God in more ways than just Father, especially if we want to avoid endowing God with a male body, a beard, and other human male characteristics, or even more probably, culturally defined masculine characteristics. We may safely conclude that if we are to be faithful to the New Testament we must not turn Jesus' practice and teaching into the false assumption that we should address God only or even primarily as Father.

Let me press past this last point in order to state my conclusion even more strongly. We should follow Jesus' example more, not less, when it comes to naming God. To follow Jesus by duplicating only his practice may not be to follow Jesus in what he was actually teaching at the most profound level. His example was to challenge the conventional image of God by naming God in a more meaningful and startling way in the contemporary culture, bringing him into conflict with the religious ideas of his day. Calling God Father did just that in Jesus' day—and calling God Father *and* Mother does it today.

Assumption 2

Calling God Father means you can't call God Mother.

Some seem to believe that Jesus had a hidden agenda when he said to call God Father. They believe he was implicitly saying that while you may call God other names besides Father, you certainly can't call God Mother. Is this true? On the surface this is an argument from silence. Jesus never said anything about what *not* to call God. At a deeper level this argument indicates a lack of understanding of the language of simile, metaphor, and analogy.

As I pointed out in Chapter One, all analogical language is limited and says something true as well as something false. Gender language for God *can* become confused with human sexual images. One person graphically raised the issue of language and our frail attempts to talk about God when he said to me, "Smith, you keep wanting to call God both Mother and Father. You must think God is a hermaphrodite!"

But God can most certainly be like a mother and like a father without having to think in sexual terms as we would with human beings. We don't seem to have this problem with mixing our metaphors when we call God both Rock of Ages and Holy One. We know God is personal even when we call God our Rock. We understand that everything about God cannot be contained in any one word picture, easily making this distinction because Rock and Holy One are not as "loaded" as are gender terms such as Mother. We do not have centuries of prejudice and power issues wrapped around the word Rock as we do for Mother.

The qualities of both a mother and a father coexist in perfect balance and harmony in God. Until we grasp this, the same balance and harmony will continue to elude us in humankind because sexism destroys the visibility of both the divine and the human feminine.

Assumption 3

If Jesus had wanted us to call God Mother,
he would have said so.

This assumption is based on the belief that Jesus and the New Testament writers said everything God wants us to know about everything for every situation in every culture for all time.

Jesus did *do* it all. He fully accomplished his work on the cross by giving his life for us and opening the path for the restoration of our lost relationship with God. But while Jesus did it all, he didn't *say* it all. He not only didn't tell us all we would eventually need to know, he didn't even tell us all the things he wanted to say. We know this because he told us precisely that: "I still have many things to say to you, but you cannot bear them now. When the Spirit of truth comes, he will guide you into all the truth" (John 16:12–13).

Why didn't Jesus look ahead, see we would be arguing about calling God Mother in the twentieth century, and tell us what to do? There are two reasons that the New Testament did not resolve all the implications of the Gospel or even apply them fully to their situation in the first century.

God Works Progressively in History

God usually does things in gradual stages, both in the Scriptures and in our lives. As someone said, "Time is God's way of everything not happening at once." The Old Testament witnesses to progressive revelation, as God is seen patiently working with people in order to bring them to the next stage. Jesus didn't come until the "fullness of time" (Gal 4:4). The word became flesh and God came to dwell bodily and uniquely in the person Jesus (Col 2:9).

The Old Testament sacrificial system and elaborate ceremonial laws were planned, chosen, and communicated by God. They were divinely intended and revealed. But they were also eventually discarded as inadequate by the prophets, and then by Jesus and Paul. Why didn't God bypass this imperfect and (looking back from a place of salvation by grace through faith) even dangerous stage? Why couldn't we move immediately to the real thing? I don't suppose we can know all the reasons, but clearly God's way of operating was progressive. It is important to note that Israel's sacrificial system was similar to other pagan cultures' but different in some respects. What seems apparent is that this kind of system was culturally understandable and prevalent in those centuries and, therefore, as imperfect as it was, it was able to communicate something true to God's people. But God did not intend for that system to remain unchanged, even though it was a divinely sanctioned system.

There is an easy way to show the error in the assumption that if Jesus had wanted us to call God Mother and Father, he would have said so. It is to apply that line of reasoning to some of the foundational doctrines which evangelicals and charismatics hold very dear.

- If Jesus had wanted us to pray to him, why didn't he say so instead of only telling us to pray to the Father?

- If Jesus had wanted us to believe in the Trinity, why didn't he say so explicitly, rather than implicitly?

- If Jesus had wanted us to believe he was God, why didn't he say so directly rather than indirectly? (Why didn't he say "I am God in person—worship me," instead of "The Father and I are one," as in John 10:30?)

- If Jesus had wanted us to abolish slavery, a practice prevalent in his day, why didn't he say so?

- If Jesus had wanted men to treat women as equals and partners, why didn't he say so?

- If Jesus had wanted us to know we were saved by grace through faith, why didn't he say so, instead of waiting for Paul to clear it up?

- If Jesus had wanted us to immerse, or dip, or sprinkle, why didn't he say so instead of leaving us with the bitter battles over baptism through the centuries?

- Why didn't God foresee the great divisions and fights over interpretation of Scripture, and say it all in such a way that it would have been unmistakably clear?

- Why didn't God see that Christians would divide over doctrines about the Lord's Supper and therefore give a definitive word so our symbol of unity would not cause so much division?

- For that matter, why did God wait so long to send Jesus?

All these questions presume God has done everything in the first fifty years of Christianity that needs to be done in terms of the outworking of the gospel in every situation—forever—and has recorded it all in the Bible. This makes the Bible a lifeless book and is not a realistic understanding of either how God works, or the intent of biblical revelation. The Spirit has been left with us to apply the gospel in many more situations than were present in the first century. The preceding questions may have been some of what Jesus was referring to when he said that he had more things to say but the disciples could not "bear them now" (John 16:12).

I believe another one of those "many things to say" areas is the challenge of expanding our male-only image of God. Its time has come in God's progressive working.

God Starts with Us Where We Are

Some things would be such a break with the past they would have made no sense in the culture of Jesus and Paul.

This can easily be seen with slavery. To call for moving a large portion of the population from slavery to freedom would have been impossible at that point and would have totally disrupted the progress of the gospel. Issues of patriarchy, intertwined in culture and language, were even more deeply embedded than slavery. Even so, Jesus moved in a startling way to confront that patriarchy, as Brian Wren says:

> In other words, Jesus knew and named God as Abba/Father in the context of a patriarchal society, but in such a way that the patriarchal order was itself called into question. Being faithful to him therefore, means naming and praising God in ways that point us toward the loving community he inaugurated, and call our patriarchal order into question. In Jesus' time, women had no hope of emancipation from male control, and to name God in female terms was not an option. It would have been an incomprehensible break with the past. 'Father' was close enough to past usage to be accepted, but Jesus' characterization of Abba was innovative enough to provoke new insight. At that moment in history, seeing God in terms suggestive of a male head of household who risks himself in costly acts of unexpected love was a clear way of signaling radical change from over-under relationships to a community of equals with only one Abba.

> Our moment in history is very different. Naming God as Father is still one important way of meeting God as our caring, loyal, and forgiving parent. Yet that name no longer has the power, *in our context,* to subvert patriarchal norms: indeed it is angrily invoked in defense of them. In Western society at least, women have made their first strides toward emancipation. For the first time in Christian history, women are gaining access to theology as a public forum for seeking to understand our faith, and many are ministering with full status in Christian churches. In our context, naming God in female terms is in line with

Jesus' intention. By demonstrating the equality of women and men, and the fitness of women to image the living God for us, it calls our own patriarchal society into question as nothing else can.[5]

Assumption 4

We mean the same thing Jesus meant by Father.

If we do not first ask what a biblical word meant during the time it was written, we will end up with a false conclusion every time. Restoration, returning to the Bible again and again to uncover the original meaning and intent, is crucial to the renewal of the church. I find it disturbing that some Christians make pious pronouncements about how we must call God only Father and never Mother without ever exploring the question, "What did the word 'father' mean in first-century Middle Eastern culture?" Perhaps it is especially tempting to bypass that question about a word so familiar and universal to all cultures, assuming it means the same thing in every culture.

The use of the word father as a metaphor for God is clearly not one of physical or sexual characteristics: God did not have sex with Mary and impregnate her. The metaphorical use of father especially requires us to uncover those qualities originally associated with fatherhood, its role, and its symbolic meaning. There are at least seven strategic ways in which the word father in Jesus' day meant something different from what it means in our culture today.

1. Father as Corporate Personality. The father was the *corporate personality* of the patriarchal family. In ancient Israel there was a distinctive mentality in which the group functioned as a single individual through any of its members which it thought of as representing it. This person is referred

---

[5]Brian Wren, *What Language Shall I Borrow?* (New York: Crossroad, 1990) 186–87.

to theologically as the "corporate personality."[6] We see Paul using this idea in 1 Corinthians 15:22 when he says "As in Adam all die, so also in Christ shall all be made alive" (RSV). When the Philippian jailer asked what he must do to be saved, the reply was "Believe on the Lord Jesus, and you will be saved, you and your household" (Acts 16:31). The assumption was that the jailer spoke for his entire family and when he was converted they would all be converted.

In ancient times the father represented all the family in a way that our individualistic society can hardly comprehend. He spoke and acted for them legally and socially, with wife, children, and servants being regarded as extensions of the father.

The father was the root summation of authority and value in a patriarchal society. This is why Paul could say, "For this reason I bow my knees before the Father, from whom every family in heaven and on earth takes its name" (Eph 3:14–15). The analogy of father as understood in first-century Middle Eastern culture gives us a wonderful picture of our dependence on God for authentic meaning and existence, just as the patriarchal family derived from its father.

But this corporate sense of the father of the household is lost in contemporary society, unless one lives life patterned after "Father Knows Best." Our heightened sense of individuality today precludes this meaning from being readily available in any one word, but father and mother together come closest to something of this sense for today's family.

2. Father as All-Powerful. The father was *all-powerful* in the family. In Jesus' day the men had most of the legal, social and religious rights. In the patriarchal ordering of society, the father was lord and owner of his wife (or wives) and his children.[7]

---

[6]H. Wheeler Robinson, *Corporate Personality in Ancient Israel* (Philadelphia: Fortress, 1980). Especially see Jean de Fraine, *Adam and the Family of Man* (Staten Island, N.Y.: Alba House, 1965).

[7]Jürgen Moltmann, "The Motherly Father: Is Trinitarian Patripassianism Replacing Theological Patriarchalism?" in *God as Father*, edited by Johannes-Baptist Metz and Edward Schillebeeckx (New York, Seabury, 1981) 52.

- Jewish women could not testify in court since they were socially considered liars and legally considered minors.[8]

- The one-time Pharisee Josephus said, "The woman, according to the Law, is in all things inferior to the man."[9]

- The right to divorce was exclusively the husband's.[10]

- If a man died, his property went to his sons, not to his wife.[11]

- In case of danger to the lives of both wife and husband, the husband must be saved first.[12]

- A wife was the husband's property and absolutely subordinate to him.[13]

- In case of a divorce, children remained with the father.[14]

- If you had a mother, but no father, you were legally considered an orphan.[15]

- Jewish women took no part in public life and it was preferable in general for them not to go out at all.[16]

- Usually only men were taught the Torah, not women.[17]

- Women were forbidden to teach.[18]

---

[8]M. *Shebu.* 4.1, Sipre Deut. 19.17, 190; b. *B.K.* 88a; *Ant.* 4.219; *Yalqut Shimeoni* 1.82, Vilna ed. 1898, 49a.

[9]Josephus, *Apion,* 2.201.

[10]Joachim Jeremias, *Jerusalem in the Time of Jesus* (Philadelphia: Fortress, 1969) 370.

[11]Joyce Hertzler, *The Social Thought of the Ancient Civilizations* (New York: Russell & Russell, 1961) 274.

[12]M. *Hor.* 3.7.

[13]Hertzler, *Social Thought,* 285.

[14]Jeremias, *Jerusalem in the Time of Jesus,* 371.

[15]*Encyclopaedia Judaica,* no ed. listed (Jerusalem: Keter, 1971) 1478.

[16]Jeremias, *Jerusalem in the Time of Jesus,* 359–60.

[17]Leonard Swidler, *Women in Judaism* (Metuchen, N.J.: Scarecrow, 1976) 93. Cf. however Susanna, whose parents taught her according to the law of Moses (Susanna 1:3).

[18]M. *Kidd.* 4.13.

In most industrialized countries today both mother and father, at least ideally, share these rights and powers.

3. Adoption. Of the many male prerogatives, *adoption* was particularly significant for Christian theology since adoption was entirely in the hands of fathers. Only men could adopt children; women could not.[19] One of the primary associations of God as Father in Paul's writings is that of adoption, "so that we might receive adoption as sons. And because you are sons, God has sent the Spirit of his Son into our hearts, crying, '*Abba!* Father!' So through God you are no longer a slave but a son, and if a son, then an heir" (Gal 4:5–7, RSV). He makes the same point again in Romans 8:14–15, RSV. Notice that both male and female are called "sons" because it was the son in the patriarchal society who had the place of honor and priority. Paul's point was not to slight daughters but to use the metaphor that communicated the greatest honor, which was "sons." Because sons and daughters are both valued now, the NRSV translates "sons" as "children."

The same is true for Paul's use of the word "Father." He did not intend to dismiss mothers, but in his day only fathers had the power of adoption, and it would have made no sense to talk about adoption and God the Mother. *"Father" was the only appropriate parent word in that culture for a God who adopts.*

Since adoption is a primary association in the New Testament use of the word father for God, today we must recognize that the word mother communicates the same meaning.

4. Transmission of Wisdom. Transmission of wisdom was a primary task of a father and his son. A son was taught the meaning of life and the secrets of the family trade by his father, as the knowledge of making a life and making a living were passed down from father to son, generation after generation. Jesus understood the human father-son relationship of his day in spiritual terms when he said, "I must be about my Father's business" (Luke 2:49, KJV).

---

[19]*International Standard Bible Encyclopedia*, vol. 1, Gen. Ed. Geoffrey Bromiley (Grand Rapids: Eerdmans, 1979) 54.

How far removed this is from our society since the Industrial Revolution, when the father's job began taking him away from the home, withdrawing him from much of childhood training. Today a son seldom learns his occupational skills from his father in our modern technical and diversified job market where education is primarily the task of the school. Today we don't think of the father as the one who transmits knowledge but rather as the one who has physically produced a son and may or may not have anything to do with raising him. We simply don't think in terms of passing on a trade or the wisdom for life when we use the word "father" today. Instead, the mother has often become a primary source of training for the family's children. Some of us are at work today in the men's movement to restore the *father and child* ties so both mother and father can share the important creation-mandated responsibility of raising the children.

5. *The Son's Responsibility to Obey.* The special responsibility of the son to his father was to *obey.* The father's absolute authority resulted in the demand for absolute obedience on the part of the children. Mother was to be obeyed but only as a representative of the father. Today both fathers and mothers teach their children to obey them and both directly represent authority. While the actual working out of this takes different forms according to various personalities and family systems, most people recognize that in today's culture healthy parenting means mother and father jointly carry through on setting limits and disciplining their children. Parental authority no longer resides solely with the father.

6. *Rights of a Father.* The father was *free* while the rest of his family was not free. He had full rights over his family, which saw themselves as his subjects, while they had no rights over him. The fathers, as men, were free to do as they wished, and the state, the Fatherland, was governed politically by these free men. The father was to rule strictly but benevolently from his position of power and freedom.

Women, on the other hand, were definitely not free in first-century Palestinian Judaism. Unmarried women were kept indoors and married women were limited in their public appearances, and even then always went out with head and face entirely covered except for one eye. It would be appropriate to speak of a quasi-harem existence for women of this time period.[20]

In our society, to the extent that patriarchy has truly crumbled, both mother and father are "free."

7. *Abba*. Finally, Jesus did not use the usual word for father that was sometimes applied to God. It was not a new idea to call God Father. The Old Testament does so about a dozen times as did others in Jesus' day. The Greeks called Zeus father. Jesus' use of a special name for God was startlingly different and may have been unique to him. In a culture where people were very sensitive to the distance between God and humanity, God was so holy and majestic that at various times in Jewish history certain names for God were not even to be pronounced. Into this context Jesus comes with remarkable authority, experience, and creativity, and calls God "*Abba*." This Aramaic word meant something like papa, daddy, or dear father in our language. It was an everyday, homey word, and totally counter-cultural in its use as a name for God.[21]

---

[20]Swidler, *Women in Judaism*, 121.

[21]Using the word "daddy" as an acceptable meaning for *abba* has been debated in scholarly circles. While Jeremias never actually comes out and says *abba* means "daddy," he implies it so strongly that it has become somewhat popular. Barr disagrees with him. However, what everyone seems to agree on is that *abba* was a word used both by the youngest child, one of the first words spoken by an infant, and by adult children for their fathers as a term of respect.

We probably don't have one word that adequately says all that *abba* meant in Jesus' day. Perhaps "dearest father" or "papa" may also say something of what it means. However, to say that *abba* does not mean *something* of what we mean by "daddy" is to ignore its use by the smallest child. No matter how much we might repeat it to them, little babies do not come into the world blurting out "dearest father" in our culture. Aided by our prompting, they start their linguistic journey with "mommy" and "daddy." It seems to me this is parallel to *imma* and *abba* in Jesus' day. So when I call God "Daddy" I am surely saying something of what *abba* means, although certainly not everything. I called my father "Daddy" until he died at age 76. This meaning of *abba*

Something of the feel of this word may be sensed when we realize that the first time Jesus used the word *abba* was not for God, but for his own daddy. It was probably one of the first words he spoke as a baby, since the first words of the children in Aramaic lands of Jesus' day were often *abba* and *imma*, daddy and mommy. The word *abba* implies the deepest trust of child for father.

"You're better than just a father.
You're a DADDY!"

Reprinted with special permission of King Features Syndicate ©

Abba was not only a term of endearment for father used by young children, it was also retained by adult children as a title of affection and respect. It therefore carried a breadth of relationship from young to old, dependent child to autonomous adult.

---

also seems quite congruent with Jesus' movement towards an astounding counter-cultural intimacy with God.

Therefore, to say *abba* does *not* mean "daddy" in any sense is to ignore its use by the smallest child. To say it *only* means "daddy" may perhaps be to ignore its use by adults as a term of respect.

See G. Kittel, *"abba," TDNT*, 1.6; G. Schrenk; *"patēr," TDNT*, 5.982–1014; Joachim Jeremias, *The Prayers of Jesus* (London: SCM, 1967) 56–65; Joachim Jeremias, *New Testament Theology* (New York: Scribner's, 1971) 64–67; Barr, "Abba Isn't Daddy," 28–47.

God is like a good daddy relating to his son as the people of Jesus' day understood the father and son relationship. It emphasizes a *personal, close, comforting, caring relationship* to God (Gal 3:23–4:7; Rom 8:12–30). It speaks of God's *approachability, protection, and forgiveness.* It underlines the ethical responsibility of the son as one who is to do the will of the father.

Abba is an important name for God precisely because it does not convey intimidating and fearful ideas of power and transcendence, but rather nearness and intimacy. An essential part of the good news is that Almighty God is accessible. God is not aloof, angry and sullen, but comes near to us in the closeness of a caring parent. Jesus' innovative use of the word abba focused the relationship on trust and intimate caring rather than dominating authority. It centered Jesus' mission on the reign of God not as Almighty Ruler King, but rather as a caring, merciful father. It must have shocked Jesus' contemporaries because it was initially a subversive term which broke down barriers of patriarchy. Jesus chose to use a word that weakened any sense of male domination or masculine distance.

One scholar has written an entire book on this one Aramaic word, *abba*, and he makes this important observation: "For Orientals, the word 'Father,' as applied to God, thus encompasses, from earliest times, something of what the word 'Mother' signifies among us."[22] Jesus was rooted in an Oriental culture, and *Abba* was his culture's most intimate and motherly word for father.

There is no sense today in which the word father includes mother, but rather it has taken precisely the opposite direction. We think of father in a highly individualized way, separate from mother, and mother as separate from father. We even consider it psychologically unhealthy for a mother or father to speak for one another. Parents who are emotionally entangled with the other do not function well, and arriving at a sense of emotional separateness is a valued psychological goal.

---

[22]Jeremias, *Prayers of Jesus,* 11.

We must ask if father is really the best translation of the word *abba* today since there are so many ways it is different, particularly in the characteristics which are important in its original intent in describing God. The word "parent" could technically be used in place of "father" and "mother," but it fails to communicate a sense of warmth and closeness, the very qualities that *abba* conveys. There is a discernable difference between "My parent hugged me," and "My daddy hugged me!" We cannot avoid male and female words because the sense of what is personal for humans only comes in these two forms.

In conclusion, Jesus saw God as like the best of what a father meant in his culture:

- Corporate representative of the family.

- All-powerful.

- One who adopts children into his family.

- Transmitter of wisdom to his children.

- One to be obeyed.

- One who is free.

- Personal, close, comforting, caring, approachable, protecting, and forgiving.

If by calling God Father, Jesus meant to teach us that God is male or masculine, then we must not call God Mother. But if Jesus' intent was to convey something of these seven qualities, then in our culture either father, or mother, or both, can serve a similar purpose.

In my mind this change in the meaning of the word father is one of the most compelling reasons to include Mother along with Father in some way in our praying, worshipping, and speaking about God. *The meaning of the word abba in Jesus' day is simply not available to us today in the one word father.* If we continue to use Father for God in the context of its meaning today, without qualification, we seriously distort its biblical intent.

What father used to mean 2000 years ago in a patriarchal culture, mother and father together now come closest to meaning in our more egalitarian society. Rather than attempting to remind ourselves and everyone listening of the seven points in this section each time we use the word Father for God, it seems much easier to me to simply speak of God as both father and mother.[23]

---

[23]The quote on the following page is taken from Donald G. Bloesch, *The Battle for the Trinity* (Ann Arbor: Servant Publications, 1985) 53–54.

The God of the Bible is . . . not only Lord but also Friend, not only Father and Brother but also Mother and Sister. . . . On occasion we may address God as "Holy Mother, Wisdom of God" or something similar, for such usage has a measure of support, not only in the Bible, but also in orthodox church tradition.

—Donald Bloesch

The War on Women 4

We must make no mistake: there is a war on women.

If country A decided to take over country B, usurping its freedom, power, and voice in decision making, we would call it war.

If nation A overrode nation B, treating the citizens of the invaded country as mere property and violating their social and economic freedom, we would call it the oppressive occupation by an invading army.

If the citizens of country A systematically abused, raped, and murdered the citizens of country B, we would call it not only war, but a brutal war, violating even the Geneva convention standards of warfare.

If country A rewrote all the history books so that references to country B and the accomplishments of its people were eliminated, we would consider it arrogant revisionism and a violation of the dignity of an entire nation, the extermination of a people's identity.

If country A methodically spread the idea that the people of country B were inferior to those of country A and should be treated as subordinates, we would call it bigotry and prejudice.

If the people of country A exploited the religious symbols and language of country B to make it clear that the God they all worshiped resembled the people in country A more than the people in country B, we would judge it to be wicked manipulation and an ultimate claim of superiority.

It would be unlikely that every citizen of nation A would be malicious in their treatment of the conquered nation B. Nevertheless, if they advocated the idea that people A should be in charge of people B, then they would be implicitly supporting the conditions that allow for the abuse, rape, and murder of people B. Some people in country A might even be against the war but say nothing. However, they too would share the responsibility for the war because they did not speak and act against it.

Whenever one country goes to war against another, the leaders of the invading country must make a case for their right to do so, marshalling all the moral reasons they can to justify the violence that must occur when the bodies, minds, and emotions of others are plundered. They utilize anything that looks like a just cause, but especially high moral grounds. Almost universally, the claim is made that God is on their side. Those in power have made this war, the one against women, appear reasonable, right, natural, and especially religious. All the major religions of the world are patriarchal,[1] justifying the war on women. Christians especially have baptized this war by claiming it was God's idea from the very beginning of creation.

The war on women is the longest running, most destructive, and most pervasive war on earth. It is the direct result of Satan's war on heaven and humankind. While the war on women has been waged for centuries all over the planet, only

---

[1]Mark Gerzon, *A Choice of Heroes* (Boston: Houghton Mifflin, 1992) 223.

recently has the existence of this war been seriously acknowl-
edged, named, and openly challenged. Marilyn French is one
of an increasing number of writers who expose this war with
pointed prose:

> As long as some men use physical force to subju-
> gate females, *all* men need not. The knowledge
> that some men do suffices to threaten all women.
> Beyond that, it is not necessary to beat up a
> woman to beat her down. A man can simply re-
> fuse to hire women in well-paid jobs, extract as
> much or more work from women than men but
> pay them less, or treat women disrespectfully at
> work or at home. He can fail to support a child
> he had engendered, demand the women he lives
> with wait on him like a servant. He can beat or kill
> the woman he claims to love, he can rape women,
> whether mate, acquaintance, or stranger; he can
> rape or sexually molest his daughters, nieces, step-
> children, or the children of a woman he claims to
> love. *The vast majority of men in the world do one
> or more of the above* (italics hers).[2]

Many Christians are so oblivious to the war on women that
they do not see how they participate in it—for many, every
time the church meets. We are so accustomed to our church
habits and have them so religiously justified we do not see
the male domination in our church leadership and religious
language.

Men Are Not the Cause of the War on Women

The feminist movement has seen women as being oppressed
and they are right. Woman experience pervasive powerlessness and life-long discounting. However, we have assumed
that if women didn't have the power, then men must have it.

---

[2]Marilyn French, *The War Against Women* (New York: Summit,
1992) 182.

But this is not true—we have seen that men also experience powerlessness and oppression in their own way.

Our problem in wrongly assigning blame is our definition of power. If we define power in terms of economics and job opportunity, then men have more power. But if we define power as the ability to control one's own life, then men experience powerlessness also. We become pawns of the same system that insists we be in charge.

When a woman is divorced, has two children, no alimony, no child support, and no job experience, that is her experience of powerlessness. When a man is in the hospital with a coronary bypass operation caused by the stress of working two jobs to support two children his former wife won't let him see, and he feels no other women will get involved with him because of those very circumstances—that is his experience of powerlessness. Both feel lonely and trapped. The same rigid stereotypes of masculinity and femininity make both men and women feel powerless. Men are told that they have the power, but what does that mean to an eighteen year old who is registering for the draft when his sister does not have to?

Men are told they need to risk their lives for women. In her confirmation hearings for Supreme Court Justice, Sandra Day O'Connor was asked about women in combat roles. Her reply was, "I would hate to see women coming home in body bags." The question I would like to ask Mrs. O'Connor is why does she see men as disposable. Why is it any more acceptable to see men coming home in bodybags than women? This is one of men's experiences of powerlessness.

I have found that most men do not see themselves as powerful dominating figures. On the contrary, we see ourselves as struggling to survive and if possible, grow, despite the mounting pressures of making a living and trying to figure out what it means to be a man in today's society.

The war on women is not a war of men against women. We naively assume that this war has been declared by and caused by men. That's the big lie! This war is being fought against both sexes, against all of us. Men are not the author of this war, Satan is. The cause of the war on women is Satan, who uses the fallen powers and principalities of this world to keep us in oppressive traditions and structures. Jesus has taught us to know that the enemy is always the Enemy!

Everyone loses in Satan's war on our sexuality, because the war on women is a war on humanity. If we assign stereotypical qualities of being in charge, assertiveness, reasoning, and initiation to men, and gentleness, patience, feelings, and receptivity to women, then both men and women have each lost half of their humanity. In this war, women have lost the feeling of power, and men have lost the power of feeling. Women have lost their confidence in the public sphere and men have lost it in the private family sphere. Men have won the illusion of control. Women have won the illusion of security. Although the focus of this chapter is the effect on women, the war on women oppresses all of us.

We have called humankind's longest war by various names: the battle of the sexes, male supremacy, the divine right of kings and men, the "natural order" of things. Perhaps most often it is called patriarchy.

Patriarchy Is the Name of the Deadly Game

According to the dictionary, patriarchy is: "a form of social organization in which the father is the head of the family, clan, or tribe . . . in which power is held by and transferred through males (and) the principles or philosophy upon which control by male authority is based."[3]

The biblical definition of patriarchy is succinctly stated in Genesis 3:16: "Your desire shall be for your husband, and he shall rule over you." Here was God's accurate description of women's unreciprocated desire for intimacy. This resulted in women's tendency to use relationships as an excuse to reject responsibility and abdicate the exercise of their own authority.

---

[3] *Random House Webster's College Dictionary* (New York: Random House, 1991).

It also described men's desire to dominate and tendency to abuse power, seeing themselves as solely in charge of everything, rejecting God's plan of partnership. This was not God's desire or *prescription* for what should happen, but rather a *description* of what would happen.

Patriarchy is the most widespread form of social organization among human beings all over the world. It is in no way unique to "Christian" cultures, but is instead the dominant form of social organization in almost all non-Christian cultures also. It is a cultural phenomenon, not a Christian one.

Patriarchy is fundamentally a system of ownership—the ownership by fathers of all other humans who are not fathers (children and women), property, language, productivity, and the means of decision-making which control the lives of everyone.

A vestige of blatant patriarchy is seen in the custom of "giving the bride away" in weddings. Twenty years ago I began refusing to ask during the wedding ceremony, "Who gives this woman in marriage?" with the expected answer to come from her father. This custom is the barefaced transfer of the father's property, the bride, into the ownership of her husband. If something traditional sounding needed to be said, I suggested something like, "Who gives their blessings to this marriage?" with the response coming from the parents of both couples.

Patriarchy is the direct result of the fall of humankind and the effect of the curse due to sin. Patriarchy is the overdependence of women upon men and the control of women by men. It always results in the valuing of masculine over feminine, however a culture defines those qualities.

A Biblical History of Patriarchy

The first two chapters of Genesis describe the full and equal partnership of man and woman. Both were put in charge of creation and were to mutually share the responsibil-

ities of bearing and raising children (Gen 1:26–28). There is
not one hint of male dominance.[4]

The creation of Adam before Eve does not denote his authority over her, and no such conclusions are even hinted at in
Genesis. If the order in which things were created was meant
to indicate authority, then the animals would be in charge of
Adam!

While God observed that it was not good for the man to be
alone, this does not mean that Adam was lonely and needed a
companion, or sexually frustrated and needed a lover. The
context of Eve's creation in Genesis 2:15–17 was work. The
man had work to do and God saw he needed a "helper" who
was to be the man's colleague and partner in the work of creation, and later on, in the work of redemption.

The word "helper," *ezer,* which is used to describe woman
in Genesis 2:18, is never used of a subordinate, and in the Old
Testament "helper" most often refers to God (1 Sam 7:12, Ps
121:1–2).

Both man and woman participated in the Fall. Adam and
Eve were both responsible (Gen 3:6; Rom 5:12–21; 1 Cor 15:21–
22). A direct result of the Fall was the curse of Adam ruling
over Eve. After the Fall, gender mutuality was disrupted and
woman became dependent on man and man became an authority over woman. Sin, not God, destroyed the partnership
between man and woman. Patriarchy is worshiping the curse.[5]

Some claim that the words "he shall rule over you" do not
describe the results of the Fall but God's prescription for the
way things should be. If this is true, then consistency demands
that the other results of the Fall stated in the same passage,
such as the hard work for the man in bringing forth crops (Gen

---

[4]I have relied heavily upon the statement *Men, Women, and Biblical Equality*, published by Christians for Biblical Equality, 7433 Bor-
man Ave. E., Inver Grove Heights, Minn. 55076. This significant
theological statement on the equality of men and women in leadership
in church and home has been widely circulated and has been signed
by over 200 well-known evangelical teachers, scholars, and leaders.
The complete, two-page statement and list of signers are available
from this address.

[5]Broadway Baptist Church member Richard Stanley's term.

3:17–19) and the pain of childbirth for woman (Gen 3:16), must also be considered God's will and we should make no efforts to reverse those effects lest we thwart God's intended plan. Men need to give up labor saving farm machinery or any efforts to make their work easier—a direction sure to meet resistance by the male half of the population. And women need to accept the pain of childbirth and not attempt to make it less painful. It was just such logic that was used to deny women anesthesia in labor when it was first discovered.

It was because of sin that culture came to value male over female, establishing patriarchy as the norm.[6] In the Hebrew culture, the masculine gender came to express value and honor given to an object. For instance, in 1 Samuel 6 two milk cows are attached to a cart carrying the ark of the covenant. As soon as the cows are put into holy service, the writer converts them to the masculine gender in Hebrew!

Scripture truthfully records the ravages of patriarchy in Old Testament "texts of terror,"[7] portraying the effects of the Fall in sexist violence against women (Gen 16:1–16; 21:19–21; 2 Sam 13:1–22; Job 31:7–11; Judg 11:29–40; 19:1–30). Even though they are not disapproved of in the text itself, these accounts do not mean God approves of these actions, but rather that God chooses to work within the framework of a sinful culture in such a way that eventually that culture is changed.

There are notable exceptions to the diminishing of women in the Old Testament, with some women in positions of prom-

---

[6]Elisabeth Badinter traces this process from the viewpoint of a secular historian in *The Unopposite Sex. The End of the Gender Battle* (New York: Harper, 1989). Drawing an interesting parallel to Genesis, she says that for the first 30,000 years of humankind there was shared power and a complementary relationship between the sexes. Moving from prehistoric times to the beginning of recorded history there is a shift to male ascendency. She indicates that our recent system of male domination began in classical Greece in fifth century BC and that the French revolution stripped patriarchy of its logic, so that it has been declining for the last two centuries and has just about collapsed in the last 20 years.

[7]Trible, *Texts of Terror.*

inence and leadership (e.g., Ruth, Esther, Miriam, Deborah, Huldah).

Jesus Christ came to redeem women, as well as men, and to restore the original partnership between the sexes. Through faith in Jesus Christ we all become children of God, joint heirs to salvation without reference to racial, social, or gender distinctives (John 1:12–13; Rom 8:14–17; 2 Cor 5:17).

After fulfilling the priestly role, Jesus did away with the special class of priests altogether and made everyone who entered the new community of God priests, men and women alike (1 Pet 2:5; Rev 1:6).

Jesus acted very differently from the other men of his patriarchal society (Mark 10:42–45; John 4:27; 13:5). Women were expected to be nurturing, kind, patient, healing, humble, self-sacrificing, self-giving, relationally oriented, sensitive, and non-violent. But these words also describe Jesus, and that was as radical then as it is today. A woman acting in these ways would have been doing what women already did in that day. Jesus' actions as a man and his treatment of women shattered the precepts of patriarchy (Luke 8:1–3; 13:34; 15:8).

The twelve men Jesus chose for his initial leadership team were given prominence in part because the patriarchal culture of the day would not have given women the freedom to teach and lead. The twelve men probably were also symbolic in some fashion of the twelve tribes of Israel. But the fact is that Jesus' innermost traveling company included women, some of whom provided the financial support for his mission (Luke 8:1–3).

Jesus taught us to "Call no one your father on earth, for you have one Father—the one in heaven" (Matt 23:9). He did this in the context of denouncing the patriarchal practices contained in the abusive religion of the scribes and Pharisees. "The new kinship of the discipleship of equals does not admit of 'fathers,' thereby rejecting the patriarchal power and esteem invested in them."[8] Jesus' use of the word father for God was a rejection of patriarchal authority in all of society, rather

---

[8] Elisabeth Schüssler Fiorenza, *In Memory of Her* (New York: Crossroad, 1988) 150.

than a reinforcement of it as some claim today. There is only one father for humankind—God.

At Pentecost the Spirit came on men and women alike and gave gifts to all without gender restrictions (Acts 2:1–21; 1 Cor 12:7, 11; 14:31). Women and men are called to develop and use their spiritual gifts, and both are to minister to the whole body of Christ (1 Pet 4:10–11; Acts 1:14; 21:9; Rom 16:1–7, 12–13, 15; Phil 4:2–3; Col 4:15).

Women, as well as men, are to teach, and lead and, despite opposition from the extreme patriarchal setting of the New Testament, some women began to emerge in these capacities: Priscilla taught Apollos (Acts 18:26), and Phoebe (Rom 16:1) was recognized as a "deacon" and leader.[9]

In Romans 16:7 Junia is commended as an outstanding "apostle." Junia was universally assumed to be a woman by all commentators up to the Middle Ages, when the name Junia was changed to the masculine form, Junias. James Dunn says, "The assumption that it [Junia] must be male is a striking indictment of male presumption regarding the character and structure of earliest Christianity. . . . We may firmly conclude, however, that one of the foundation apostles of Christianity was a woman and a wife."[10] John Chrysostom, a historian of the fourth century known for his misogyny, praised this woman apostle Junia by saying, "Oh, how great is the devotion of this woman, that she should be even counted worthy of the appellation of apostle!"[11] Origen, Jerome, and others also considered Junia to be a woman. It was Aegidius of Rome, in the thirteenth century, who decided she should be a man.[12]

---

[9] *prostatis pollōn*—often translated "helper of many" but the verb *proistēmi* occurs eight times and usually connotes governing or ruling. Reicke concludes that the verb has the primary sense of both "to lead" and "to care for" (*TDNT* 6.702).

[10] James D. G. Dunn, *Romans 9–16* (WBC; Dallas: Word, 1988) 894–95.

[11] John Chrysostom, *Homily on the Epistle of St. Paul the Apostle to the Romans XXXI*.

[12] Aegidius, *Opera Exegetica*, Opuscula I in *Journal of Biblical Equality* (July 1992) 44.

Other women of note are Philip's daughters (Acts 21:8–9), Tryphena and Tryphosa (Rom 16:12), Persis (Rom 16:12), and Euodia and Syntyche (Phil 4:2–3).

The few passages that appear to restrict women's roles must not be interpreted apart from the rest of Scripture. Rightly understood, they are Paul's *defense* of women in partnership with men, both in church and the home, and not a suppression of that mutuality (1 Cor 11:2–16; 14:33–35; 1 Tim 2:9–15, Eph 5:21–33). I will deal briefly with these passages in the following sections.

Husbands and wives are to be co-participants in a relationship of mutual submission and shared responsibility (1 Cor 7:3–5; 11:11–12; Eph 5:21). The husband's role as "head" is to be understood as a source of self-giving love and nurturing life, and not as "boss" or "authority over."[13]

Paul's stunning vision of the removal of sinful social barriers is stated in Gal 3:28: "There is neither Jew nor Greek, slave nor free, male nor female, for you are all one in Christ Jesus" (NIV) This was possibly meant to correct the Jewish daily prayer, "I thank God I am not a Gentile, an uneducated man, or a woman,"[14] which was the enshrinement of the three sinful systems of racism, classism, and sexism.

The liberation of women from traditionally subservient roles was soon reversed in early church history, and the church returned to sinful patriarchy where it has remained until recently.[15]

---

[13]Gordon Fee, *The First Epistle to the Corinthians* (NICNT; Grand Rapids: Eerdmans, 1987) 503; Berkeley and Alvera Mickelsen, "The 'Head' of the Epistles," *Christianity Today* (Feb. 20, 1981) 20–23; F. F. Bruce, *1 and 2 Corinthians* (Grand Rapids: Eerdmans, 1980) 103; Stephen Bedale, "The Meaning of *Kephalē* in the Pauline Epistles," *Journal of Theological Studies* (Oct. 1954) 2111–14; Gilbert Bilezikian, Stanley Gundry, and Roger Nicole in *Men, Women and Biblical Equality*.

[14]B. *Ber.* 136b.

[15]Evidence of the church's efforts to restrict this early women's liberation movement continues to surface, and reveals that women in leadership were more prevalent than previously thought. *The Wisconsin State Journal*, June 9, 1990, reported that Giorgio Otranto, professor at the University of Bari, in a paper to be published by Harvard Divinity School, cited a fifth-century papal letter ordering bishops to stop

Calling patriarchy God's will is like calling pornography God's will. The analogy between patriarchy and pornography is quite fitting because the two are very similar in their effects. Pornography objectifies persons by turning them into property to be owned, demeans the feminine, trivializes sexuality, and perpetuates violence toward women. This is also precisely what patriarchy does. Patriarchy treats women as objects, demeans and trivializes them, and provides a subtle theological framework for the right to abuse women. Calling patriarchy God's will is theological pornography![16]

Four New Testament Passages

Traditional interpretations of four New Testament passages legitimize patriarchal practices in many of today's charismatic and evangelical churches. Other interpretations of these passages are now making their way into standard conservative scholarly commentaries and offer a framework for understanding which is more consistent with the entire New Testament.[17] I will summarize some of these in the next four sections.

1 Corinthians 11:2–16

This passage deals with women's head coverings or hairstyles in the public worship setting, and there are an extra-

---

ordaining women as priests, and a ninth-century Italian bishop who stated that women shared the priestly ministry equally with men.

[16]I found this idea first in Mary Hunt's article "Theological Pornography" in *Christianity, Patriarchy, and Abuse* (ed. Joanne Carlson Brown and Carole R. Bohn; New York: Pilgrim, 1989) 89.

[17]For instance, J. I. Packer observed in *Women, Authority, and the Bible* (ed. A. Mickelsen; Downers Grove: InterVarsity, 1986) 298: "The burden of the proof regarding the exclusion of women from the office of teaching and holding authority in the congregation now lies on those who maintain the exclusion rather than on those who challenge it."

ordinary variety of interpretations concerning this practice. Some women were apparently disregarding the custom of praying and prophesying with their head covered by a veil or perhaps were having their traditionally long hair cut short. The fact that prostitutes typically shaved their heads had created a serious problem of miscommunication by women who wore short hair, not unlike when, in the 1960s, long hair for men became associated with drug use. Women were coming into new freedom in the new reign of God inaugurated by Christ, and conservative Jewish Christians had difficulty understanding its implications, just as some conservatives do today. To deny women freedom was to deny the gospel, but to pursue a rate of change that was unrealistic would throw the Christian community into disarray and obliterate its already dubious reputation with the outside community. Paul argues from custom, shame, and creation in order to *protect* the public ministry of women in prayer and prophecy. A complete interpretation of this passage is beyond the scope of this study, so I will only examine those parts which have been used most often to limit women's roles. Gordon Fee (in his commentary on 1 Corinthians) provides an excellent survey of the major views.[18]

> Christ is the head of every man, and the man is the head of the woman, and God is the head of Christ (11:3, NRSV footnoted reading of "the husband is the head of the wife").

There are two reasons this opening triad is not meant to imply some kind of hierarchy. First, the order is not: God is the head of Christ, Christ is the head of man, man is the head of woman. Rather, the humans are sandwiched in between the divine. Second, the word "head," when used metaphorically in the New Testament, means "source of life and nurture" and never "authority over."[19] The discussion is not about a chain of command but about derivation, and reads like this: Christ

---

[18]Fee, *1 Corinthians.*
[19]See note 13.

is the source of man, man is the source of woman, God is the source of Christ.

> . . . but woman is the glory of man. Indeed, man was not made from woman, but woman from man . . . (11:7–8, NRSV footnoted reading of "woman is the reflection of man").

Gordon Fee says: "Although at first blush these sentences sound as if they indicate her subordination to him, vv. 11–12 make clear both that Paul did not intend them to be so, and that he also realized that they could (incorrectly) be taken so. How does Eve coming from Adam make her his glory? Man by himself is not complete; he is alone, without a companion or helper suitable to him. The animals will not do: he needs one who is bone of his bone, one who is like him but different from him, one who is uniquely his own 'glory.' In fact, when the man in the OT narrative sees the woman he 'glories' in her by bursting into song. She is thus man's glory because she 'came from man' and was created 'for him.' She is not thereby subordinate to him, but necessary for him. She exists to his honor as the one who having come from man is the one companion suitable to him, so that he might be complete and that together they might form humanity."[20]

> A woman ought to have a symbol of authority on her head (11:10).

Most contemporary commentators, even those who advocate patriarchy, agree that this authority which the woman must show is her own authority and not the man's authority. This entire passage must be seen overall as a defense of women's ministry of prayer and prophecy and in no way a suppression of it. Paul wants enough custom to be observed that women's ministry may continue as a blessing rather than as a source of disruption.

> Nevertheless, in the Lord woman is not independent of man or man independent of woman. For

---

[20]Fee, *1 Corinthians*, 517.

just as woman came from man, so man comes
through woman (11:11–12).

In case any of his previous reasons may be construed to
mean that men are in charge of women—as his arguments
certainly have been throughout much of church history—Paul
sets the record straight. In an extraordinarily clear statement
he perfectly balances male and female with one another in the
restored partnership of Genesis 1–2. Then Paul further elabo-
rates on the idea of "head" from v. 3 as "source" in affirming
that, while Eve was made from Adam, from that time on every
man has come from a woman. Creation and nature model the
balanced and equal partnership of male and female. Paul reminds us that Adam's creation prior to Eve does not mean his
authority over Eve because, from then on, every man has come
from a woman.

1 Corinthians 14:33–35

(As in all the churches of the saints, women should
be silent in the churches. For they are not permitted to speak, but should be subordinate, as the
law also says. If there is anything they desire to
know, let them ask their husbands at home. For it
is shameful for a woman to speak in church. . . .)

Some scholars believe Paul is quoting what some at Cor-
inth were teaching, and he sternly rebukes them in vv. 36–38.
The Greek text and 1 Corinthians 7:1 and 14:26 suggest this
also. The NRSV places this entire passage in parentheses. Others
observe that the constant interruption by the newly liberated,
but uneducated, women asking questions made it difficult to
continue the services. Paul tells the women to catch up by
asking their questions at home.

An increasing number of well-known, conservative commentators, including Dale Moody, Gordon Fee, and F. F. Bruce,[21]

---

[21]Dale Moody, *SBC Today* (October 1989): Letters to Editor; Fee,
1 Corinthians, 708; and F. F. Bruce, "A Mind That Matters," *Christianity
Today* (April 7, 1989) 25.

have concluded that this is one of the few places in scripture where words which Paul did not originally write were added to an early manuscript. The passage is found in different places in early manuscripts, giving textual reason to doubt its authenticity. Also, the passage itself contradicts what Paul has just said in Chapter 11, where he is defending women's right to speak out in prayer and in the very powerful and highly regarded ministry of prophecy. If it is disgraceful for women to speak in church in this passage, how can doing so be considered a good thing three chapters earlier? What "law" says this? The Greek text, grammatical construction, and content of the passage itself all lead them to conclude that it is not authentic and therefore is not binding for Christians.

I believe the weight is on the side of the last interpretation. This is not simply a way to discard the passage, but rather it is based on the same textual principles that evangelicals have accepted in other disputed passages (Matt 6:13; Luke 11:2–4; John 5:3b–4, 7:53-8:11; Mark 16:9–20; 1 John 5:7). However one understands this passage, it must be consistent with the rest of the New Testament and interpreted in the light of the other clear passages which are not in doubt textually.

Ephesians 5:21–33

> Be subject to one another out of reverence for
> Christ (5:21).

This is the key sentence of a new section and states that submission is for everyone. But how does this look in the rigid hierarchical relationship of slavery and patriarchy of Paul's day?

> Wives, be subject to your husbands as you are to
> the Lord (5:22).

This verse is grammatically bound to the previous verse because verse 22 has no verb. The verb "be subject" is borrowed from verse 21, and therefore verse 22 is the beginning of the explanation of how all are to submit. The new thing is that the culturally-based legal and social submission, which was often in outward form only, is now to be done from a spiritual base. This is revolutionary subordination, moving from mere outward compliance to genuine inner attitude.

> For the husband is the head of the wife just as Christ is the head of the church, the body of which he is the Savior (5:23).

How can Paul phrase the submission of husbands to wives in a way that is not disruptive of the social order of the day? He again chooses the word "head," which in this case means "source of life and nurture," to describe the husband's relationship to his wife. This word has been incorrectly defined in some lexicons as meaning authority, and popularly understood as "boss over." Head in our day can mean boss or chief, but this is not its meaning here. Speaking of the headwaters of a river is a contemporary usage that fits with Paul's meaning. A number of scholars now define "head" as "source."[22] This fits more accurately with its use in other passages that call Jesus head of the church, meaning source of life, rather than authority (Col 1:18, 2:19; Eph 4:15). Jesus is, of course, also Lord of the church, but that is not the point in this passage. Therefore, the husband is a source of life and nurture to his wife, not her boss. This is further accentuated with reference to Christ as Savior rather than as Lord. If "authority over" was the point here, then Jesus as Lord would have been the better analogy.

> Husbands, love your wives, just as Christ loved the church and gave himself up for her (5:25).

Paul again chooses words that still allow the husband to fit into a hierarchical pattern but now infuse that pattern with Christ and his model of self-giving love. The result is a way for husbands to submit to their wives within the cultural context without unduly disrupting the established social patterns for that day. I do not know if these wordings were a conscious choice by Paul, or entirely the result of the Spirit's transcending Paul's natural understanding. However, this very com-

---

[22]See note 13.

mand plants the seeds for the eventual liberation from the pattern of patriarchy that placed men over women.

Backing away from this passage, one gets the impression that Paul has just taken a subtle, but revolutionary, position and reversed the role of wife with husband. The wife was socially considered to be the source of nurture, but Paul assigns that job to the husband and reinforces it with Jesus as the model of the nurturing source of the body of Christ!

The seeds of mutual love and submission are to flower one day into a church that promotes full and open partnership between husband and wife and where both of them love and submit to one another in mutual interdependence.

1 Timothy 2:11–15

Part of the context of 1 Timothy was a crisis created by false teaching in Ephesus. This accounts for the many references to false teachers.[23]

A woman should learn . . . (2:11, NIV).

Paul does not say that women *may* learn or should be *allowed* to learn, but rather this is a command that women *must* learn. Women were not taken seriously as religious students, not taught the Torah, and in general were uneducated. But now in Christ they have come to a new freedom and are "to learn" (*manthanō*) which particularly signifies study in a rabbinic school.

. . . in quietness and full submission (2:11, NIV).

To us this sounds like something you would say to a child: "Be quiet and listen." But in this case, the word "quietness" is the same word, *hesuchia*, used earlier for everyone (2:2), and means an ideal state of peaceful living. This silence does not have to do with speaking, but connotes respect and lack of disagreement. This is the way all rabbinic students were to

---

[23]Most material in this section adapted from Aida Spencer, *Beyond the Curse* (Peabody: Hendrickson, 1985) 71–95. This is an excellent resource.

learn, and Paul is treating the women in respectful and equal fashion.

I permit no woman to teach (2:12).

This is not a command as is the previous "should learn," but instead a present active indicative is used for the Greek word "allow." This form principally denotes continuous present action and may be more precisely translated, "I am not presently allowing." Because of the context and tense of the verb we know that this is a temporary condition imposed on women until they can be fully taught. The sentence is connected to v. 11 by an adversarial participle which indicates that these two instructions are contradictory. What one expects of those being taught is that some of them will eventually become teachers. Paul expects this also, but in this particular case he slows the process down by keeping the women from teaching until they themselves are fully taught.

. . . or to have authority over a man (2:12)

The word translated "have authority" (*authentein*) occurs only here in the New Testament. There are other words for authority that Paul uses elsewhere, but here he chose a very special word. In contemporary Greek it means "to commit a murder." Josephus used it to describe those who were the assassins and murderers of Galilean Jews. Therefore, in this context, a more accurate translation is "to domineer" or "wrongly take authority" over someone.

. . . she is to keep silent (2:12).

This is the same word (*hesuchia*) used before where it was translated "quietness." The two verbs "have authority over" and "keep silent" are antithetic parallel verbs, and therefore, this domination is exactly the opposite of living a quiet life. At no time should any teacher, or anyone for that matter, be domineering over anyone else.

For Adam was formed first, then Eve (2:13).

Now Paul uses an analogy to illustrate his previous instructions. There has been a great misunderstanding of

Paul's meaning here because we read our patriarchal assumptions back into the Genesis creation account. A careful examination of the first two chapters of Genesis shows that there is not one hint of the man being "in charge" in any way that the woman was not also "in charge." Both Adam and Eve are instructed to multiply and to subdue the earth. They are both told to rule over creation. In Genesis 2, the difference that Adam's being created first makes is that he is the one who receives the instructions about the garden directly from God. The basic issues in Genesis 2 are learning, teaching, and deception, which are the same issues Paul is dealing with in Ephesus. Eve had not received the teaching from God that Adam had and, presumably, picked up her information from Adam later on. She therefore enters into the temptation experience with some false beliefs. She believes that if she touches the fruit of the tree she will become like God and not die (Gen 3:3–5). Yet God had never forbidden touching the fruit, only eating it. And Eve did die. It was Eve's uneducated position that was dangerous as she then sought to teach Adam. Nowhere does Genesis indicate that the meaning of Adam's being created first is that he has authority over Eve.

This understanding is further sustained by use of the verb *plassō*, "to form, mold, shape," (presumably in spiritual education) and not *ktizō*, "created first." Paul's argument, then, is based on the "order of education," not the "order of creation."[24]

> ... and Adam was not deceived, but the woman
> was deceived and became a transgressor (2:14).

Adam was deceived shortly after Eve's deception and also became a sinner. In other places Paul places the blame for the Fall on Adam and not Eve (Rom 5:12–21; 1 Cor 15:21–22). Since the point here is the order in time, Paul stays with the idea that Eve was the first to be deceived because she was not correctly educated.

The analogy between Adam and Eve and the Ephesians is that the women of Ephesus were like Eve in the garden. These

---

[24]Walter Kaiser, Jr., "Shared Leadership," in *Christianity Today* (Oct. 3, 1986) 12–I.

women, like Eve, had not been taught correctly and therefore
were open to deception. They were then presuming to teach
the men in an authoritative way the false doctrine they had
learned. Adam did his own part in being deceived, and if we
were trying to make a case for who had the more difficult
situation it would surely be Eve. Eve had to contend with Satan's deceiving her, while Adam only had to contend with Eve's
deception.

Paul wants to save the Ephesians from a similar fate, even
the destruction of the church at Ephesus because of false
teaching coming from people who have not been adequately
taught themselves and are wrongly assuming the authority of
teachers.

> But women will be kept safe through childbirth
> (2:15, NIV, 1978 edition).

What does this seemingly disconnected reference to having babies safely have to do with Ephesus or the preceding line
of reasoning? Does this mean women who don't have children
will not be safe? Or that Christian women will never die during
labor? This passage only makes sense if we understand its vital
link to the previous illustration about Eve.

Paul is continuing the same argument, but some translations do not make this clear because of their choice of available meanings for the words. Paul is saying this ban on women
teachers is not final because, even at the same time Eve was
deceived and sinned, she was given the promise of redemption through her children, and in particular, through Jesus.
"And I will put enmity between. . .your offspring and hers; he
will crush your head . . . " (Gen 3:15, NIV).

This meaning is further emphasized in Greek by the use of
the singular article to modify "childbirth." It is literally "the
childbirth," and suggests the most significant birth to Christians, the Child born to Mary.

The word translated "kept safe" also means "to be made
whole." Eve sinned in the Fall and yet she herself was to be
liberated from the effect of that Fall through her childbearing
function. She was both the mother of the human race and also
the mother of the Savior who was going to redeem her. She

held within herself the means of the salvation of the world and herself.

This is reminiscent of Paul's argument in 1 Cor 11:12, where he points out that as woman originally came from man, now all men come from women and there is a balance between the sexes.

> . . . if they continue in faith, love and holiness with propriety (2:15, NIV).

This liberation from not teaching is not automatic. The women of Ephesus must be discipled and taught. They must learn to exercise good judgment based on correct education so, at some point, they will exhibit the qualities of sound teachers. Then they will be free from the temporary restriction of not teaching.[25]

This entire passage, when read in a traditional way, comes out sounding something like this:

> Women should be quiet and never teach or be in charge of anything that involves men. The reason for this is that man was created before woman and, therefore, he should be in charge. Since the woman was the one deceived, women are not smart enough to teach or be in charge. Women will make it safely through having babies if they act sensibly and properly.

In the light of the preceding line by line analysis, here is my paraphrase of 1 Tim 2:11–15:

> Women must first learn. And like everyone, they should learn from a peaceful place. Currently, I am not permitting your women to teach anyone, and certainly never to be domineering over men and they are never to be domineering in the exercise of authority. An illustration of your situation is found in Adam being formed and educated first, while Eve was formed later. Since Eve was

---

[25]Bruce, "A Mind That Matters," 25. Bruce says this passage is "merely a statement of practice at a particular time."

only partly educated, she was easily deceived and wrongly assumed to teach Adam. But women will be able to emerge from this restrictive condition because Eve is the mother of both the human race and of the Savior who redeems her. This will not happen automatically but requires women who are willing to grow in faith, love and holiness, and to learn good judgment.

Question

What is the primary argument
made by scholars who oppose your position?

The most reasonable and scholarly book I have found which presents another viewpoint is Donald Bloesch's *The Battle for the Trinity*.[26] He argues that "God is not a man, but, for the most part, he chooses to relate to us as masculine."[27]

He says the "controlling symbol" for the Christian understanding of God is the image of God as Father.[28] This means that God has chosen to relate to us primarily in masculine terms of authority, power, and initiative, rather than in feminine attributes of nurture and receptivity.

There are three problems with this approach. First, his case falls apart if masculine and feminine are no longer defined in these stereotypical ways. The old idea that women may not initiate, have power, and exercise authority and that men may not nurture and be receptive has crumbled. Defining masculine and feminine in such rigid terms does injustice to every man and every woman. In our worship service recently

---

[26]Bloesch, *Battle for the Trinity*. See also William Oddie, *What Will Happen to God?* (San Francisco: Ignatius, 1988) and Vernard Eller, *The Language of Canaan and the Grammar of Feminism* (Grand Rapids: Eerdmans, 1982).

[27]Bloesch, *Battle for the Trinity*, 33.

[28]Ibid., 34.

we sang "Rejoice Ye Pure In Heart" in which the second verse contains the line: "strong men and maidens fair." As I later reflected on that line, I wondered what a person would think at that point in the service if they were not a "strong man" but a ninety-five pound weakling? What if you weren't a "fair maiden" but a really homely one? How about making the line "puny men and maidens ugly"? Or why not strong maidens and men fair? Better yet, let's drop the caricatures and narrow definitions. Such stereotyping of men and women is not helpful to either those who fit the mold or those who do not.

Some traditionalists say we must have well-defined pictures of how men and women should look and act. I disagree. There are certainly psychological as well as physical differences between male and female, but authority, power, initiative, nurture, and receptivity are human qualities that should not be divided by sex. Jesus' choice to call God "*Abba*," the most motherly word for father in Eastern culture, can be a powerful argument to show that he was combatting just such cultural stereotypes.

Second, Bloesch does not wrestle with the effect of patriarchy on fallen language. How does a patriarchal culture talk about God, the Being of Supreme Worth? If masculine language is the way one speaks of ultimate worth, then that culture must primarily use masculine language to talk about God. In a patriarchal society where only male was honored, to speak about God as female in any direct way would not be possible. This idea that honor and importance equals male and masculine was so deeply embedded that God's feminine aspect could only be represented indirectly through occasional feminine imagery. The truth from God is authoritative over our lives, but the vehicle for the truth is not. Since language is fallen and all metaphors are limited, we must carefully distinguish between the true and the false in all our language for God.

Third, while some like Bloesch may think that God has chosen to relate to us primarily in terms of power, authority, and initiation rather than receptivity and nurture, this formulation does not take the Trinity seriously. If the Jewish Father is all there is to God, then God's "masculinity" may be set forever. However, if Jesus is fully God, then we have a God who submits, nurtures, and relates within the Godhead—one who exhibits what some may label feminine characteristics.

Bloesch allows for referring to God in female images as long as the masculine terms are the "controlling" ones,[29] fitting Bloesch's position on patriarchy.

I agree with Bloesch that Father is a controlling analogy, but the controlling content is around parenting qualities of care, protection, intimacy, acceptance, boundaries, limits, nurture, training, and reliability—qualities now hopefully and ideally shared by both mother and father.

Question

Isn't the Trinity ruled by God the Father, showing that patriarchy is grounded within God's very being?

Most theologians understand Jesus' subordination to the One he called Father to have been temporary and restricted to the incarnation.[30] The idea that Jesus was eternally and forever subordinate to the First Person of the Trinity was rejected as the heresy of subordinationism by the early church councils. The Son was "begotten of the Father," but this has nothing to do with some sort of hierarchy within the Trinity. Rather, the Eternal Christ shares fully in the authority of the Godhead and is not a Junior God. The Trinity doesn't have a boss. Rather, God contains within Godself all polarities of authentic masculine and feminine, no matter how they are culturally defined.

---

[29]Ibid., 53–54.

[30]See Benjamin Warfield, *Biblical and Theological Studies* (ed. Samuel Craig; Philadelphia: Presbyterian and Reformed Publishing Co., 1952) 55–59; also Royce Gruenler, *The Trinity in the Gospel of John* (Grand Rapids: Baker, 1986) xiii–xxi.

The Trinity models mutuality and partnership as the Father, Son, and Spirit share fully in the divine qualities of give and take, initiative and receptivity.[31]

Question

*Does it bother you that many Christians
who also reject patriarchy and accept God as both
Mother and Father often seem to hold other beliefs
with which evangelicals strongly disagree?*

Sometimes it does bother me. Perhaps this is because I want everyone to believe and behave just as I do. Other times it is because I don't like the hard work of separating the true from the false as I understand God's call for me. We tend to like package deals and are most comfortable with groups which believe and behave just as we do. But life is seldom that tidy.

Sometimes God wants to teach me something through a group with whom I mostly disagree. Because some feminists who call God Mother and Father may believe Jesus is not as essential or unique as I do doesn't mean I shouldn't call God Mother and Father. It just means I must work through those issues that I believe and don't believe about Jesus that may be different from what others believe.

Years ago I came to realize that if I were to oppose any particular belief or practice because it is held by a group with which I do not agree on other issues, I would end up not believing in anything! Just because other religions believe in prayer or one God, doesn't mean I cannot. I am not about to stop evangelizing just because some evangelists are coercive in their approach and give evangelism a bad name. Some Christian communicators on television have been manipulative and dishonest in asking for money to support their cause, but that doesn't mean I should stop asking for money for the

---

[31]See Gruenler, *The Trinity in the Gospel of John*, for a fuller exposition of this understanding.

cause of Christ, although I may be extra careful about how I do it.

Christians share parts of a common agenda with many other groups in the world. Other groups believe in such things as peacemaking, care for the hungry and homeless, justice, belief in heaven and hell, sexual morality, prayer, some of Jesus' teachings, monotheism, the sanctity of life, and environmental concerns. Some may reject patriarchy and call God Mother because they operate from an ideological position of political correctness. Others may call God Mother because they think one name is just as good as another for God. Some may call God Mother because they are advocates of some pagan religion. I reject patriarchy and call God Mother and Father because I want to be faithful to the meaning and the message of the Bible.

Guilt by association is intellectually dishonest, morally lazy, and an unreliable criterion for deciding the truth of an issue. Those who oppose some belief or practice merely because of its association with those with whom they disagree in other areas will almost certainly end up opposing something God is for.

Question

If we allow women to lead and call God Mother, won't we end up with a "feminine" church which is even less inviting to men?

This is an important concern. Having women in more leadership roles and recognizing the feminine face of God along with the masculine could move the church, which is already strongly feminine in style and population, to be more so.

In many churches there is already a gender gap. It is symbolized in Sunday morning services where only men are visible up front—male leadership and a masculine God—while in the back are the men who are ushering and taking care of things, and outside are the rest of the men smoking or waiting to pick up their wives. Filling the pews in between the male-dominated front and back are mostly women. The question being asked is: "If we take away the male-dominated front, will the men leave altogether?"

Church growth consultant Lyle Schaller recently declared that the trend which most concerns him is the "feminization" of the church in almost all denominations. With the general population of our country 53 percent female and 47 percent male, Sunday worshippers are 62 percent female and only 38 percent male. He asks, "Where are all the men?"[32]

To push this concern even further, male leadership and spirituality in general seem to have become excessively "feminized," using that term in its stereotypical meaning of nurturing, receptive, in touch with feelings, and relational. "Masculine," as commonly used, points to outward, goal-oriented separation and initiation.

Often the men who are present in church seem to be those most comfortable with "feminine" qualities. Some may have even lost their sense of the masculine. The "dresses" of the priests and the "Protestant smile" of the clergy are perhaps only two signs of a church that has majored on being "pleasant" rather than on engaging the world and aggressively pursuing disciple making.

Many men think being Christian is synonymous with being "nice." The church has come to a curious place where we are patriarchal in structure and language but often lacking in strong men who are at home with deep spirituality. The new generation of men in our culture often seem to be more in touch with their feelings, but they may not be as in touch with outgoing, assertive energy. One result may be that more women than men have been attracted to the church.

Some have argued that because of this situation we need enlightened patriarchy now more than ever lest the women take over completely! I agree with the assessment, but not the solution.

---

[32]Quoted in Gordon Dalbey, *Healing the Masculine Soul* (Waco: Word, 1988) 175.

The authentic solution to a church which is moving toward being excessively female in population and feminine in style does not reside in maintaining male domination. *The solution is not to limit women but to liberate men!*

The goal of men and women in partnership will be absolutely unworkable if men do not come into their own personal potency. Women's lib must be accompanied by men's lib. The men's movement is not a reaction to the women's movement, but rather women's new awareness has paved the way for the men to get past the false macho image.

Men are often afraid of women, insecure, and timid. Some cover it up by a false masculine or macho swagger, but it all stems from the same insecurity. Speaker and author Gordon Dalbey says:

> Certainly, we men do not fantasize before *Playboy* centerfolds because we are so courageous before real-live, three-dimensional women, but rather, because we fear them; we do not beat up women because we are so strong, but rather, because we feel so powerless before them; we do not impregnate women and leave them to consider an abortion because we are so self-reliant, but rather, because we feel inadequate to be responsible fathers and husbands. In a word, our masculine soul is torn—so badly that we cannot recognize the One who comes to heal us.[33]

These journeys of liberation, while different for men than for women, must be equally pursued. The church's movement into male and female partnership in leadership and language must parallel a personal movement by both men and women into their own inner healing journeys.

Jesus modeled both "masculine" and "feminine" qualities within himself. He was both relational and goal-directed. He was at home with both the inward and the outward journey, inner space and outer space. He could cry and get angry. He could be nurturing and assertive. He could be warm and wild.

---

[33]Dalbey, *Healing the Masculine Soul,* 21.

We have much more to learn about these deep journeys into authentic personhood as men and as women.

Question

*Don't men need Father God to
help them separate from their mothers
and form their identities as men?*

Yes, they do, and this is another reason we must not give up the male image of God. But any argument along this line is also an argument for calling God Mother as well. The best response to this question might be another question: "Don't women need Mother God to help them form their identities as women?" And the answer here is the same as for men—yes, they do.

We are increasingly aware of men whose relationship with their father has been severely damaged. The epidemic of weak or absent fathers in our culture has led to sons who have not been called away from their attachment to their mother. These "mother's boys" remain in what has been called a "soft masculine." These men lack freedom, assertiveness, and vitality. They may especially need to know how God is like a father.

However, the same must be said of those whose relationship to their mother was damaged. Some have not bonded well with their mother, and therefore struggle with issues of abandonment. They also need a redeemed relationship with the God who is like a mother, and who will never leave or forsake them. Ultimately, we all need an emotional dimension of a parental relationship with God which is like the best of both a healthy father and a healthy mother.

Psychologically men need Father God differently from the way that women need Father God. Men need Father God to call them away from mother and into manhood, while women need Father God to affirm their importance and infinite worth. Similarly, men need Mother God in a different way than women need Mother God. Men need Mother God for a certain dimension of comfort (male nurture may seem different in some ways from female nurture), for the redemption of the faulty male view of the feminine, and to call them into the inner spiritual and emotional journey. Men are often emotionally damaged in our culture because we are frequently split off from our feelings. Women are not as separated from their feelings but they are more abused and demeaned as persons, conditioned to believe their femininity is bad or inferior. They are taught to let men invade them. Therefore, women need Mother God to strongly affirm that they are made in God's image and to set healthy boundaries around their physical and emotional selves, their personhood. I believe women can only go to a certain point in their spiritual journey without coming to see the feminine side of God. Only healthy mothering, both human and divine, can release women from the Genesis curse of excessive and unhealthy dependence on men and into their own spiritual journeys.

Question

Aren't we inviting a fourth member of the Trinity, Mother God, to go along with Father, Son, and Spirit?

Any liturgy that says "in the name of God, the Father and Mother, Son, and Spirit" may give this impression. Although the placement of the "and" between Father and Mother is an attempt to avoid a fourth person, I think it can be too easily misunderstood, and therefore I avoid such ambiguous phrases. Just as with calling God Father, we must carefully make clear what we mean and do not mean when we call God Mother. Scripture reveals God to us as tri-unity, not quad-unity, so in replacing the name "Father" with "Father and Mother" for God we must speak and write in such a way that the impression of four persons is not given.

Thinking of Mother God as a different person from Father God within the Divine Triune Family seems to occur mostly with those who cannot image God with multiple metaphors. When we limit ourselves to only one image of God we confine God to a prison of one symbol. The Bible does not do this, and neither should we.

Question

In confronting patriarchy don't we have to guard against pagan goddess worship?

Yes, we do. Guarding against female goddess worship is as important as guarding against male god worship.

It is a common but false assumption that the Old Testament was careful to use only male imagery for God to keep it distinct from pagan Canaanite religion. A respected scholar in the field of ancient religions and Director of the Department of Biblical Civilization for the Reconstructionist Rabbinical College, Tikva Frymer-Kensky points out that the ancient Canaanite religion was not female-centered and that the pantheon of gods was officially headed by El, father of the gods, and dominated by the storm god Ba'al. The goddesses were marginal figures and goddess worship did not necessarily involve fertility concerns, nor was ancient pagan religion essentially sexual.[34]

However, in the search for meaning in our society, there is a resurgence of spirituality which often embraces New Age beliefs and pagan rituals. Some worship a female goddess called the Great Mother or other variations which tend to make mother *into* God rather than seeing mother-like quali-

---

[34]Tikva Frymer-Kensky, "The Bible, Goddesses, and Sex," in *Daughters of Sarah* (March/April 1990) 16–19. Frymer-Kensky has developed these ideas into a book, *In the Wake of the Goddesses* (New York: Fawcett Columbine, 1992), pointing out that although polytheism did accord females an important role, the strict division between male and female deities actually served to keep women in a subordinate position. This dualism was displaced by the Bible, in which women were not considered to be inherently inferior.

ties *in* God. Christians through the ages have always had to differentiate their God from others. Yahweh had to be differentiated from the male god Ba'al and the female god Ashtoreth in the Old Testament. False female goddesses must be rejected with as much vigor as we reject false male gods.

Question

In calling God Mother, aren't we running the danger of making God sexual?

Some object to feminine metaphors for God based on a belief that the Old Testament rejected any feminine naming of God because the pagan gods were feminine. Such metaphors, they say, inevitably lead to a goddess religion and the deification of nature and the self.[35] God as male, they say, is not sexual, but God as female is sexual. They are mistaken.

As I pointed out in the previous section, a closer look shows that the religions of the day had both male and female gods. The Canaanite sky god, El, was an autocratic father figure, and Ba'al was a male god. Zeus was even called father and had female consorts with whom he fathered the other gods. There was no concern at all about the maleness or femaleness of God in relationship to any of these pagan gods.

Concern that the feminine of God will be bound up with "Mother Earth" and "nature goddess spirituality" is based on patriarchal assumptions. The ground we walk on is not "Mother Earth," and "Mother Nature" betrays a false assignment of the feminine to nature. Feminizing nature is sexist projection, and Christians should confront it as such.

Brueggemann says, "Biblical faith is quite uninterested in questions of God's sexuality, masculine or feminine, or even in God's asexuality but is singularly and passionately concerned with God's covenanting and the implication of covenanting for

---

[35]Alvin Kimel, Jr. *A New Language for God?*, Episcopalians United, 3645 Warrensville Center Rd. Shaker Heights, Ohio, 44122, 1990, 6.

human history. In its singular concern, it is free to use various images to articulate that paradigm of covenanting. While every language is transformed by the paradigm it articulates, every image also retains something of its own primal power."[36]

Christian doctrine has historically and consistently taught that God is spirit, and therefore without sexuality. This is in contrast to pagan religion, which saw the primal creative force as sexual in nature. In Genesis God has no female partner and the earth and humankind were created by the will of God, not procreated by some kind of sexual god.

By the fourth century some Christians began taking the metaphor of Father-Son in a human or sexual way in reference to God and Jesus. This theological movement, called Arianism, argued that since the Son was "begotten" of the Father, the Son must be a creation of the Father and not really one with the Father, and therefore subordinate or inferior to the Father. The Council of Nicea in 325 attempted to resolve the Arian controversy by stating that the Son was "eternally begotten of the Father" and is of "one being with the Father." They interpreted the name "Father" in a philosophical and metaphorical way to remove any confusion that it should be taken in some literal or sexual way. An eternally begotten Son cannot be thought of in sexual terms, nor does that present any barrier to thinking about the Father and Son being one. On a human level, a son is a different and completely separate person from the one who fathers him, but at the divine dimension Jesus and the Father are of "one being."[37]

This traditional position on the nonsexual nature of God is once again being weakened by a technicality when some say that God is not male but "he" is masculine.[38] The word "male" is replaced by "masculine" and "sex" is replaced by "gender." Therefore, some have arrived at the strange position that God

---

[36]Walter Brueggemann, "Israel's Social Criticism and Yahweh's Sexuality," *Journal of the American Academy of Religion*, supplement (Sept. 1977) 739.

[37]James E. Griffiss, *Naming the Mystery* (Cambridge: Cowley, 1990) 36.

[38]Bloesch, *Battle for the Trinity*, 33.

is not male but God is masculine, and God has no sex but God has gender.

I agree that there is a danger of making God sexual. However, the threat comes not from me, but from those who oppose recognizing the feminine face of God. Traditional language about God is not non-sexual. It is male sexual, and *those who advocate patriarchy make God into a sexual being—male and masculine.* My cause is to maintain the traditional, historical, and biblical stance that God is not sexual, but includes and transcends male and female.

We have a Trinity where the Third Person has been sentimentalized, the Second Person has been spiritualized, and now, the First Person is being genderized. This must not happen.

Question

*Will the next thing be to say that
Jesus should have been a woman?*

It's already been said. Feminine images of Jesus have been used down through church history by respected and orthodox teachers.

> The Word [Christ] is all to the child, both father and mother, and tutor and nurse (Clement of Alexandria [AD 150-215] *The Instructor*).[39]

> Just as a woman nurtures her offspring with her own blood and milk, so also Christ continuously nurtures with His own blood those whom he has begotten (St. John Chrysostom [AD 347–407]).[40]

---

[39] *The Ante-Nicene Fathers: The Writings of the Fathers down to A.D. 325*, ed. Alexander Roberts and James Donaldson, vol. 2 (New York: Charles Scribner's Sons, 1908) 220.

[40] St. John Chrysostom, *Baptismal Instructions LXV* (trans. Paul Harkins; London: Longmans, Green and Co., 1963) 62.

He who has promised us heavenly food has nourished us on milk, having recourse to a mother's tenderness. For just as a mother, suckling her infant, transfers from her flesh the very same food which otherwise would be unsuited to a babe, ... so our Lord, in order to convert His wisdom into milk for our benefit, came to us clothed in flesh (Augustine [AD 354–430]).[41]

But you also, Jesus, good Lord, are you not also Mother? Are you not Mother, who are as a hen who gathers her own chicks under her wings? Truly, Lord, you also are Mother. For that which others have been in labor with and have born, they have received from you (Anselm [eleventh century]).[42]

We realize that all our mothers bear us for pain and for dying, and what is that? But our true mother, Jesus—All-love—alone bears us for joy and for endless living, blessed may he be! Thus he sustains us within himself in love and hard labor, until the fulness of time (Julian of Norwich [fourteenth century English writer]).[43]

Christ was humankind's foster-mother, enduring with greatness and strength of the Deity united with your nature, the bitter medicine of the painful death of the cross, to give life to you little ones debilitated by guilt (Saint Catherine of Siena [Dominican tertiary and activist of the fourteenth century, given the title Doctor of the Church in 1970]).[44]

---

[41]St. Augustine, *On the Psalms*, vol. 2 (Westminster, Maryland: Newman Press, 1961) 20–21.

[42]Anselm, "Oratio LXV ad Sanctum Paulum Apostolum," *Opera Omnia, Patrologia Latina*, ed. J. P. Migne, vol. 158 (Paris, 1863) cols. 981–982.

[43]Julian of Norwich, *Revelations of Divine Lord* (trans. M. L. del Mastro; Garden City: Doubleday, 1977) 191–92.

[44]St. Catherine of Siena, *The Dialogue of St. Catherine of Siena* (trans. Algar Thorold; London: Kegan Paul, Trench, Trubner, 1907) 68–69.

Nineteenth-century evangelical literature also contains references to God as mother and Jesus imaged as woman. Hannah Whitall Smith, author of the widely read *The Christian's Secret of a Happy Life*, was a popular Bible teacher and advocate of women's education. One of her Bible studies in *The Open Secret* is entitled "God As Our Mother." She speaks of the "many . . . ways in which God is like a mother" in order to "open our eyes to see some truths concerning Him, which have been hitherto hidden from our gaze."[45]

A. B. Simpson, founder of the Christian and Missionary Alliance, said in *Echoes of the New Creation*, "His humanity was unique and different from all other humanity. He is not a man, but He is the Man. He is not male. He is just as much a woman as He is a man."[46]

Jesus was not averse to casting himself in a female image as in Luke 13:34 where he pictured himself as a mother hen longing to gather her brood under her wings. I am not saying Jesus was confused as to his sexual identity, but rather just the opposite. Because he was so secure in his male identity, he could use a female image to express his passionate care.

Jesus also fashioned a profound feminine metaphor in his words to Nicodemus

> "Very truly, I tell you, no one can see the kingdom of God without being born from above." Nicodemus said to him, "How can anyone be born after having grown old? Can one enter a second time into the mother's womb and be born?" Jesus answered, "Very truly, I tell you, no one can enter the kingdom of God without being born of water and Spirit. What is born of the flesh is flesh, and what is born of the Spirit is spirit. Do not be astonished that I said to you, 'You must be born from above' " (John 3:3a–7).

---

[45]Quoted in Donald W. Dayton, *Discovering an Evangelical Heritage* (Peabody: Hendrickson, 1988) 95.

[46]Ibid.

What a striking female image of spiritual regeneration! Southern Baptist chaplain Jann Aldredge Clanton says, "The Hebrew Bible's images of God as a woman in labor reach their culmination in the New Testament picture of the Spirit giving new birth through the suffering love of Christ. The image of God as a Mother bringing forth life serves as a unifying strand throughout biblical revelation."[47]

The Old Testament word for the Spirit (*ruach*) of God is feminine and the New Testament Greek word (*pneuma*) is neuter. With Jesus' close association of the Spirit's work with birthing, perhaps it would be more accurate to sometimes refer to the Holy Spirit as "she" rather than exclusively as "he." Tony Campolo, in a talk at the 1992 Youth Specialties Conference, had excellent biblical and linguistic grounds when he said, "And then there is a Holy Spirit that fills. And when she fills us . . ."

However, at the heart of Christianity is a male human being, Jesus. In Colossians 1:15 Paul makes this remarkable statement: "He is the image of the invisible God." How are we to understand this idea? Does it mean the image of God is Jewish and male? Is Jesus' maleness basic to his role as God Incarnate and our Savior? If so, then where does it stop? Is Jesus' Jewishness basic? Is having brown eyes important (assuming Jesus' eyes were brown)? Is his being unmarried basic in the scandal of the incarnation? Is his being a carpenter essential?

Something is wrong when we cannot conceive of the Messiah coming from a different cultural setting or being of a different race or gender. Does this mean the picture of a black Jesus displayed on the wall of Saint Sabina Catholic Church in Chicago is blasphemy? Of course not.

It is probably less difficult to imagine Jesus as Chinese or black than it is to see Jesus as a woman. However, the one is no more historically incorrect than the other—the difference is our prejudice against women.

---

[47]Clanton, *In Whose Image?* 34.

Some people have violent reactions to my picture of "Christa," a sculpture of a female Jesus hanging on the cross. There have always been strongly negative reactions wherever Edwina Sandys' original "Christa" sculpture has been displayed. But there are also other equally strong responses to this sculpture such as this anonymous handwritten poem which was found taped to a bulletin board at the Cathedral of St. John the Divine in New York during an exhibition of "Christa."

> O God,
> through the image of a woman
> crucified on the cross
> I understand at last.
>
> For over half of my life
> I have been ashamed
> of the scars I bear.
>
> These scars tell an ugly story
> a common story,
> about a girl who is the victim
> when a man acts out his fantasies.
>
> In the warmth, peace and sunlight of your
>   presence
> I was able to uncurl the tightly clenched fists.
> For the first time
> I felt your suffering presence with me
> in that event.
> I have known you as vulnerable baby,
> as a brother, and as a father,
> Now I know you as a woman.
> You were there with me
> as the violated girl
> caught in helpless suffering.
>
> The chains of shame and fear
> no longer bind my heart and body.
> A slow fire of compassion and forgiveness
> is kindled.
> My tears fall now
> for man as well as woman.

You were not ashamed of your wounds.
You showed them to Thomas
as marks of your ordeal and death.
I will no longer hide these wounds of mine.
I will bear them gracefully.
They tell a resurrection story.
   "By His Wounds You Have Been Healed"[48]

—Anonymous

I have another picture of Jesus hanging on my wall which, from a distance, looks like a fairly traditional rendering of Jesus as a Jewish man with a crown of thorns and a cross in the background. But up close one can see the image is actually composed of 48 faces representing women and men of all races and ages. It is not historically accurate but it is theologically true: Jesus represented all of humanity.

The New Testament itself paves the way for such physically incorrect but theologically true images:

> I saw one like the Son of Man, clothed with a long robe and with a golden sash across his chest. His head and his hair were white as white wool, white as snow, his eyes were like a flame of fire, his feet were like burnished bronze, refined as in a furnace, and his voice was like the sound of many waters. In his right hand he held seven stars, and from his mouth came a sharp, two-edged sword, and his face was like the sun shining with full force (Rev 1:13–16).

Sometimes I hear an argument against women being pastors which goes like this:

> Jesus was a man and appointed only men to be part of the Twelve. These facts lead us to conclude that we should stick with this pattern and limit leadership to men.

But it does not seem to be as obvious that Jesus was also a Palestinian Jew and only appointed Palestinian Jews to be his

---

[48]Reprinted by Susan Thistlethwaite, *Sex, Race, and God* (New York: Crossroad, 1991) 92.

first apostles. If all of our pastors have to be male Palestinian Jews we're in deep trouble!

Yet in another sense Jesus' maleness was of great importance in what it communicated in his day. His definition of masculinity was a direct contradiction of the contemporary, male-dominated culture. He did the things only women were supposed to do, such as serving and washing feet. Only a man could have modeled such a counter-cultural life-style.

So while the incarnation needed to be in Jewish and male form for historical and cultural reasons, was the preexistent Christ a man? Is it really true that "in the beginning was the Word and the Word was male?" Or, "Before Abraham was, I was male?" Really? Is the Risen, transcendent Jesus Christ a Jewish male? Is the Eternal, Cosmic Christ a man, or does Christ's maleness fade to the background after the ascension? Perhaps Jesus' teaching, "In heaven there is no marrying and giving in marriage," indicates that gender may not be significant in our risen state.

The essence of the incarnation is God becoming human, not God becoming a male Jew. Since Jesus as Christ, Messiah, Savior and Redeemer transcends sexual identity, I wonder if it is wise to continually refer to the Risen Christ in masculine terms. Surely Jesus' maleness recedes into the background of eternity as our Risen Savior.

I personally try to avoid using masculine pronouns for the Risen, transcendent Christ except when I am speaking of him during his time here on earth before his ascension.

Question

Why didn't Jesus call God Mother?

In one sense he didn't need to. Since calling God Father was not meant to convey sexual characteristics, there was no reason to call God Mother when the Palestinian word for daddy, *abba*, communicated the very qualities of power, authority, freedom, value, nurture, protection, comfort, and closeness which Jesus saw in God. It was an ideal term for God in a patriarchal society. However, the existence of a patriarchal society reflects the fall of humankind and its resulting war on women, not God's will. So the fact that father described God better than mother in Palestinian culture reflected the conditions of wartime, i.e., male-dominant structures, not a male God.

In another sense, he couldn't call God mother. It would have been too great a break with the existing culture. A society which ascribes ultimate worth to maleness and not femaleness will certainly use many more male analogies for God than female. *Calling God mother in a culture which considered women the property of their husbands would be like calling God "slave" instead of "master."* But, of course, Jesus was about to change even the slavery image because he took on the form of a slave and forever changed our understanding of God. But naming God more directly as Mother waited upon the results of Jesus' transforming model, the challenging of the war on women, and a culture where both mother and father are beginning to share the qualities and powers that were only ascribed to fathers in Jesus' day.[49]

---

[49]The statistics on the following page are taken from Lori Heise, "The Global War Against Women," *World Watch*, reprinted in *Washington Post*, April 9, 1989.

Is there a war on women? In the twelve seconds it took to read these last few lines, one more woman in the United States has been beaten by a man, three hundred every hour. Over 1,300 women are murdered each year by their husbands or boyfriends. Sounds like a war to me.

Why It's Important to Call God Mother 5

Centuries of assault on the nurturing, maternal, and compassionate images of God have resulted in the virtual abortion of the feminine in much of the church today. This dismemberment and discarding of the feminine in leadership and language is the most pressing theological and social agenda within the American church today. The abortion of the feminine from our language about God is the foundation of the war against women within the church.

But language about God is important not only to those of us who are calling for an end to the battle of the sexes. Someone said to me, "But this language thing about God just isn't very important. Why don't we move on to something more significant?"

I replied, "If how we speak about God isn't very important, then you wouldn't mind if I called her Mother would you?"

With great intensity he shot back, "Oh no, you can't do that!"

Suddenly it seemed very important to this person that I not do any such thing. At times like that I wonder just what people mean when they say this subject isn't very important. It seems to be rather important to many of us, both to those who agree and to those who disagree. In this chapter I want to explore how we attempt to evade the significance of the language problem and eight reasons I believe calling God Mother is important for the church today.

Evading the Problem

Problems, whether personal or social, from alcoholism to poverty, are often dismissed in one of three ways. One way is to *deny there is a problem.* "I may get drunk every weekend, but I'm not an alcoholic." Or, we pretend the problem doesn't exist: "This poverty thing is just another way for the government to take our money. I don't know any poor people, at least none who couldn't make more money if they wanted to."

Another way to discount a problem is to *deny its significance.* "I may get drunk and drive, but I haven't killed anybody yet." Or, "I'll admit there are people who want to work and can't find a job, but not many compared to the number of people who have jobs." We admit there may be a problem but trivialize it by claiming it is only of minor significance.

A third way to discount a problem is to admit there is a problem but to *deny there is a solution.* "I've been drinking all my life, and I've tried to quit but no one can help me." Or, "Jesus said that we will always have the poor with us. It's just a fact of life; besides, I don't have any money left over from my paycheck, so there's nothing I can do about it." We believe that while there is a problem, solving it would be too much trouble or is beyond our personal resources, and therefore we are justified in ignoring it.

I have heard these three approaches sometimes used by those who oppose calling God Mother. Some say there is no problem: "I think women are treated just fine. There's no sexism in our language. Christians have always called God 'Father' and 'he,' and if those women with their feminist agendas would just become Christians, we could all go back to the way it has always been."

Some deny the significance of the problem: "I'll admit our language about God may need to change, but this is nothing to stir up a fuss about. It is too controversial to bring up. It's not worth the conflict." When language is examined as both an instrument of oppression and a potential tool of liberation, many men close their ranks and defend their inalienable right to manage controversy. They trivialize the discussion. "I just don't understand why we should quibble over words." Sometimes it is women who discount the importance of the issue, saying, "It doesn't bother me." While an honest answer, it is also a self-centered answer and implies that if the problem is not mine, it must not be very important.

Finally, some say the solution is too difficult: "Why, we'd have to change the way we pray and talk about God. We'd have to rewrite our hymns, and people wouldn't like that. Most of our theology books, commentaries, and Christian literature are written in masculine language. People are just too set in their ways to make such vast changes, and most Christians would never do it."

We must challenge ways of thinking which discount the problem, its significance, and its solvability. I believe not only that there is a problem today in our language about God but also that it is of major importance—and solvable.

The Priority of the Church

Aren't such concerns as evangelism, missions, poverty, racism, militarism, the environment, and the breakdown of the family much more important than arguing over religious words?

These are important problems. The church is called to produce world-class disciples who are theologically, psychologically, and spiritually equipped to wrestle with all the contemporary challenges of spreading the gospel and opposing injustice, discrimination, and the misuse of creation.

Jesus faced similar issues in his day: people without the gospel, political corruption, rampant immorality, poverty, oppression of every kind (including massive enslavement of entire populations), and the breakdown of family life. Yet Jesus gave himself to the fundamental task of establishing a new and revolutionary community of the redeemed, even as he laid the groundwork for making disciples who embraced a justice ethic that, among other things, challenged the sexist stereotypes of his day. It was from the love and righteousness modeled within this new community that wisdom and truth would flow into the rest of the world. Jesus did not let the world's agenda keep him from giving priority to the church's agenda. The image of God is part of the church's agenda.

Paul faced both the great need to spread the gospel and the social problems of his day with a similar approach. He considered the church his priority in working out the challenges of evangelism, missions, and justice. He outlined the church's most pressing theological and social agenda in the magnificent charter of Galatians 3:28:

> There is no longer Jew or Greek, there is no longer
> slave or free, there is no longer male and female;
> for all of you are one in Christ Jesus.

Of these three sets of social relationships, Paul's first priority was how Christian Jews and Christian non-Jews (Greeks) were to relate. While stating the need to redemptively re-work the relationship between Jew and Greek, slave and free, and male and female, he fully addressed only the Jew/Gentile problem. He dedicated major portions of his letters to wrestling with how Jews and Gentiles were to relate to one another, fashioning a theological foundation for how to interpret the Hebrew Scriptures in light of the revelation of Christ, providing practical guidelines, and calling Christian Jews and Christian Gentiles into a revolutionary new community of sharing. Paul left it to succeeding generations to do the same with slave and free and men and women—it took eighteen hundred years for the church to confront the challenge of slavery.

We are now called to do with female and male what Paul did with Jews and Gentiles—work out a theological foundation in light of the Scriptures, provide practical guidelines about how women and men are to relate, and call people into a revolutionary community of justice and love. We clearly have not addressed the male/female issue yet because the church itself continues to be one of the prime perpetrators in the war on women.

The most pressing theological issue within our American churches today concerns the relationship of male and female.

Will we allow women to use all of their God-given gifts without the restrictions temporarily placed on them in another time and culture? Will we stop excluding the feminine in our language? Will we recognize the feminine face of God? Will we wrestle first with injustice and discrimination within our own house so that we can authentically deal with it elsewhere?

Blindness to our sin within the church limits our ability to work redemptively with sin outside the church. For instance, the rape of our ecosystems can be convincingly shown to be a result of macho masculine values of domination, materialism, and war. When we remove the balancing dimension of the feminine from the masculine, no matter how a society defines feminine and masculine, we have removed one of the prime avenues for a more redeemed world. Many of our evangelical and charismatic churches have been oblivious to such connections because we have bought into the same male-dominating values. As we become aware of the intricate web of theological seduction and injustice in an issue lived out in our church and family, we open the way for greater sensitivity and creativity in solving other crucial issues. Once we begin to see how blind we have been to the evils of male supremacy within the church, we begin to see racial, economic, family, and ecological challenges with greater clarity.

Underlying the challenge of how men and women are to relate is the image of God. Until there is peace between male and female in our image of God, there will be no peace between male and female in the church. Here are eight reasons that affirming the feminine image of God in our language, along with the masculine, is so important.

Religious Language Profoundly Shapes Our Image of God

Dear God,
Are boys better than girls?
I know you are one,
but try to be fair.
    Sylvia

Years ago I thought this little girl's letter to God[1] was amusing and would quote it in sermons, evoking smiles and laughs. Now I think it is profoundly sad, and I feel anger and grief every time I see it. In these two sentences we are stunningly confronted with the heart of the God-language problem.

Why did Sylvia believe that God was a "boy" and therefore wonder if boys are better than girls? Because our religious language taught her this with single-minded clarity, unquestioned authority, and incredible repetition.

Our image of God is not formed by mental concepts as much as it is by images that produce a "feltness" about God. David Seamands points out that inside every one of us is a picture of God which we usually think of as a concept or mental picture. But in our image of God "the most determinative factor is our 'feltness' of who God is."[2] This feltness has been formed by all of our education, experiences, and memories, including those seemingly insignificant social signals such as masculine language for God. *Every time we use, hear, or read exclusively masculine language for God we receive another tiny imprint on our internal "felt" picture of God that God is masculine.*

In *Brave New World*, Aldous Huxley wrote "Sixty-two thousand four hundred repetitions make one truth." Many more times in the lifetime of the average Christian, perhaps millions of times in the lifetime of the serious Christian who reads Christian books and listens to numerous sermons, God is called Father, King, he, him, his, and himself. And each time, the deeply-imprinted, "felt" masculine picture of God is subtly reinforced. No amount of explanation or reassurance that "we all know God is not male" can prevent this felt image from profoundly embedding itself in our psyche. The sheer magnitude of the repetition of masculine words prevents any other image from getting a foothold.

---

[1] Eric Marshall and Stuart Hample, eds., *Children's Letters to God* (New York: Pocket Books, 1966), quoted in *Reader's Digest*, March 1967, 97.

[2] David Seamands, *Healing of Memories* (Wheaton: Victor Books, 1985) 95.

Language is as observable and concrete as radiation, cable systems, and computer chips. Because language is fallen, it is always a loaded gun ready either to protect or destroy. Nazi leaders understood the power of words when they called their facilities for carrying victims to the killing centers "The Charitable Transport Company for the Sick," and when they defined their mass killing of the Jews as "the final solution." Democritus taught that "word is a shadow of deed." Plato said the same thing, only negatively: "False words are not only evil in themselves, but they infect the soul with evil."[3]

We form our words and then our words form us. We see the long tradition of the power of changing language to change one's condition in Shaw's *Pygmalion*. Professor Higgins changed the rough Eliza Doolittle into a lady by altering her speech patterns, and her low self esteem was transformed by a new vocabulary and a different rhetoric.

Our perception of reality is shaped by words because "language is being's house" (Heidegger). The words Sylvia had heard, even in the short span of her life, were powerful shapers of her own identity and how she imaged God. She believed God was male.

What do you believe? Or more specifically, what does the "feltness" sensed by the little child in you tell you about your picture of God?

Our Image of God Is the Key to How We Relate to God

What does calling God father mean to me? Well, first of all, I know what it should mean. It's supposed to mean love and caring and protection like Jesus talked about. But what does it really mean to me? It means rape, physical abuse, and abandonment because that's what my father did to me.

A twenty-four year old woman
considering Christianity

---

[3] Guy Condon, "You Say Choice, I say Murder," *Christianity Today* (June 24, 1991) 20.

We could easily find someone else who suffered abuse at the hands of his or her mother. "Mother" and "Father" are potent words, evoking some of the most powerful memories and meanings we ever encounter. Our first experience of "godness" is always Mom and Dad, or whoever served as the primary caretaker in our first few years of life. Jesus' identifying God as like a heavenly parent further reinforces this natural formation of our spiritual lives. Seeing God as a parent, therefore, has its blessings as well as limitations, and the journey to spiritual and emotional maturity always involves sorting through the distortions that our earthly parents brought to our image of our heavenly Parent.

Gender distortions about God may produce feelings of fear, distance, sexual abuse, abandonment, and a pervasive sense that God can't be trusted. My father was usually angry at me and often distant, rarely spending any time with me. I had another set of problems with my mother, who was anxious, panic-prone, borderline schizophrenic and emotionally smothering. Much of my spiritual journey has been in understanding how God is not like my earthly father and mother and letting God transform my image of both.

But my feltness of God has changed more dramatically in the last four years than in all the previous fifty-four. God the Mother has opened up a new nurturing closeness and a brilliant transcendence in my journey with God that is sometimes breathtaking.

- I feel the nearness of my Mother God in joyous tenderness. I bow before the majesty of my Divine Mother, protected by her fierce maternal strength.

- I treat women differently. They are made in God's image.

- I read the Scriptures differently, moving more easily past the cultural situations and fallen language to find God's word for me in its transcendent power.

- I am more passionate for justice because I feel liberated in a way that I could not fully grasp while still wrestling with a patriarchal image of God. I instinctively knew my understanding of justice issues was clouded by a male-dominant God, but I couldn't get a handle on it until I also saw God as Mother.

- My greatest surprise has been a profound transformation in my masculine images of God when they became freed from patriarchy. When I used only masculine word pictures for God, the only language of intimacy available to me was the old, rigid, distant, male images which have failed. God was about as close as a football buddy or an army comrade. But when I freely began using other word pictures for God, such as mother, sister, and female friend, then a new and biblical range of describing and expressing my intimacy with God became possible. God as masculine became more meaningful and nurturing when I was liberated from the my false macho images.

We Become Like the God We Worship

If we worship a white, middle class God, then we justify our white, middle class existence. If we believe God is fair and just, we will make our country, workplace, neighborhood, and family that way. If we believe God makes no value distinctions in race or gender, we will work to make it so in life. We become like the God we worship.

If our God is loving we will become loving. If our God is harsh and judgmental, we will be, too. If we believe the Trinity is an all-male club with the Father in charge, we will see to it that our churches and families are dominated by all-male power groups. If the male dimension of God dominates the female dimension, then men will dominate women. If God is male, then male is more important than female; men will feel more important than women, and women less than men. The rallying cry of male supremacy is: "God is male and in him there is no femaleness at all!" We become like the God we worship.

I believe there is a certain point in a woman's spiritual journey in this day and in culture beyond which she cannot go without coming to embrace God as Mother too. If God is only likened to male, and not female, then women will reach a barrier in the image of the God they worship that prevents further spiritual development.

Because Jesus Was Male We Must Be Exceptionally Clear That God Is Not

The REAL question is this: How do we know what God is really like? (Billy Graham, Evangelist).[4]

When I think of God, it's pretty hard not to think of His Son, Jesus Christ. God sometimes seems way out there and you're not really sure about Him, but when you focus on Jesus, you get a much clearer picture of what God is really like (Tom Landry, former coach of the Dallas Cowboys).[5]

He [Jesus] is the image of the invisible God (Col 1:15).

As evangelicals and charismatics we joyfully proclaim the man Jesus Christ of Nazareth as our Lord and Savior. We are quite aware, as were the first Christians, that the title "Lord" is also the Old Testament name for God. In naming Jesus as our Lord we are also gladly proclaiming him as our God. Along with the first Christians who worshiped Jesus and proclaimed him as God in human flesh, we say, without flinching, that Jesus is uniquely God incarnate.

But this core affirmation of our faith can be dangerous if left without boundaries or theological qualifications. One of these dangers is that, because Jesus was a man, we may receive the idea, if only subconsciously, that God is male.

---

[4] *What Do We Mean When We Say God*, compiled by Dierdre Sullivan (New York: Doubleday, 1991) 116.
[5] Ibid., 61.

There are those who believe Jesus' maleness made an extremely important statement about God. In January of 1977 the "Vatican Declaration" argued that only male priests can represent Christ here on earth because "Christ himself was and remains a man."[6] C. S. Lewis also argues against women being ordained for the priesthood because Christ was incarnate as a man. Lewis argues:

> Suppose the reformer stops saying that a good woman may be like God and begins saying that God is like a good woman. Suppose he says that we might just as well pray to 'Our Mother which art in Heaven' as to 'Our Father'. Suppose he suggests that the Incarnation might just as well have taken a female as a male form, and the Second Person of the Trinity be as well called the Daughter as the Son. . . . All this, as it seems to me, is involved in the claim that a woman can represent God as a priest does.

> Now it is surely the case that if all these supposals were ever carried into effect we should be embarked on a different religion. Goddesses have, of course, been worshipped: many religions have had priestesses. But they are religions quite different in character from Christianity.

> . . . Christians think that God Himself has taught us how to speak of Him. To say that it does not matter is to say that all the masculine imagery is not inspired, is merely human in origin, or else that, though inspired, it is quite arbitrary and unessential. And this is surely intolerable: or, if tolerable, it is an argument not in favour of Christian priestesses but against Christianity.[7]

---

[6] From "Vatican Declaration," Origins, N.C. Documentary Service, VI (February 3, 1977) 522.

[7] C. S. Lewis, *God in the Dock: Essays on Theology and Ethics*, ed. W. Hooper (Grand Rapids: Eerdmans, 1970) 236–37.

I would argue that the conclusions of the Vatican and C. S. Lewis about the importance of Jesus' maleness are a theological and social disaster.

The Word became flesh in male form for historical and cultural reasons, not because God is masculine. Jesus lived in the transitional time between Old Testament Judaism and the inauguration of the reign of God. Jesus had to be a Jewish man to represent the great high priest in Judaism (Heb 2:17; 5:10). As the Lamb of God, Jesus had to be male since only an unblemished male lamb could be the sacrificial offering in the Jewish sacrificial system (Heb 9:12). Jesus was fulfilling a role in the Old Testament metaphor of priesthood and sacrifice (Heb 8:6–13; 9:12).

Jesus' maleness also sent a powerful message to men. He modeled servanthood in a culture where only women were expected to serve. What a revolutionary message to men! It is interesting to see Jesus hammering home servanthood to the men who followed him, yet as far as we know, never telling a single woman to become a servant—they were already immersed in a life of constant service. The challenge for women, then as today, was to acquire more of the rights and freedoms that men expected and received as a matter of course. Jesus had intellectually stimulating conversations with women and saved some of his most profound teachings for them (Luke 10:38–42; John 4:1–42; 11:17–40, 12:1–8). In contrast to the culture of the day, which denied women any religious education, he made a point of teaching them and affirming their new status as students of spiritual matters. Thus, a male incarnation was, in part, a prophetic judgment on patriarchy. Jesus was a feminist in his day!

However, Jesus' maleness was not theologically important in the sense that it was saying anything about God. It carries no more theological meaning than the color of Jesus' hair or the fact that he spoke Aramaic. The very fact that Jesus was male means we must be especially careful not to infer that God is male. Because of the pervasive misunderstanding today that God is masculine, we must pointedly call attention to this error by using feminine metaphors of God even as we speak of the man Jesus Christ.

The Bible's Message of Justice and Love Calls Us to Affirm The Feminine in Both Humanity and God

In this country, if you're one of those things—poor, black, fat, female, middle-aged, on welfare—you count less as a human being. If you're all those things you don't count at all. Except as a statistic (Johnnie Tillman, Chair of National Welfare Rights Organization [1970s]).[8]

People call me a feminist whenever I express sentiments that differentiate me from a doormat or a prostitute (Dame Rebecca West, English journalist [1892–1983]).[9]

I'm just a person trapped inside a woman's body (Elaine Boosler).[10]

Seventy-two years ago women got the vote. Boy, does time fly when you're being repressed (Lily Tomlin).[11]

I know little about His or Her form, but a great deal about God's ways. . . . When one finds peace by making a commitment to the eternal values of peace, justice, and love, one understands a second dimension of God (Heslip M. Lee, American Baptist minister and Member of Fundamentalists Anonymous).[12]

Our language about God affects not only our personal relationship with God but also how we treat others. Those who would reduce the impact of Jesus on their lives to internal feelings of peace and joy and the sure knowledge of escape from hell have missed much of Jesus' mission and message.

---

[8]*And Then She Said*, 4.
[9]Ibid., 17.
[10]Ibid.
[11]*Kansas City Star*, July 17, 1992, E-1.
[12]Sullivan, *What Do We Mean*, 120.

The Christian faith is both personal and social. The resurrection was also a political statement, meant to affect every part of our lives, including our social and political structures. There has been a tragic division of American Christianity between the inner journey and the outer journey, between a personal relationship with Jesus and loving others, and between personal salvation and social justice. All of these are dimensions of our relationship with Jesus.

Our image of God has vast social ramifications. If God, who is creative, all-knowing, powerful, and dominant is characterized exclusively as male, then male must be more like God than female. Males must therefore be strong, creative, all-knowing, powerful and dominant. The implication is that females must be the opposite—weak, uncreative, ignorant, powerless, and submissive.

According to a survey commissioned by the American Association of University Women, girls emerge from adolescence with a poor self-image, relatively low expectations from life, and much less confidence in themselves and their ability than boys. For example, when elementary school boys were asked how often they felt "happy the way I am," 67 percent answered "always." By high school, 46 percent still felt that way. But with girls, the figures dropped from 60 percent to 29 percent.[13]

Language reflects power in relationships. The "Whites Only" sign on the restroom door or drinking fountain is a more obvious power play than singing "Good Christian Men Rejoice," but the same power structure and subordination based on physical characteristics is at work. Neither is just, both are deadly. How shall we talk about God today if we do not want the sign on God to say "Male Only"?

The brokenness over the masculine and feminine in our world today directly affects many areas of life ranging from the "glass ceiling" in the workplace to the stained glass ceiling in our churches. It includes absent and confused fathers and ha-

---

[13] *Kansas City Star*, Nov. 11 1991, E-1.

rassed single mothers. More than 75 percent of all people living in poverty are women and children.[14]

One woman complained to me, "We should not get our theology and social justice issues mixed up." That's exactly the problem. We have failed to integrate them, and people with a heart for justice can't reconcile a patriarchal-based theology with their social conscience, and people with a heart for theology don't get concerned about social issues because they don't understand how theology is inescapably intertwined with social and political actions.

I had a comparatively minor experience with the injustice of linguistic invisibility during a workshop led by a woman in our church. She told us she was deliberately going to use only female pronouns and images as an experiment. After an hour of "When a person works, she is doing well", and, "God, she . . ." I was climbing the walls. Not because of the strangeness of the language, but because nobody seemed to know or care that I was there. It was as if the male half, *my half,* of the human race suddenly didn't exist. I became linguistically invisible and, because I was not a part of the workshop leadership, I couldn't do anything about it. My voice had no authority. In this setting I experienced a tiny fragment of what women have experienced in gigantic doses for centuries.

I was discussing this subject with an intelligent man who is ardently opposed to racism. He said, "Language about God doesn't seem very important." I replied, "How long has it been since you used the word 'nigger'?" He winced as he realized the gulf between his awareness of the agenda of racism and the issues of sexism.

Sexism, like racism, is evil, inhuman, and anti-Christian. Limiting ourselves to male leadership and predominantly masculine images of God is a disservice to men as well as women. It denies a part of ourselves, regardless of the way in which a culture defines masculinity and femininity.

---

[14]*Kansas City Star,* May 22, 1992, C-4, from report of talk by Mary Azzahir, director, National Network of Women's Funds.

The Christian community is deformed to the extent it practices the injustice of sexism. I have decided that I will no longer participate in the war against women. I refuse to knowingly use sexist language of any kind.

Sexism Perpetuates Violence Against Women

> There is definitely a greater force that can screw people over, a main guy who controls the time clock. Also, God is certainly a man. It's a man's world. He's set it up so maleness controls. Don't misunderstand me. There's an advantage to being female. Females can see through maleness. But nature is wild and dangerous. It's very male to be aggressive and make people feel threatened. Human interaction is what softens and smooths and that comes from women.[15]

> The boys never meant any harm against the girls. They just wanted to rape.[16]

An attitude of patriarchy is fundamentally at the root of a culture that allows women to be beaten and abused. Violence against women, including assault, mutilation, murder, infanticide, rape, and neglect, is one of the most pervasive, yet unrecognized, evils in the world. *The pervasive evil of patriarchy is given legitimacy by the idea of a primarily male or masculine God.*

Where male is valued over female, women suffer not only psychological harm but physical abuse and death as male violence towards women continues in crisis proportions all over the world today. In Bangkok, Thailand, 50 percent of married women are beaten regularly by their husbands. In Nicaragua, 44 percent of the men admit to beating their wives or girl

---

[15]Marian Salzman, Age 31, Media Executive, New York City, in Sullivan, *What Do We Mean*, 101.

[16]Joyce Kitbira, deputy principal of St. Kizito's boarding school in Kenya, where 71 schoolgirls were raped and 19 others died when a group of boys raided the girls dormitory, in *New Woman*, January 1982, 122.

friends. In Nepal, female babies die from neglect because parents value sons over daughters. The pressure in India and China to bear sons is so great that women have begun using amniocentesis as a sex identification test to selectively abort female fetuses. Indian sex education clinics boldly advertise that it is better to spend $38 now on terminating a girl than $3,800 later on her dowry. Of 8,000 fetuses examined at six abortion clinics in Bombay, 7,999 were found to be female. Several million little girls are missing in China as newly released 1990 census data supports previous suspicions that 5 percent of all infant girls born in China are unaccounted for.[17] In Brazil, primarily a Catholic country, a husband can kill his wife on the grounds of his honor being violated if she allegedly has been unfaithful.[18] Under English common law, a husband had the legal right to discipline his wife. Judicial decisions in the United States upheld this right well into the nineteenth century.

Today, in the United States, the single largest cause of injury to women is violence by the men they live with. A woman is beaten every 12 seconds, and each day four women are killed by their abusers. Women are more likely to be abused and killed by their husbands and boyfriends than all other sources combined.[19] More women are murdered at work than die on the job from traffic accidents, machinery mishaps, plane crashes, falls, and suicides combined. Forty-two percent of on-the-job fatalities for women are murder. By contrast, the homicide rate for men accounts for only 12 percent of all on-the-job deaths.[20]

There is widespread economic violence. According to a 1992 assessment and as noted above, more than 75 percent of all people living in poverty are women and children, and 90 percent of the world's refugees are women and children. Single

---

[17]Lori Heise, senior researcher at World Watch Institute, "The Risk of Being Female," *Kansas City Star*, April 30, 1989.

[18]America Watch segment of "All Things Considered," PBS program aired on Oct. 6, 1991.

[19]Lori Heise, "The Global War Against Women," *World Watch*, reprinted in *Washington Post*, April 9, 1989.

[20]*Denver Post*, March 2, 1990, B-5.

mothers are the fastest growing segment of the homeless population. Professional women earn 68 percent of what their male counterparts receive.[21] At every educational level women make less money than men with the same amount of schooling. Women with four years of college earn roughly the same salary as men with a high-school diploma, according to government statistics released in 1991.[22] The "feminization of poverty" is even more widespread at the lower end of the economic scale.

It is naive to deny the pervasive social, legal and, as we have seen, even religious framework which promotes this violence against women. One part of that framework is the insistence by Christians that God is primarily masculine. Christianity has been a major force in leading women to accept abuse. By the church's misunderstanding the picture of Jesus on the cross as meaning women should accept physical abuse as did Jesus, and by the church's misinterpreting the idea of "submission" as meaning women must do whatever men tell them, Christian women have been taught to accept the suffering that comes from abuse as their role in being good followers of Jesus.

One's picture of God validates certain attitudes and confronts others. Men have reported that including God's feminine side has had an interesting effect in their attitudinal violence against women. For example, it has made it more difficult to lust. If God is masculine, then "good ol' God wouldn't mind a little lusting after women, would *he*?" But if God can also be likened to women in some ways, "she might get real upset at the treatment of women as sex objects." When men see the feminine in God, they value women more, and it becomes more difficult to treat them in demeaning ways.

Changing our language and incorporating the feminine image of God are critical components of changing our attitudes and patterns of violence towards women. The old saying, "Sticks and stones may break my bones but words can

---

[21] *Kansas City Star*, May 22, 1992, Mary Azzahir (see note 14).
[22] *Kansas City Star*, Nov. 4, 1991, A-1.

never harm me" may be one of the greatest falsehoods ever passed down from one generation to the next. Words can not only harm us, they can break our hearts, and eventually kill us.

Sexism Hinders Evangelism

> In Japan we are taught to fear fire, earthquakes, typhoons, and fathers. When Christians came and told me about Father God, this was the last religion in the world I wanted to accept. I almost didn't become a Christian because of that. I still can't call God Father (A Japanese man).

The witness of the church is tarnished when we are sexist. While the church's agenda must not be culturally determined, it must be culturally sensitive as we seek to communicate in today's world. Increasingly, the world's criticism of Christians is not that we follow Jesus, but that we fail to follow him. The irreligious person knows instinctively that being sexist cannot be Christian and will increasingly reject any church that is.

Twenty-five million children are abused each year in the U.S., most by their fathers or other men. The image of God as father is a terrible picture to them. How shall we evangelize them if we insist they relate to a God whom we only image as father?

Many in the new generation of baby boomers who attempt to return to church have embraced the equality of the sexes, and they have real problems with a sexist church. And an increasing number of those already in church are finding themselves having to leave their churches in order to remain Christian! Mistreating women in the name of Christ is so contrary to what intelligent, spiritual people understand about Christianity that they avoid any church which devalues women.

I was leading a workshop for about a hundred pastors and invited any who wished for me to pray for them individually to stay after the break. About half of them returned and two of our church's healing prayer team members and I prayed with them for healing for the next three hours. A woman pastor from a very liberal denomination hovered around the fringe of the group as we prayed for most of the pastors there. Finally, she moved to the center of the group, and I asked, "Is there anything in particular you would like us to pray about for you?

She replied, "I'd like to know Jesus."

What a wonderful request to these old Southern Baptist ears. Wouldn't it be great if people would come up to us every-day and say that! Since she was the pastor of a church, I asked her, "What is behind your request?"

She responded, "I want to know the kind of Jesus you know."

She told her story as we stood there in the middle of the room. She had grown up in a rigid church with an angry, dom-ineering pastor who had told her she couldn't use her teaching and leadership gifts because she was a woman, subjecting her to abuse cloaked in the name of Jesus. She finally rejected them and their Jesus and went into a very liberal denomina-tion so that she could "still be a Christian but not have to deal with Jesus." I had made the point in my talk to the pastors that I believed in God the Mother as much as God the Father, sev-eral times referring to God as Mother and she, and this had made her feel safe in coming to me for prayer. We prayed and one of our other pastors, Marcia, who was praying with me, saw a picture of Jesus picking up this woman as a little girl and sitting her on his lap. Then Jesus picked up a Bible and said, "I want to read this book to you for the first time like I meant it to be read."

It was a wonderful healing picture and we were all in awe at what God was doing in her life at that moment. After we finished I asked her on behalf of all Southern Baptists to for-give us for the way we had treated her. We both wept as she let go of years of hurt and anger, and then we hugged each other. Inclusive language is the language of evangelism.

The most revolutionary change taking place in many countries today is the changing role of women. Recent socio-logical studies by the Southern Baptist Home Mission Board have shown that the number of "angry" women has reached a critical mass of 12 million in this country, or about 15 percent of the total population. Southern Baptist denominational researcher Orrin Morris points out that these 12 million women are the equivalent of all women age 18 and older in the states of Alabama, Georgia, Kentucky, Louisiana, Mississippi, North Carolina, South Carolina, Tennessee, Virginia and West Virginia.[23] Many of these are women who have rejected the church as oppressively patriarchal and, in so doing, have also rejected the gospel. Often not even willing to hear the gospel except from another woman, they are certainly not about to set foot in a church service where the language and symbols of worship all contrive to pretend that women are not really there. They correctly perceive that religion is being used to perpetuate the status quo rather than to challenge it as Jesus did. A growing number of men are also beginning to perceive the same realities about our sexist church life, realizing that the oppression of any group is actually the oppression of us all. Who will evangelize this growing number of people who need the gospel?

When I share this statistic I sometimes hear an angry reaction like: "Since when are we letting a bunch of angry women tell us how to evangelize." The attitude reflected in that response is one of the reasons these women are angry! Angry women, unlike angry men, are constantly written off in our society. If we are truly interested in presenting the gospel to all people, it has to include angry people, too, even angry women.

Paul encouraged women to observe proper dress and hair standards so that their ministry would not be misinterpreted by the cultural standards of the day (1 Cor. 11:2–16). Paul's primary concern was always the progress of the gospel in his time; anything that would hinder the spread of that gospel had to take second place. Just as directly *attacking* patriarchy and slavery in Paul's day would have brought the gospel into disrepute, so today *advocating* slavery or, in our case, patriarchy,

---

[23] *Word and Way* (Missouri Southern Baptist State newspaper) June 23, 1990, 4.

now brings the gospel into disrepute. How long will churches put up barriers to hearing the gospel simply because those who have already heard it do not want to change from the familiar and comfortable?

We are in the midst of a spiritual heat wave, with contemporary people interested in spirituality more than ever, exploring new religious experiences as never before. The Christian church is often seen as irrelevant, squabbling over denominational differences, stuck in the religious language and culturally defined patterns of the past. Our faith is not a memorial to sentimental feelings and the nostalgia of past experiences, meaningful though they may be. What are those of us within the church willing to change in terms of nostalgia and familiarity for the sake of those on the outside who need the gospel?

If people are going to reject the gospel it should not be because we are sexist, but because the truth of Jesus Christ has been rejected. The offense of the gospel should be the cross, not sexist language.

Men's Liberation Requires That They Also Understand God As Mother

Men and masculinity are under attack. Our humor reveals that men are now getting what they have given for centuries—sexist ridicule. We laugh at female stand-up comics as they joke about men, but our laughter is uneasy.

- I refuse to consign the whole male sex to the nursery. I insist on believing that some men are my equals.[24]

- If you catch a man, throw him back.[25]

---

[24]Brigid Brophy, quoted in *And Then She Said*, 26.
[25]Australian Women's Liberation slogan quoted in *And Then She Said*, 26.

- Hell hath no fury like a man scorned.[26]

- Men with pierced ears are better prepared for marriage—they've experienced pain and bought jewelry.[27]

- What do you call a man with half a brain? Gifted.

- My ancestors wandered lost in the wilderness for 40 years because even in biblical times, men would not stop to ask for directions.[28]

- On cover of a "when you care to send the very best" Hallmark card:

  Men are scum.
  (On inside)
  Excuse me. For a second there, I was feeling generous.[29]

Men feel confused, oppressed, guilty, and bewildered as the spotlight has shifted from them to women. Male oppression of women has been so obvious historically that we feel apologetic. The man's role is no longer clear. Even less clear is the extent to which it differs from the woman's role, or if it even should. Every aspect of our lives—romance, social relationships, marriage, business, church, and family—is being called into question as patriarchy crumbles and women come into their own liberated womanhood. As men search for a new self-image, we are reaching for new models of what it means to be men because the old ones no longer work and actually never did.

The current task of men's work is to differentiate manhood from patriarchy. Until we men separate being a man from dominating women we will wander around aimlessly, alternating between Rambo and wimp. The road to this goal is a difficult one because it centers on learning to listen to our inner self, the soul in other men, and the deep heart of God. For those of

---

[26]Bartlett, *Ms. Bartlett's Familiar Quotations*, 9.
[27]Rita Rudner, "Sauce, Satire and Shtick," *Time* (Fall 1990) 62.
[28]Elaine Boosler, "Sauce, Satire and Shtick," *Time* (Fall 1990) 62.
[29]This card has since been recalled and discontinued because of protests.

us who have been taught to suppress the most sensitive appa-
ratus for listening we have, our feelings, this is a monumental
challenge. It takes a lot of testosterone to move into the unfamiliar territory of authentic manhood!

Perhaps one of the most profound changes in this journey
comes when we abandon the old patriarchal divine images
and come alive to God as Woman—mother, sister, grand-
mother, friend, and lover. Until we understand the feminine
side of God we don't know how to embrace the masculine side
without getting entangled again in the old patriarchal images
of divinity.

It may be even more difficult to grasp the "feminine" dimension of Jesus, because we have read the Gospels with
so many patriarchal assumptions about Jesus—which do not
hold up under scrutiny. Men longing for authenticity cannot
fully embrace Jesus as our male hero until we see Jesus' liberating attitudes towards women, lest we fall back under the
spell of the false masculine.

Why were women so strongly attracted to Jesus? Perhaps
it was due in part to such things as his kindness to children,
his rejection of violence, his ability to have meaningful and
intellectual conversations with them, and his refusal to discount the feminine in his day. When the men lacked courage
to stay with him near the end, the women stood by with emo-
tion-filled loyalty (Luke 23:27).

We are searching for more biblical and trustworthy images
of divine masculine so we can be liberated to find them for
ourselves. One writer offers five new models for our time to
counter five traditional models of masculinity connected to
patriarchal values: frontiersman, soldier, breadwinner, ex-
pert, and lord can be replaced by healer, mediator, companion, colleague, and nurturer.[30] Another offers us King, Warrior,
Magician, and Lover, redefining them without their patriarchal connotations.[31]

---

[30]Gerzon, *A Choice of Heroes.*
[31]Robert Moore and Douglas Gillette, *King, Warrior, Magician,
and Lover: Rediscovering the archetypes of the mature masculine* (San
Francisco: HarperSanFrancisco, 1990).

The journey away from macho man begins with rejecting the false ideas of manhood and getting in touch with a new image which may appear more "feminine" at first. But this is only because of our bad habit of ascribing certain qualities to men and others to women which properly belong to all persons, such as nurture, feeling, relationality, interdependence, cooperation, assertiveness, achievement, thinking, and movement towards a goal. There is no other way to get to true manhood except by first rejecting the false version of male domination.

Our journey at the church where I serve typifies this process. When I came to the church thirty years ago I immediately began men's groups for sharing, support and prayer. Then our wives wanted their own groups, which we provided. But eventually it seemed clear the health of our marriages required meeting as couples. Over a period of a year, almost all of the married men moved from men's groups to couple's groups, and that it how it has been until the last few years. As we came to believe patriarchy was unfit for human consumption, we moved to women and men partnering in leadership and teaching in the church. Two of our men sensed a new urgency for men to come together, this time on the other side of our gender revolution. They initiated a men's group and almost immediately, and with little effort, four or five men's groups started. Once a week men explored their feelings; roaring like lions, openly crying, shouting, releasing pent-up frustrations, and doing anger work in the group. They gave each other back rubs and shared their deepest secrets and struggles at a much more intimate level than the men's groups of thirty years ago. I felt I had witnessed the power of men rejecting patriarchy and then, sensing the vacuum needed to be filled with something more, taking a risky step to come closer to listen to the souls of other men.

As we men redefine the shape of our manhood, we must continue to guard against returning to the old images of power and domination, and disenfranchising women once more. Yet we must also be free to explore our desire to initiate, to be aggressive and assertive. Men need an appropriate place and way to be loud—and earthy. Real men don't always have to just say "baloney." We need to find ways that Jesus can be our male hero without denying he can also be women's hero, even as we recognize the leap to hero is not as direct with women. We must not hesitate to embrace Jesus as male for ourselves. All of this can only be done in its fullest and deepest manner when we, both men and women, can embrace the "feminine" within ourselves, in humanity, and ultimately in God.

There is one more reason why recognizing the feminine image of God is important. We are called to be healers of broken hearts just as Jesus was, and this heart mending is such a significant facet of God's image that I will devote the entire next chapter to it.[32]

---

[32]The quote on the following page is taken from Leanne Payne, *Crisis in Masculinity* (Wheaton: Crossway, 1985) 83.

It was as if I were a little child rocked in the arms of Christ, at once God the Son and a mothering, nurturing, healing God. . . . The images are both masculine and feminine because ultimate masculinity and ultimate femininity are rooted in Him. God is truth. The God who is pregnant with all that is real, out of whose uncreated womb all creating is birthed . . . because God holds all real good with Himself, the images we have of Him will contain both the masculine and feminine.

—Leanne Payne

"It's a girl!"

Inner Healing 6

We are all wounded in some way.

The most obvious wounding in Jesus' day was physical, so Jesus went about healing bodies. God has provided remarkable channels of healing today through the medical sciences, but God still heals now, as then, through the power of the Spirit. I regularly participate in the monthly healing services of our church and see both gradual and instantaneous physical healings through prayer.

However, the most obvious wounding today is emotional. In our nation of dysfunctional families, more and more adults are finding themselves unable to cope with their inner pain and "emotional demons." I believe the leading edge of Jesus' healing ministry today is not the physical body, but the wounded child within. A fundamental part of our disease is the alienation of masculine and feminine not only in humankind and in the image of God, but within each of us individually.

"You're Getting Too Old for That"

Bob[1] wrestled for over twenty years with his woundedness in the form of depression, hopelessness, homosexual affairs, thoughts of suicide, and addiction to Valium. As a young boy he became aware of having strong feelings of attraction for other boys, and as is usually the case, didn't know what to do except feel ashamed. Growing up in a Christian home and active in church he wrestled with being "different." After a year at Bible college he returned to his home church and unloaded all his frustrations and burdens on his pastor. Unknown to Bob, the pastor had secretly tape-recorded his confession and presented it to the deacons, including Bob's father, at their next meeting. Bob was devastated by this betrayal of confidentiality. Somehow it seemed his sins were less acceptable than other sins and he moved into years of addiction to sex and drugs to anesthetize his inner pain.

Then at age forty-seven, Bob discovered Second Chance Ministries, a support group and ministry to gays who want to find healing and change their lifestyle. About the same time he also found our church and the personal ministry of one of our pastors, Marcia. Here in his own words is one of his inner healing breakthroughs.

> A childhood memory that had long been crammed into the recesses of my mind was awakened by the Holy Spirit last week. It brought new meaning to the verse found in Isaiah 49:15, "How can a mother forget the baby at her breast and have no compassion for the child she bore. Though she may forget, I the Father will not forget you." I revisited the memory of the first time I mourned the absence of my mother's love and compassion.
>
> We were gathered for a noon meal in the kitchen of our farmhouse and I demonstrated that day, as

---

[1] Bob gave me permission to tell his story and helped write it.

I did everyday, my affection toward my mother with a kiss on the cheek as I hurriedly went outside to play. A farmhand sharing the meal with us commented how wonderful it was to see this kind of warmth between us. Then my mother turned to me and said, "Big boys don't need to kiss all the time. You're getting too old for that. So stop it!"

I left the house feeling so ashamed and guilty that I had wronged my mother. Meal times became terrible as I plunged into the deep dark despair of my soul. I did not receive a kiss from my mother until twenty-two years later, standing in the reception line following my wedding ceremony when she leaned over and kissed me on the cheek.

Reliving the memory of this experience, I once again felt deep loneliness and sadness. I prayed for her forgiveness and mine, and that the Father would pour out his healing love into this memory. I prayed that God would be revealed as the "Perfect Parent" I so desperately needed. On the following day while walking through a small courtyard near my place of employment I stopped to rest and relax. I prayed the simple prayer that I often pray: "Father, I love you. Abba Father, I love you. I truly love you." Walking away from the courtyard two words came to my mind: Mother God!

Mother God! Mother God! At that moment the Holy Spirit brought a head knowledge of Abba Father down into the courtyard of my inner being. Now, in the sanctuary of my soul, Mother God resides not only to heal the memory, but to nurture, to hover, to woo, and to cuddle me as only a "motherly father" can. Isaiah 66:13 says, "As a mother comforts her child, so will I comfort you" [NIV]. True to the biblical promise, I received the comfort and healing I needed for the despair I felt in my relationship with my mother and a new sense of God's care and presence.

What Is Inner Healing?

One of several significant gifts the charismatic renewal has made available to the church is the ministry of inner healing. Inner healing, or healing of memories as it is sometimes called, deals primarily not with the sins we have committed but with the sins which have been committed against us. Our own sins can be dealt with by repentance, forgiveness, and the disciplines of the spiritual life. But injury to our inner child[2] of the past from the sins of others does not respond to these remedies.

I was privileged to attend a number of sessions offered by the School of Pastoral Care with Agnes Sanford, an early pioneer of a new model of both physical and emotional healing. She would often remind us that "Isaiah 53:4 says 'Surely He hath borne our griefs and carried our sorrows' [KJV]. And this includes those hurts buried deep within our subconscious."

Deeply buried traumatic incidents from the past, repeated abusive treatment, and unmet needs from our childhood, if unhealed, cause great emotional pain and reduce our capacity to function as disciples of Christ. Jesus came to "let the oppressed go free" (Luke 4:18). A part of this oppression comes from fallen political and social structures, but some of it is personal and internal. Not all the homeless are walking the streets. Many of us grew up as emotional orphans and have discovered a homeless child living inside of us who has been rejected, abused, or traumatized in some way, who cries out to be healed and freed from the pain of the past.

---

[2]The "inner child of the past" terminology has been made popular by John Bradshaw (*Homecoming: Reclaiming and Championing Your Inner Child,* New York: Bantam, 1990). The phrase refers to the early developmental experiences and memories of what Transactional Analysis defines as the child ego state. David Seamands, retired professor of pastoral ministries at Asbury Theological Seminary, calls the process of healing this inner child of the past the "healing of memories." He says it is a "form of Christian counseling and prayer which focuses the healing power of the Spirit on certain types of emotional/spiritual problems" (Seamands, *Healing Memories,* 24).

"I Don't Feel Close to God"

A visitor to our church, whom I will call Susan, came to see me because she couldn't feel close to God. All of her life a satisfying sense of God's presence had eluded her. At Broadway Baptist she became especially aware of this absence because she was surrounded by so many others who enjoyed a very real awareness of God's presence.

We had only a few minutes in between services, so after she told me her problem, I asked her if she was open to my praying for her. When she said she was, we sat down in one of our counseling rooms where I suggested that she not pray at all for the next few minutes but rather relax and let me do the praying. Often those who come to us for help have prayed and agonized with God so much about their problems that praying has become an exercise in anxiety and disappointment. I find people are most able to receive the ministry of the Spirit if they relax and stop trying so hard to make something happen.

Almost immediately a picture came to my mind of a little girl who was being bounced on her daddy's lap and snuggled. It seemed to be a beautiful picture but something felt wrong about it. I asked God what my sense of evil was and immediately the picture moved to one of sexual abuse. At this point I had to decide if this was to be shared, because a picture that comes to us in prayer may or may not be from God, and even if it is from God, it's not always one that should be shared. It seemed appropriate in this case to proceed, so I asked Susan if she had ever been mistreated by her father. She took a startled breath and said she had. I asked her if she had been sexually abused. She began crying and said yes and that she had never told anyone about it. Although it takes a victim of sexual abuse an average of seven months in therapy before they can recall or admit to being sexually abused, in this case the gifting of the Spirit in a "word of knowledge" (1 Cor 12:8, KJV), moved us along in a remarkable way.

I asked if she was comfortable with my touching her as I continued praying for her (female victims of sexual abuse are often too vulnerable to feel comfortable with a man touching them). Normally, I would have been part of a healing prayer team of two others including at least one woman, but this was an unplanned time and I didn't have any others praying with me. She agreed and I lightly placed my hand on her shoulder and asked the Spirit to begin ministering to her. After a minute of quiet another picture came to my mind. It was God as a fiercely protective mother who rushed into the first scene, put herself in between the little girl and her abusive father and chased him away. I asked Susan if her mother had been aware of what her husband had done. Susan was sure she had been and did not understand why her mother had let this go on. I shared the picture of Mother God coming in to protect her and there was an explosion of grief and tears as Susan received a touch of healing for some of her abusive past. She became quiet again and sat with her eyes closed. I prayed for her, saying quietly out loud, "Holy Spirit, minister to Susan in any way that you want to right now." Almost immediately she slumped back in the chair, peacefully resting in the Spirit. I quietly left her there so she could continue to soak up the healing presence of God. Later, I encouraged her to get some professional counseling and further inner healing prayer, which she did. She also reported to me that she felt a new sense of God's presence immediately after we prayed and it increased in the following months as more healing took place.

The abuse by Susan's parents had damaged her inner "receptors" that would normally allow her to sense God's love and presence. Inner healing is a process of reconstructing those receptors through personal prayer and the Spirit-led prayers of others. Healing of memories through prayer is not an attempt to bypass the wisdom found in psychological understanding or an attempt by untrained Christians to play "therapist." Rather, it is an additional and uniquely spiritual channel which enhances personal growth through the ministry and gifts of the Spirit directly in a person's life in the context of prayer.

In this prayer journey the painful memories and destructive patterns of abuse from the past are brought into the light of Jesus' presence. We "relive" the experience but this time with the resources of grace and the presence of the Spirit that we were not able to let in at an earlier time. This must usually be repeated a number of times until the various layers of the wounding experience have been healed and "completed" in a positive way, releasing the emotions that have been painfully frozen in the old trauma. Then the love of God can move from being merely God's theological responsibility to being a powerful sense of personally felt love.

Everybody Needs a Mom and Dad on Earth —And One in Heaven Too.

Since most inner healing deals with the wounding of the inner self from childhood, it is obvious that the absence of healthy loving parenting is the primary cause of such trauma. There is no debate that in God's plan human parenting should come in two dimensions: mothering and fathering. Far from attempting to remove all distinctions between the genders, good psychology recognizes how crucial it is that we receive both maternal and paternal love from our earthly parents. The debate is whether we also need both paternal and maternal love from our Heavenly Parent. It seems obvious to me that we do.

G. Campbell Morgan, a biblical expositor in early 1900s, appreciated the truth of a balanced gender image for God when he said: "In God there is a Father—"like as a Father pitieth His children;" and there is Mother—"as one whom his mother comforteth."[3]

John Wimber, founder of the Vineyard churches, author and teacher on the phenomena of signs and wonders today, recognizes the need for a maternal side to God when he says:

---

[3] Morgan, *The Gospel According to John,* 47.

Some of us often have a difficult time relating to
the Father image of God. Remember that God is
not just Father, he is also Mother. There are both
characteristics to be found in the makeup of God.
If you are unable to relate in an intimate way to
God as Father because of a poor role model, try
relating with your mother in mind. The overall
tone is to relate as a son or daughter to a parent.[4]

Theologian Donald Bloesch, even though he opposes public feminine language for God, has a place for calling God
Mother in personal devotion and prayer. He says, "Yet this
does not mean that on occasion, especially in our private de-
votions, we cannot address God as 'Holy Mother, Wisdom of
God' or something similar, for such usage has a measure of
support, not only in the Bible, but also in orthodox church
tradition."[5] In a remarkable admission, Bloesch states, "The
God of the Bible is . . . not only Lord but also Friend, not only
Father and Brother but also Mother and Sister. . . ."[6]

Leanne Payne, author and teacher of healing prayer, speaks
of God as "Mother-Father-Savior,"[7] and shares wonderful stories about Mother God like: "From being held by Esther, she
went right into the arms of God, and He became both mother
and father," and " 'Heavenly Father' became your mother and
healed you."[8]

She articulates the masculine and feminine of God in the
context of inner healing prayer:

It was as if I were a little child rocked in the arms
of Christ, at once God the Son and a mothering,
nurturing, healing God. . . . The images are both
masculine and feminine because ultimate masculinity and ultimate femininity are rooted in
Him. God is truth. The God who is pregnant with

---

[4]John Wimber, *Teach Us to Pray* (Anaheim: Mercy, 1986) 90.
[5]Bloesch, *Battle for the Trinity*, 54.
[6]Ibid., 53.
[7]Leanne Payne, *Restoring the Christian Soul Through Healing
Prayer* (Wheaton: Crossway Books, 1991) 119.
[8]Ibid., 135.

all that is real, out of whose uncreated womb all creating is birthed. . . because God holds all real good with Himself, the images we have of Him will contain both the masculine and feminine.[9]

Notice in this quote that the impact of her beautiful depiction of the feminine side of God is entirely canceled out by her use of not only masculine pronouns for God, but capitalized ones! Because Payne deals so much with inner healing and gender identity problems she cannot avoid recognizing the need for the maternal side of God. Yet she does not quite come out into the open and affirm this in her writing style, or in the majority of her writing.

None of these teachers have made it a practice to use feminine language for God, and therefore their points about its usefulness often appear to be theoretical and not fully available to the people to whom they minister. *It is almost as if they are saying it is good to affirm the feminine face of God as long as we keep it a secret!* Yet Wimber's Vineyard movement has fostered deeper intimacy with God by both public expressions of worship and tender songs sung to God. Here are some of the words from one such worship song expressing the need for God's paternal face.

> I need you to hold me like my daddy never could.
> And I need you to show me how resting in your
>   arms can be so good.
> Oh hold me father. Never let me go. Hold me
>   tight. Hold me closer still. . . .
> In your arms is where I need to be. I need you to
>   walk with me.
> Hand in hand we'll run and play. And I need you
>   to talk to me.
> Tell me again you'll stay.

> (*I Need You To Hold Me* by Brenda LeFave,
> Copyright © 1991, Mercy Publishing.
> Used by permission.)

---

[9]Payne, *Crisis in Masculinity*, 83.

If there is recognition of the need for God's fatherly closeness, why is there no similar recognition of God's motherly closeness? Only the very naive would believe that mothers have provided perfectly for their children while fathers have not, and therefore only the father image has been distorted.

I was listening to a popular Christian radio program offering psychological advice to its callers. The counselors were highly qualified, evangelical Christians who offered excellent help, but I noticed they constantly spoke of God only as Father. Father seemed to be their word of choice for God and no other. I could not imagine how they reconciled their deep understanding of psychological needs with an image of God that was only masculine. Were they aware of what that does to people's self-image and how diminished their emotional help was because they neglected a fuller picture of God?

In the traditional church setting, which is impoverished by exclusively masculine references to God, there is no permission to think of God in any way other than masculine. Or if maternal images do come up they are quickly dismissed. Bob and Susan, mentioned at the beginning of this chapter, were able to move further in their healing because our church community invites a more balanced image of God. God is the gender-transcending Parent of our Savior Jesus Christ, who welcomes all who come. Neither motherly or fatherly images of God are sufficient. But both are appropriate, and even necessary as the Scriptures demonstrate in offering multiple pictures of God: father, mother, shepherd, king, suffering servant, mother bear, and others. A pathway for healing can be to pray: "O God, my Father and Mother in heaven, hallowed be your name."

Hungry for Mom

I mentioned that Bob found a mentor in his journey to wholeness in one of our pastors, Marcia. She is also a powerful preacher and an open channel of the Spirit in prayer. Her prophetic gifts are very strong and she bubbles up with amazing pictures of healing every time we minister together. One reason God uses her so richly is because she is a wounded healer and traveling on her own journey of inner healing. Here is some of Marcia's story.

> In the past few years my healing process has centered around the relationship I had with my mother. I always envied the relationship she had with my oldest sister and competed fiercely for her attention. I seldom got what I wanted emotionally from Mom and was often left with a nagging sense of inadequacy.
>
> I have fought being overweight most of my life. Two years ago, several months after my mother died, I went for counseling to try to get to the point of my constant hunger. The significant image in meditation that appeared to me was that I was on a lonely dark path leading around the side of a mountain. I felt scared and all alone. As I came around the corner of the mountain there was my mom. I was so glad to see her and she said she would always be with me. That felt comforting but, for some unknown reason, not completely satisfying.
>
> One night as we worshiped in our healing service, I found myself on that path again on the inner screen of my imagination. This time, when I came around the corner of the mountain, it wasn't my mother who was waiting for me but my Mother God—the Healing Parent. She wasn't my mom at all but the Completely Other Mom. I felt overwhelming joy as She saw me. And She was joyful, too. I ran to her. She ran to me and received me and held me. I knew then why the other image of my real mom had not been totally satisfying. It carried the burden of our wounded relationship: my rejection, my shame, my inadequacy. Now I was being received with total joy, acceptance,

and love. The inadequacy and shame melted away. Now it was not just Mother God but Mom God.

Later I received prayer during the Healing Service ministry time. Paul, without knowing my need at the time, prayed that I be "filled with what I was hungry for." I knew right away that I was hungry for Mommy God. I never got enough of my mom's mothering love. I've been hungry all my life. I moved into a time of knowing the presence and peace of the Holy Mom who quietly talked to me, combed my hair, held me, played with me, and loved me in total acceptance and joy.

Some Christians may be uncomfortable with Marcia's story because they have been warned about "New Age" guided imagery and are suspicious or afraid of pictures and images in their minds—even about spiritual things. This is very unfortunate and quite opposed to biblical thinking. The wonderful metaphors throughout the Old and New Testaments and Jesus' own parables were exactly this—word pictures of God designed to evoke vivid internal images symbolizing how God looks and acts. "The LORD is my shepherd" says the Psalmist. It is quite difficult to read this and not think of God as a shepherd! Hosea 13:8 presents God as ferocious as a bereaved mother bear. "I will fall upon them like a bear robbed of her cubs, and will tear open the covering of their heart." Should we place a warning label on this passage so that no one would be tempted to image God as a fierce she-bear?

But more importantly for our subject, the language Marcia uses to describe the images the Spirit gives her are counter-cultural enough that some may find themselves uneasy. Many Christians seem to be uncomfortable with the nearness of God, much as we are sometimes uneasy with the mystical saints down through the centuries and their use of lover's language to describe the ecstasy of union with God. But surely speaking of God as "Daddy" or "Mommy" in the innermost place of our hearts gets to something of the meaning of *Abba.*

A Flawed Search for the Divine Maternal

The Catholic Church for centuries has instinctively reached out for the healing, maternal face of God but continues to miss it by focusing on Jesus' mother, Mary. In *Our Father, Our Mother*, Catholic biblical scholar George Montague paints a beautiful picture of the biblical basis for the maternal face of God and our need for just such an image. But then the Roman Catholic Church's unyielding commitment to patriarchy leads him to reject the direct recognition of that image in God and he advocates Mary as its fulfillment. He proposes the "Fatherhood of God and the Motherhood of Mary" and says, "Her love is rather the instrument of the Father's own maternal love, which was only implicit in the biblical term 'Father' but is clearly and beautifully mediated in a unique way through Mary. She is not a metaphorical appendage but a revelation in person of the maternal face of God."[10]

Perhaps Mary can be a picture of the motherhood of God, but she is not a substitute for God our Mother. When an important spiritual need is not allowed to be met in a legitimate way, then it will almost always be met in an illegitimate way, in this case loading the figure of Mary with more theological baggage than she can legitimately carry.

Ruth Carter Stapleton was one of the pioneers of inner healing in the early 1970s and a personal friend whom I greatly admired. But in leading several conferences with her, and praying for others in numerous inner healing sessions together, I found it somewhat unsettling that she would let the figure of Mary serve as an agent of healing for those who needed a motherly sense of God. She would always ask us not to tell anyone because she was in enough trouble with some of the male leaders of the charismatic movement who were uncomfortable with anything that looked "mystical," especially with a woman doing the teaching. We talked about it and I thought,

---

[10]George T. Montague, *Our Father, Our Mother, Mary and the Faces of God* (Steubenville: Franciscan University, 1990) 139.

even then, there should be some way to let the maternal love of God into the healing times, and Mary seemed to be the best we could come up with. I experimented with this two or three times in praying for others, since often the healing situation needed a motherly figure of divine power. But I stopped because this was so unsound biblically and theologically, even though it seemed to bring a measure of healing to others. This was before the full emergence of evangelical feminism, and years later I realized it simply had not occurred to either one of us that God herself could directly fulfill that healing role. I know now God the Mother can directly let in God's mothering love. We do not need to resort to any other resource.

Personal Healing Disciplines

Because of this intensive masculine conditioning, some of us have adopted deliberate counter-balancing rituals and practices. These allow a fuller and more adequate image of God to gradually sink down into our subconscious and do its renewing work.

I have personally refrained from speaking about God in masculine terms for four years now. I have slipped up about a dozen times, but that's not bad considering that talking about God is my occupation! It takes some quick juggling of words and phrases in teaching and conversations to avoid masculine pronouns, but it is possible. While I advocate balanced gender language I have temporarily adopted this discipline to counter the constant stream of masculine language from what I read and hear from others. When I hear others say something like "God is great and he really loves us," I inwardly respond with, "Yes, she does!"

When I am involved in praying for others I often see motherly images of God and share them. They seem to have a healing impact that is quite striking. I also see fatherly images, but they do not have quite the same effect, perhaps because they are so familiar. When I anoint with oil for healing I say: "I anoint you in the name of the Father, Son and Holy Spirit, the One God who is Mother to us all."

I have participated in my church's experimental, inclusive language worship services and have seen the tears of those who found liberation just from the corporate singing of a hymn that included feminine language for God. These men and women waited all their lives to have the feminine face of God recognized and affirmed, and when it was, they were healed.

Every morning I exercise vigorously, one day on my stair climber and the next on my treadmill. One of the disciplines I practice during this time is to reflect on the two large pictures of the crucifixion which I have hanging in our exercise room at home. Neither are the usual scenes. One is Salvador Dali's *Christ of St. John of the Cross* where Jesus is surrealistically hanging on a cross suspended in mid-air over the Sea of Galilee (actually the Sea of Spain in this picture). Is this an accurate picture? No, but then no representation of the crucifixion is entirely accurate since we don't know what Jesus looked like. However, this one captures something true for me that other representations do not. It moves my mind to think of the Transcendent, Cosmic Christ encompassing the entire world in God's loving and dying for all humankind.

The other is a large print of Edwina Sandy's *Christa*, a four-foot sculpture of a naked woman hanging as from a cross and wearing a crown of thorns. Is it accurate? No, of course not. But then again, its effect may be legitimate. Thinking of Jesus as a naked woman nailed to the cross shocks me into realizing again the length to which God went in my redemption. A woman seems especially helpless and vulnerable, and my culturally-conditioned religious self still recoils. I am daily impacted by this reminder that Jesus died for women too, taking on all of their shame and grief. Jesus is not just a man for all seasons, but a person for all humankind.

The older I get, the more aware I am of wanting to protect my inner self from false or unhealthy pictures of life by discipling myself in what I hear and see. When I read, or watch movies and TV I find myself attempting to avoid several kinds of unhealthy images: violence, eroticism, profanity which uses

God's name, and exclusively patriarchal images of God. Only the last one is difficult to do because I would have to avoid going to most churches to accomplish it!

James, a gifted musician and seminary graduate in our church, prays this prayer every morning upon waking: "*Abba,* I am a focused man and I belong to you. *Imma,* I am a focused man and I belong to you." He is using the very words Jesus spoke, so significant because the first person Jesus ever called *Abba,* "Daddy," was not God, but his own father, Joseph. Later he used *abba* for what many believe was his only name for addressing God. James says, "I use *imma,* Aramaic for mommy, so I can learn to own more of the feminine side of God. I want to live long enough with the feminine side of God until I have made the shift on the inside."

The Awesome She

Here is an experience of healing brought about by the feminine face of God unfolded in the compelling prose of author and hymn writer Brian Wren.

> Twice I have experienced the immediate presence of God: at the age of 19, when I met Jesus on the cross, and last October 27, at about three in the afternoon. At that moment, I'm ashamed to admit it, I was feeling an upsurge of lust in the presence of a young woman.

> As I was wrestling with myself, trying to stop the flow of fantasy, I was interrupted by a gripping awareness of divine presence, arresting and unmistakable. For the first time in my life I met the loving God as Holy Femaleness, Awesome She. She impinged on me not as Mother, Sister, or Lover (though no doubt she can be so known) but as the archetypal power and spirit from which such personal images derive. She told me, in words I can't now frame, that the woman in my thoughts was precious to her, under her protec-

tion and someone I had better treat with respect. Faced with that powering presence, my fantasies evaporated, leaving me chastened and changed.

Between the immediacy of that presence and any conceivable representation of it lies a gulf. Her presence was sensed rather than seen, the visual element being indistinct. When I later tried sketching the impact of that presence, drawing rapidly, frustrated by lack of skill, I found myself summoning visual symbols I had not seen clearly, or seen at all in the moment of encounter. The picture that follows is therefore partly a "vision" and partly a rendering of indefinable experience into visual form.

I saw, and met, a divine presence that was toweringly female yet beyond sexuality: She was arresting and awe-inspiring. There was the impression of a great dark mask covering what was not a face. Above the mask of the face-not-a-face was an impression of hair, sweeping upwards and outwards on either side, becoming great wings, as of an eagle facing me, poised to soar upwards or beat downwards in bone-breaking fury. The hair becoming wings, was not joined to the mask, but above and close to it. Between the wings was neither shape nor form, but a dark purple fire.

Below the mask over the face-not-a-face was the impression of an iridescent robe—dark blue, purple, russet and black—flecked with gold, covering a torso whose breasts were indistinct yet immense, able to comfort someone embraced or snuff out the life of one hugged in anger.

On each side of the robe was the impression of great arms in movement, indistinct, yet with fur and forepaws clearly visible. The paws, I thought, can bless and embrace, but also seemed those of a she-bear robbed of her cubs—reaching out ready to hug or crush and rip apart in wrath: a warning from fierce love. The robe swept down for a great distance, becoming indistinct far be-

low, lost in clouds of thick darkness, with lightning flickering within and without. Beneath the
clouds were tiny figures—the women whom she
loves and protects with her power.

She is the Holy One of Sarah and Abraham, Mir-
iam and Deborah, Mary of Magdala, Martha and
John. She is Moving and Flowing Spirit, Birth-giver
Unborn. Word and Wisdom, present in Jesus, El
Shaddai, Awesome She, Protector of Women.

The presence came unasked, an encounter with
the whole being of the one God, known in that
moment as She. It was as if the complex diamond
of the divine shone at me intensely from that one
facet. In the moment of meeting there was no
time for reflection. . . . I believe I was stopped in
my tracks by the first person of the Trinity, the
source of all things. But since God is indivisible,
when we meet one person of the Trinity the others are immediately present. The Holy One who
met me certainly had something of the untame-
able wildness of the Holy Spirit. She also had
something of the fierce love for each human
being that was enfleshed in Jesus of Nazareth,
and which prompted that male Jew to treat the
disvalued and subordinated women of his time
with revaluing love and respect.[11]

In Summary

The importance of the feminine face of God cannot be
fully grasped without understanding the inner woundedness in both men and women which comes from the with-
holding or abuse of mother love and father love in childhood.
I could tell as many stories of the importance of the masculine

---

[11]Copyright © 1988 Christian Century Foundation. Reprinted by
permission from the February 17, 1988 issue of *The Christian Century*.

face of God, but that face is already available to us. The abortion of the feminine of God has prevented us from looking into the mothering eyes of God. This is a centuries old wounding which cries out to be touched.

Because of this great need it is sometimes difficult to be gracious to those who oppose recognizing the motherlike side of God. It feels like they don't care about our brokenness. At its deepest level, the image of God is not only an issue of truth but also one of deep inner healing.

In the garden, male and female were torn asunder, and in the Fall the "feminine" was dismembered and banished from God and the human community. Until the divine male and female have been reunited and the female half of humanity has been returned from exile, we cannot be healed.[12]

When we look into the face of God, what kind of face do we see? The shape of that face and the look of those eyes will determine whether we shall be healed or wounded once more.

—Lynda Shillito
Broadway Baptist Church Co-pastor

---

[12]Some phrases in this paragraph are from Gross, "Steps toward Feminine Imagery of Deity in Jewish Theology" in *On Being A Jewish Feminist*, 234.

"My pastor baptized me in the name of the Creator, Redeemer, and Sanctifier. Will I go to hell?"

"No, but your pastor will."

Why Are There Such Strong Reactions?

7

I have seen normally rational men and women become almost hysterical in their opposition to the idea of calling God Mother. Voices shake, breathing becomes heavy, faces turn red, and tension increases. I have no desire to second guess or psychoanalyze those who disagree with me, and certainly some reactions are simply strong disagreements. I don't want to discredit genuine theological objections by attributing them to emotional reactions, and I seriously considered not including this chapter. However, it seems helpful to explore these intense reactions in order to understand something of what others may be going through, allowing for a more empathetic response and, ultimately, better communication and relationships. I hope my readers do not feel that they are merely being analyzed or that their objections are being evaded in this chapter. My intent is to be caring and helpful, even if it means bringing factors into the light which may be painful to see but which need understanding, time, healing, and sometimes repentance.

I have observed a number of different factors which may contribute in various ways to some of the strong negative reactions to calling God Mother.

Culture Shock

One woman reported to me that she "felt the Spirit leave" when someone during our Sunday morning service offered a prayer which began, "Loving God, you are like a strong mother who protects her children with her fierce love." She said, "It just ruined my worship that morning and, since the Spirit left, it is surely a sign that God is not pleased with feminine God language."

It seems to me there is possibly a much better explanation of what happened—culture shock.[1] The very unfamiliarity of putting "she" and "God" together in the same sentence, in the context of centuries of male references to the Trinity, is bound to produce cognitive dissonance. The vast majority of the population in our country who say they believe in God have been primarily influenced by the traditional Judeo-Christian communication of a God who is likened more to men. When we in the church discover disregarded feminine metaphors for God in Scripture and begin to use them, we must be prepared to battle against our culture's idea of God—which is not the same as the Bible's idea.

Most counter-cultural practices seem very strange to us at first. When I first observed Christians raising their hands in worship I thought it was truly weird. I searched the scriptures and church history and was surprised to find it was a common practice in the Bible and the early church.[2] I decided to try it out in the next meeting of some of those who, in the 1960s, were called "neo-pentecostals." I went alone and sat in the far back corner. As I raised my hands in worship (trying to look cool doing it), I was embarrassed to find my hands trembling. I was

---

[1]This line of thinking was suggested by Bobbie Crawford in "A Female Crucifix?" *Daughters of Sarah* (Nov.–Dec., 1988) 24.

[2]Lifting hands to God is the most reported body language of prayer and praise in Scripture and early Christian art (Ps 28:2; 63:4; 88:9; 134:2; 141:2, Luke 24:50; 1 Tim 2:8). In today's world, raising our hands is also the most universal expression of celebration, surrender, joy, asking for help, and victory.

sure everyone in the room could see my shaking hands and was going to run out and tell all of my friends how dumb I looked. I felt anxious, stupid, and heretical. I managed a good five seconds of hand raising before I ran out of freedom.

I knew raising our hands was a modern imitation of the ancient practice, now signaling the spiritual values of surrender, asking for help, celebration, joy, and victory. It just seemed more "natural" at a rock concert than in a church! Just like the woman in our service who said, "I felt the Spirit leave," I did not sense any of God's presence as my attention moved from God to myself in these first attempts at more expressive body language.

Now, thirty years later, I have to sit on my hands to keep them from going up during praise and worship if I'm someplace where hand raising is not considered appropriate. Now it seems the most natural and "spiritual" practice I can imagine, and quite regularly it helps me become conscious of God's presence.

Becoming comfortable with feminine language for God has been a similar process for me. In my own prayer life, addressing God as Mother seemed unreal at first. In conversation I nervously smiled or laughed along with others when I referred to God as "she." It seemed like I was making an off-the-cuff joke rather than speaking seriously. At Broadway Baptist we began an alternative worship service on Sunday evenings, and for a year we used mostly feminine language for God in those times. I felt like I was participating in some clandestine underground church, practicing secret, forbidden rituals, and expecting at any moment the heresy police were going to rush in and arrest us. But these times of being with others for whom it seemed more natural also decreased my extreme self-consciousness. It took three years for me to emerge from the "weird" stage to a sense of comfortableness, and now I easily refer to God with feminine imagery when I share or lead in prayer in some smaller group where it seems appropriate.

While attending a meeting of 6,000 Southern Baptists who are open to women in ministry, I was initially startled and then exhilarated as a speaker prayed, "Dear God our heavenly

Mother." The public and corporate legitimization of what I personally had come to embrace affected me so much I finally moved from excitement to tears. Part of our moving from culture shock to comfortableness waits on this kind of public affirmation.

We must allow ourselves and others time to get over the shock of a counter-cultural image of God as the Spirit converts our culturally conditioned emotions and habit patterns.

Fear of Heresy

Often the first time a committed Christian hears another Christian seriously call God Mother it seems like the God being addressed is surely different from the God of Abraham, Isaac and Jacob, and the Father of our Lord Jesus Christ. I can easily understand such an impression and the immediate fear that this is heresy of the highest order. I understand it because that's what I originally thought also.

Being careful to avoid heresy is never a bad thing! We evangelicals and charismatics are committed to the Bible as the source and authority for our understanding of God and the Christian life. Since the predominant biblical imagery for God is masculine, we really do wonder if we are committing some kind of heresy. As I wrestled with this myself, I found it pushed me to deal thoroughly and in depth with the scriptures. As with any new area of restoration, I believe there is even a deeper understanding of the Bible which needs more time and reflection to emerge. I look forward to more and more scholars bringing their expertise and insight into this subject and seeing it develop further.

Eventually, as I searched the scriptures, the whole issue of heresy reversed, and that very fear became a primary motivation that pushed me to write this book. I have come to believe that when I call God Father and Mother I am *less* heretical and *more* orthodox than those who would limit God to only Father!

Many are not aware of the feminine imagery in the Bible. They do not realize how God's truth has come to us in language shaped by patriarchal culture, and they mistake the form of revelation for the content of revelation. We must do much more teaching and allow time for new perspectives to sink in as we come into a deeper consciousness of God's image.

Confusion Over the Role of Mother

Women, particularly mothers, are torn in the conflict of changing roles. The traditional role of homemaker and care-taker of the children is being challenged by the economic demands of a full-time job, sometimes needed for survival, and an emerging sense of responsibility to the larger world of politics, corporate America, entrepreneurship, the arts, social ethics, church leadership, and other areas beyond the home.

Is the mother image one of self-sacrifice and service or breadwinner and protector? Is it family-oriented or cause-oriented? Even in this study I have wrestled with avoiding stereotyping women as nurturers and men as workers, especially with words like "masculine" and "feminine" which are so loaded with culturally changing meanings. Perhaps some of the reactions to imaging God as mother stem from such role confusion and tension.[3]

The role of father is also changing, but patriarchy, with its rigid role definitions, is so embedded in our psyches that it may seem less confusing as well as be extremely familiar, to image God as father. It is the new which throws us into panic—unless it is clearly defined. One writer says, "Much more work will have to be done on the socioeconomic and psychological levels to make the role of mother a positive and

---

[3]Suggested by Linda A. Mercadante in *Gender, Doctrine, and God* (Nashville: Abingdon, 1990) 160, a stimulating study of the Shakers and their attempts at gender-inclusive language.

less ambiguous one, before the image of God as Mother finds a ready welcome in the church."[4]

Difficulty of Changing Deeply Ingrained Behavior Patterns, Even When They Are Abusive

I have pondered why so many women feverishly defend patriarchy, and some seem especially opposed to calling God Mother. Since one of the results of the Fall has been the tendency of women to misuse vulnerability and men to misuse power, perhaps we resist that which is unfamiliar, even though a change may be much better for us. Women are very familiar with how to use vulnerability as a tool to get their way, just as men use physical and structural power to impose their wills. It is as difficult for women to learn how to confidently assert themselves in decisive responsibility as it is for men to learn how to be vulnerable and reveal their deepest feelings and needs to others.

This resistance to unfamiliar ways of behaving is different from culture shock in that it engages deeply ingrained psychological ways of acting, which may seem safe because they are so familiar. Partnership may be resisted because we don't know how we would function within it, while we know all about working within a patriarchal system.

Why does an abused child cling to its abuser? Why do battered wives continue to return to their abusing husbands? Perhaps we tend to recreate unresolved childhood situations in adulthood, hoping to "get it right" this time. We return to old patterns, seeking to resolve them and bring relief from old pain. It takes great effort and courage for those who are being mistreated to break away from abusive systems because abused people at least know what is expected of them. The fear of abandonment can be greater than the fear of mistreatment,

---

[4]Ibid.

and the fear of the unknown future may be greater than the fear of present pain.

Invalidating Previous Ministry

Women who have functioned amazingly well under a male-dominant system do not want to be called foolish. They played by the rules, often accomplishing a great deal, and are now being invited to believe they contributed to an abusive system. A new awareness does not invalidate what has been accomplished in the past, and women who have functioned well under the limitations of traditional ministry practices are to be commended, not put down.

Even while calling God "he" all of their lives, many who have dedicated years of ministry to a lost and needy world in the name of Christ may resent any idea that they missed something or hindered the gospel. We must all come to value our past in such a way that we can remain open to learning the new thing God is teaching us.

Fear of Losing God as Father

We live in an age of the absent father. The Industrial Revolution has taken fathers out of the home, away from their wives and children, and placed them in inaccessible factories and offices. They are missing physically and psychologically. Men no longer spend long hours alongside their daughters and sons in the family business or on the family farm. Today many of us live with a great father wounding, especially those of us who are sons. We long for our missing fathers, someone to initiate us into the world of manhood and breathe into us an understanding of what it means to be a man. The male soul has been left shriveled and unaffirmed for want of good fathering.

It is because of this void that some perceive calling God Mother as a great and tragic loss. They fear that this means we will stop calling God Father or lessen the importance of God as Father. Some men believe the last vestige of hope they have for affirming their masculine identities will be gone forever. This fear is often capitalized on by the hysterical writing and teaching of some who warn of just such dire consequences.[5] Even though I and others constantly point out that we should continue to call God Father, advocating an expansion of that name, not a substitution for it, some continue to believe we want to stop calling God Father altogether.

Those who desperately need God as Father must hold fast to what they know they need, and relate to God in that very way, as father. It is safe to do that, as I will elaborate later on, only when one has removed male domination from the image of God. As long as the maleness of God dominates the female-ness of God, the image is a dangerous one because it provides the underlying rationale for male supremacy and violence against women. Advocating God as Mother frees us up to embrace God as Father in even more credible and healthy ways.

Of course there is also a real loss for many men and women. This loss is one of losing a God who is likened to men, which changes the rules of patriarchy—those connected with male importance and privileged position, and female help-lessness and a desire to be taken care of. Such a major change in the power rules of life is sure to be resisted by some men and women alike. But, indeed, we must lose the macho God and accept a true divine fatherliness which does not dominate women.

Such a loss needs to be faced, grieved over, and worked through. However, the idea that we will lose God as authentic father is simply not true. I want to expand our image of God, not further reduce it. When we see it, really see it, and feel it, really feel it, then God is more father than father and more mother than mother.

---

[5]I found Oddie's *What Will Happen to God* to be just such a book in its extreme caricatures.

The Image of Women as Evil

The pervasive and sometimes subtle attitude that what is feminine is somehow inferior and evil—an integral part of our religious and cultural history—makes referring to God as female or feminine seem like we are accusing God of something bad.

The early church fathers as well as Jewish and Greek philosophers of the early church era represented women as, at best, less than men, and at worst, evil. Socrates said, "Do you know anything at all practiced among mankind in which in all these respects the male sex is not far better than the female?"[6] Aristotle said, "We should look upon the female state as being as it were a deformity."[7]

The sayings of the religious leaders of Jesus' day also provide insight into attitudes toward women:

> A man should be careful not to walk between two women, two dogs, or two swine.[8]

> All women are potential adulteresses unless carefully guarded and given much busywork.[9]

> Conversing with a woman is likely to result in gossip or lewdness.[10]

> It is well for those whose children are male, but ill for those whose children are female. . . . At the birth of a boy all are joyful, but at the birth of a girl all are sad. . . . When a boy comes into the world, peace comes into the world: when a girl comes, nothing comes. . . . Even the most virtuous of women is a witch. . . . Our teachers have said: Four qualities

---

[6]Plato, *The Republic* (trans. B. Jowett; New York: Modern Library, 1941) 176.

[7]From *Generation of Animals* (trans. A. L. Peck; Cambridge: Harvard University, 1953) 459–61.

[8]Kitzur Shulchan Aruch quoted in *On Being a Jewish Feminist, A Reader*, 17.

[9]M. *Ketubot* 5:6.

[10]M. *Abot* 1:5.

are evident in women: They are greedy at their food, eager to gossip, lazy and jealous.[11]

Jesus ben Sirach, who wrote early in the second century BC, lamented, "Better is the wickedness of a man than a woman who does good; and it is a woman who brings shame and disgrace."[12] Josephus, who described himself as having been a Pharisee entrusted with considerable leadership, claimed, "The woman, says the Law, is in all things inferior to the man."[13] Rabbi Eliezar articulated a particularly harmful idea with, "Let the words of the law be burned rather than given to a woman."[14] Rabbi Hillel said, "Many women, much witchcraft."[15] Another rabbinical text says, "One glass is good for a woman; two are a disgrace; with three she opens her mouth; with four she solicits in complete abandon even as an ass on the street."[16]

The civil and religious literature of Jesus' day made it clear that women were classed as inadmissible witnesses, in the same category with gamblers, pigeon-racers and other persons of low character.[17] In his book devoting exhaustive research to attitudes toward women in formative Judaism, Swidler concludes:

> Simply stated, the clear conclusion . . . is that in the formative period of Judaism the status of women was not one of equality with men, but rather, severe inferiority, and that even intense misogynism was not infrequently present. Since the sacred and secular spheres of that society were so intertwined, this inferiority and subordination of women was consequently present in both the religious and civil areas of Jewish life.[18]

---

[11]Leonard Swidler, "Jesus Was a Feminist," *South East Asia Journal of Theology* 13 (1, 1971) 103.

[12]Sirach 42:14.

[13]*Against Apion* 2.201

[14]M. *Sotah* 3, 4.

[15]M. *Abot* 2, 7.

[16]B. *Ketuboth* 65a.

[17]B. *Rosh Hashanah* 22a.

[18]Swidler, *Women in Judaism,* 167.

Jesus treated women very differently from his predecessors and contemporaries, and the early church saw the beginning of a true women's liberation movement. However, male power was so thoroughly entrenched that it moved to curtail the new teaching of valuing the feminine. Tertullian (AD 160–230), a leading Christian teacher, wrote:

> Woman, . . . do you not know that you are (each) an Eve? The sentence of God on this sex of yours lives in this age: the guilt must of necessity live too. *You* are the devil's gateway: *you* are the unsealer of that (forbidden) tree: you are the first deserter of the divine law: *you* are she who persuaded him whom the devil was not valiant enough to attack. You destroyed so easily God's image, man. On account of *your* desert—that is, death—even the Son of God had to die (translator's parentheses and italics).[19]

Reversing the strong liberation movement which had begun in the early church, the Council of Laodicea abolished the ordination of women finally and completely in AD 365.[20] In the sixth century, men went even further and debated whether or not women had souls. At the Council of Macon a vote was taken on this issue and women won . . . by one vote! This vote reveals a historical context in which women were viewed by the church fathers as defective men.[21]

Pope Leo XIII, in 1879, declared the thirteenth-century Thomas Aquinas to be the one theologian whose writings must be studied in all Catholic colleges, universities, and seminaries. Aquinas believed that woman "is defective and misbegotten." He taught that, while it is true that woman is misbegotten, it is God's intention that woman be included in

---

[19]Tertullian, "On the Apparel of Women," *Ante-Nicene Fathers* (trans. A. Roberts and J. Donaldson; Buffalo: Christian Literature, 1885) vol. 4, book 1, chapter 1, 14.

[20]Diane Tennis, *Is God the Only Reliable Father?* (Philadelphia: Westminster, 1985) 14.

[21]Ibid.

humanity, in order that she may be Adam's helper. The only help she could offer, though, was the "work of generation," because "Man can be more efficiently helped by another man in other works." Aquinas affirmed Genesis 1:27, that both male and female were created in God's image, but he argued that there are different degrees to which a person can be in the image of God. Only the man "actually or habitually knows and loves God," not the woman, "for man is the beginning and end of woman, just as God is the beginning and end of every creature."[22]

Our heroic reformers had some definitely less than holy ideas about women. Martin Luther said, "If one take women from their housewifery . . . they are good for nothing.[23] John Knox, in biting satirical commentary, proclaimed,

> For who can deny but it is repugnant to Nature that the blind shall be appointed to lead and conduct such as do see? That the weak, sick, and impotent persons shall nourish and keep the whole strong? And finally that the foolish, mad and phrenetic shall govern the discreet and give counsel to such as be of sober mind. And such be all women, compared unto men.[24]

These sinful attitudes toward women have polluted not only our theology, but also our art. Women in Western art often embody shame, evil, and sexuality (which, for much of church history, was considered sinful). Men, however, are shown as clothed, powerful, and conquering.[25]

Women are not the weaker sex, the inferior sex, or the opposite sex. They are just women, like men are just men, and all of us share the worst and best qualities of humankind. *As long as women are seen as inferior, evil, and sexually seductive, it will be impossible to see the feminine of God.* Since God

---

[22]Thomas Aquinas, *Summa Theologica*, Q. 92, art. 1.

[23]Cited in Gerzon, *A Choice of Heroes*, 152.

[24]Ibid.

[25]See Margaret Miles, *Carnal Knowing: Female Nakedness and Religious Meaning in the Christian West* (Boston: Beacon, 1989).

cannot be inferior, evil, or sexually seductive, whenever some-one calls God "she," we are brought face to face with our sex-ism. Our inability to talk about God in feminine terms cannot be resolved until we repent of these attitudes.

Rejected "Feminine" Qualities

The rejection by both men and women of the qualities of nurture, receptivity, intuition, and expression of feelings re-sults in several situations which make calling God Mother difficult.

While we are accustomed to male gender language about God, we are not accustomed to female gender language about her. Sometimes we men must deal with unconscious sexual attractions and repulsions around unfamiliar sexual imagery. The world of motherhood often brings to mind images of birthing, while fatherhood seldom brings to mind images of impregnation. God's male chest may be comforting, but God's female chest may be another matter! Calling God "he" sounds normal, but calling God "she" may sound sexual.

Perhaps many men have not yet consciously admitted to themselves how profoundly we fear a world full of powerful women. Our fear of female power may come from some sense that the feminine is evil, or possibly from unresolved child-hood developmental issues which result in difficulty trusting women.

One of our co-pastors at Broadway Baptist, Marcia Fleischman, has reflected on the unresolved inner "feminine" and says:

> Some of the resistance to the feminine face of God is that many people are afraid to face their issues with their own mothers. Fathers have been easier to deal with in one sense because they have been largely absent from the home, and that distance has allowed some safety to afford the anger one must go through in the healing pro-

cess. In our generation, mothers were often physically at home with us, although not always emotionally there for us. Getting angry at Mom in order to become separate is a greater core issue for many because being with Mom was a survival issue—lose Mom's love and you die. To an infant or small child it seems clear there is no one else but Mom to take care of you. Therefore, when someone mentions Mother God, someone who hasn't become emotionally and internally separate from their own mother, may suddenly put their mom's face on God and become afraid. How can I afford to feel the rejection, shame, or manipulation from God like I received from Mom? How can I become separate from Mom like I need to but not become separate from my divine Mom?

The worst insult to a man in any macho culture is to imply that he is like a woman. Boys hurl the name "sissy" or "wimp" at those they want to hurt because it seems the ultimate put down to newly developing physical masculinity. Calling God Mother may seem like calling God "sissy" and a challenge to God's "masculinity." This may have been what was happening with my fundamentalist friend, who said to me, "I don't like people who want to give God a sex change operation!" He believed God really was male, and some form of theological castration was taking place if we referred to God in female terms!

Much of the charismatic movement has taken a strong, patriarchal position about women being submitted to men in everything. They typically teach that husbands should be in charge of wives and women must never teach, pastor, or in any way be in charge of men. One large charismatic community I visited had been instructed in the details of radical role differentiation and subordination, not as a matter of social grace or custom, but as religious "truth." The men were always to open doors for the women and never women for men. When walking into a public place the women should walk behind. Men were told not to wear anything pink (gays were thought of as preferring the color pink), and when any of the leaders (all men) entered the room, everyone should stand! Why has militant patriarchy so often been characteristic of the charismatic movement, which Peter Wagner of Fuller Seminary has termed the "second wave" of the Spirit in this century?[26] (Interestingly, "first wave" charismatics, or classical Pentecostals, seem to have escaped much of this, perhaps because from the very beginning they affirmed women in leadership.) Charismatics often say the Bible commands patriarchy and this is why they are carefully working out what it means in today's society. But I believe this does not entirely account for why one particular interpretation of the Bible has been chosen by many charismatics over several others which seem to be equally reasonable and faithful to the texts.

I have another possible explanation for this perpetuation of patriarchy. I have observed certain phenomena in myself and other men as a result of a new openness to the Holy Spirit. There is a new freedom to demonstrate intimacy with God in worship such as kneeling, lifting hands, clapping, and dancing, verbal expressions such as saying out loud, "I love you, I worship you," and greater emotional tenderness often shown in weeping and groaning for the pain of world. Also common is open affection with other Christians, saying "I love you" and embracing and hugging one another. The charismatic movement has clearly preceded the current men's movement in giving men permission to cry and express feelings of warmth and affection!

Many of these new freedoms are what our society would stereotypically see as "feminine" behaviors. It is my hypothesis that because these qualities of nurture, receptivity, gentleness, intuition, and expressions of feeling have been so rejected and suppressed in men, when they emerge so openly by the work of the Spirit, many men became fearful. As men fear becoming "feminized" or acting like women, they overcompensate by retreating into heavily patriarchal theology and practices. They create rigid power structures where they can maintain some of their old macho selves and not have to deal with their own inner rejection of these very human qualities. These men

---

[26]Peter Wagner, *How to Have a Healing Ministry Without Making Your Church Sick!* (Ventura: Regal Books, 1988) 11–36.

are often the most vocal about the need for men to be in charge and have the greatest difficulty in conceiving of the feminine face of God.

I am reminded of the behavior of men on the football field or in combat. They hug one another, pat each other on the rear, cry openly, or tenderly embrace a wounded buddy. The super macho context of football or combat makes it safe to behave in ways these men would never act away from the game or the war. Christian men may find it much safer to act in such expressive, nurturing ways only in the context of a rigid patriarchal structure which makes it clear by external and structural means that they are MEN and not women.

Another result of this rejection of the "feminine" can be an emphasis in worship and music on the militant power and warrior-like majesty of God. Of course, there is a wonderful place for this style of music, and many churches are dying for lack of it. However, I sometimes find endless jubilant worship does not connect with me where I am, and if I try to participate I run of out energy and feel worn out. When I come into a church service feeling vulnerable and in touch with sadness and pain, I need some songs that recognize the weakness of the human condition and God's identification with it, i.e., God's suffering, weeping, and pain, and the depth of brokenness we Christians experience. Many of us who come to worship are struggling with our own inner anguish and need a place to connect in worship with the God who understands and allows us to be where we are. The book of Psalms, the worship book of the Old Testament, models this as it alternates between pain and praise, anger and awe, grief and greatness. In some churches, the God revealed in Jesus as the suffering servant and vulnerable friend seems much less visible than the Lion of Judah who roars and conquers all. Both aspects are true and have a place in balanced worship.

I believe as these "feminine" qualities become healed, accepted, and affirmed among us, we will have both a more gender-balanced image of God and a more balanced style of worship that includes both joy and sorrow, strength and weakness—a release from the bondage of patriarchy.

Confronting the Powers and Principalities

Paul says in Ephesians 6:12 that "our struggle is not against enemies of blood and flesh, but against the rulers, against authorities, against the cosmic powers of this present darkness, against the spiritual forces of evil in the heavenly places." In Galatians 4:1–11 and Colossians 2:8–23, Paul defines these elemental spirits (*stoicheia*) as human tradition, public opinion, fearful observance of religious requirements about eating and special days and, in general, deeply embedded social, political, and religious structures, prescriptions and doctrines within which society lives and moves. They are those unseen powerful forces "in the air" which control our lives instead of God.[27]

Of the ten major changes we have made in the church where I have served for the last thirty years, I have never encountered these powers and principalities as strongly and directly as with this change. One of our men, not often given to openly expressing his emotions, came to me after a meeting where I had shared how sad I was at attending a large, dynamic, evangelical conference where all the speakers and leaders were men. This fit their policy of "affirming(?)" women but not allowing them to be in leadership. He was sobbing and could hardly speak as he related the picture God had brought to his mind as I had shared my sadness. It was a picture of a battlefield with bodies strewn all over, moaning, wounded, and dying. Pain was everywhere. It was a civil war scene and the church was battling itself, shooting at its own sisters and brothers. The powers and principalities had diverted us into this war among ourselves to keep us from battling them directly, causing trauma, tension, and even death in the church.

I often feel like I'm entering a minefield when I challenge the traditional ideas of God's image. I want to do a dangerous thing now and name some of the powers arrayed against our affirming the feminine in humanity and God. It is dangerous

---

[27]For an excellent discussion of the powers, see Hendrik Berkhof, *Christ and the Powers* (Scottdale: Herald Press, 1962).

because the principalities do not take direct attacks on their entrenched power lightly. They crucified Jesus.

There is the spirit of *blindness*. This is the biblical word for what we call denial. I often hear: "It doesn't bother me that there are no women teachers or leaders in our church," or "Calling God 'he' and never 'she' doesn't bother me." Denial says: "There's no problem here. Sexism doesn't exist. Women are not mistreated. Nobody thinks God is actually male."

There is the spirit of *confusion*. When this subject comes up, a cloud of confusion often comes over people's minds, and they can't understand what is going on. It's one thing to see the issues and disagree, it's another to disagree without understanding. Those whose minds are clouded by a spirit of confusion often have the greatest fears about the terrible things they believe will happen if we call God Mother.

There is the spirit of *bitter militancy*, often on both sides. The battle of the sexes began in the Fall recorded in Genesis 3, with the destruction of mutuality between the sexes and the shaming of our sexuality. Now in the secular world, angry radical feminists spew centuries of stored up anger against men, and male-bashing has come into vogue.

On the other side is the ancient and deep hatred of women which fuels the physical, verbal, and economic violence toward them which I have previously described. This is a volatile mix that becomes easily focused on the debate over how we shall address God.

Among Christians I sometimes experience a rigidity that quickly turns into bitterness and militancy on both sides when the subject is discussed. This destroys our ability to hear one another and meet with mutual understanding and creative dialogue. I have had to wrestle with just such feelings in myself in writing this book. I feel very strongly about the evil of patriarchy but have tempered some of my statements in order to refrain from such militancy. Some of my readers may believe I have not succeeded and may find it hard to believe that I have actually restrained myself. You should have read the first draft!

Finally there is the spirit of *idolatry*. An idol is anything which takes our devotion and trust away from God. We have spent a great deal of time (about 25 centuries) and money (patriarchy wouldn't last if it didn't make money for those in power) inventing the idol of an all-male God.

Paul Tillich once remarked that the Old Testament is the history of God's battle with our idolatry.[28] "Therefore watch yourselves very carefully so that you do not become corrupt and make for yourselves an idol, . . . whether formed like a man or a woman" (Deut 4:15–16, NIV). It is this idol, which is being shaken when we consider the feminine side of God as the Holy One of Israel, which still does battle with us. Perhaps one of the chief values in calling God "she" is that it is so shocking. Idols are sometimes more effectively shattered with lightning bolts than with endless debates.

Image breaking is a part of all true Christian theology. We must shatter all false images of God. This does not mean the end of male imagery for her. It simply means that once the idolatrous part of the image has been destroyed, then the true part can return as an authentic metaphor—a graphic or verbal image that helps us worship, but which we are careful not to confuse with God, who cannot be fully comprehended. A practical test to determine if we have a God who is only masculine, and therefore a false image, may be the degree of comfort we have with feminine references to God. When calling God "she" no longer bothers us, then it may be safe to call God "he."

Some of us often have a difficult time relating to the Father image of God. Remember that God is not just Father, he is also Mother. There are both characteristics to be found in the makeup of God. If you are unable to relate in an intimate way to God as Father because of a poor role model, try relating with your mother in mind. The overall tone is to relate as a son or daughter to a parent.

–John Wimber,
Founder, Vineyard Ministries International[29]

---

[28]Griffiss, *Naming the Mystery,* 178.
[29]Wimber, *Teach Us to Pray,* 90.

"Since we don't have any women on the faculty at the moment, you female students will be pleased to hear that Mrs. Muscovitz has agreed to be your mentor."

A Remarkable Parallel in
Acts 15

8

What institutions do best is defend themselves. Churches do it particularly well because they think they are defending God.

Most churches vigorously defend themselves against any significant change with the rallying cry of "Come weal or woe, we want our status quo." But the suggestion that it might be good to call God "Mother" may ignite some of the most volatile reaction to institutional change, especially in those churches that attempt to take the Bible seriously. Of all the changes which the church I serve as visionary leader has made over the past thirty years, this one created the most uproar. I was caught off guard because no one had warned me this issue scored so high on the ecclesiastical stress scale. Of course I was aware that theologians hotly debated the subject, but it seemed like they argue vigorously and vociferously about a lot of things. In the hundred or so books and journal articles I had read on this subject there were few pastoral warnings about the strong reaction this topic can cause in the local church or how to go about managing this kind of change.

I have listened to hundreds of pastors in the last thirty years of leading pastors' workshops and support groups. The

one thing that seems most discouraging to them is their difficulty in leading their churches to make significant changes.
Many would not even consider challenging their congregation's idea of the masculine image of God because of the
amount of conflict they expected over such a break with tradition. Therefore, any serious exploration of the subject of "God
talk" must deal with our attitudes towards conflict as well as
measures to help us cope with it.

For years I have been fascinated with the proceedings of
the Jerusalem Council recorded in Acts 15 and the creative way
the young church resolved a monumental controversy.

The Jerusalem Council

> Then certain individuals came down from Judea
> and were teaching the brothers, "Unless you are
> circumcised according to the custom of Moses,
> you cannot be saved" (Acts 15:1).

Should new male converts to Christianity who were not
Jews be circumcised, as was required of all male converts to
Judaism? There was more going on here than the practice of a
traditional religious rite, because circumcision had expanded
to become the catch-all word for general obedience to the
Law. Should the new male Gentile converts to Christianity be
required to fulfill the Law? Was Christianity a category within
Judaism so that becoming a Christian meant you were also
becoming a Jew? What was the relationship between law and
grace? Did you need only the Messiah, or did you need both
Christ and the Law to have a right relationship with God? From
our vantage point two millennia later the answers may seem
fairly obvious, but they were not so clear to the early church,
and there were many unanswered questions at this stage in
the development of Christian theology. The question of circumcision was so controversial and crucial that an historic
conference was called for everybody who was anybody in the
Christian movement, in addition to the whole church in Jerusalem which must have numbered in the thousands (Acts 15:6,

12, 22). The intriguing details of the debate and its resolution are found in Acts 15.

Recently it occurred to me that the very subject of God language itself and the anguish surrounding it today are remarkably similar to the conflict the early church faced over circumcision. These striking parallels can serve as an enlightening model for us today. The situations are similar in the following ways.

Sincere People

First, those on both sides of the controversy were sincere people. The Christian Pharisees were deeply committed to God's revelation in the Old Testament and wanted to protect it at all costs. Jesus, the Messiah himself, had said, "Do not think that I have come to abolish the law or the prophets; I have come not to abolish but to fulfill" (Matt 5:17). The members of the circumcision party were not mean people who didn't love God. They did love God and handled God's sacred word, or Torah, with great seriousness.

I believe most evangelicals and charismatics on both sides of the language debate today are also people who want to be true to God's written word. Certainly there are some legalists on one side who abuse scripture, just as there are some feminists on the other side who have left the boundaries of Christian orthodoxy. However, the great majority in the middle ardently want to protect God's revelation in the scriptures from distortion or dilution. The idea of dispensing with a male-only God must seem to many today as much a radical departure from scripture as dispensing with the Law did to those first Jewish Christians.

Deeply Embedded Perceptions about How God Acts

A second resemblance is that both situations concern strong pictures of God's nature and ways of dealing with humanity. The Law provided a picture of the orderly way God operated and what God expected of humankind in return. God was not capricious or vague, but gave clear guidelines about what righteous people should and should not do. This picture of a stable, law-giving God thoroughly permeated Jewish culture in their daily habits and collective thought patterns. According to the interpreters of the Law, the violation of the least important of its precepts was the same as "rejecting the Law, thrusting off God's yoke and denying the faith's foundation."[1]

In a comparable fashion, the anguish today is over long-held traditions deeply embedded in culture which deal with our perception of how God behaves. Does God only act like a man, or also like a woman, however society defines those actions? At first I thought those who so strongly refused to consider feminine language for God simply did not understand. But I have come to believe that some really do understand, or at least intuitively know, the magnitude of the change involved. A woman in our church who is one of the most committed, caring, and self-giving persons I know said to me, "This whole business of talking about God being feminine has shaken the very foundation of my faith." She correctly perceived we were talking about deep changes in our religious subconscious, which has been formed in part by many centuries of patriarchal dominance of language.

Drastically Affected Relationships

A third similarity is that the Law radically influenced how the Hebrew people related to all those who were not Jews. The Law's interpreters believed that one of its purposes was to "make a hedge" around the people of Israel. The Law made the men different with the bodily mark of circumcision. It limited social contacts because of kosher food requirements, mar-

---

[1]Henri Daniel-Rops, *Daily Life in the Time of Jesus* (New York: Hawthorn Books, 1962) 468.

riage restrictions, and social boundaries of clean and unclean. These requirements, originally provided to protect them from being absorbed by pagan cultures, had turned into exclusive and hostile attitudes toward those not of their ethnic group.

Their sense of being the chosen people, especially blessed by God, led to an extraordinary sense of national pride, which in turn contributed to the damaging prejudices toward others which Jesus so often challenged. A widely spoken proverb recorded in the Talmud said, "A piece of bread given by a Samaritan is more unclean than swine's flesh."[2]

I find a noteworthy parallel in the effects of patriarchy in leadership and language today. Imaging God as masculine affects the way men relate to all those who are not men, i.e., women. A pervasive and powerful sense of gender pride is created if it is assumed that masculine must be more like God than feminine. It creates exclusive closed circles of male egos basking in the "good ol' boy" network of church, business and government. "Unclean" women are not allowed into these sacred confines. Male gender prejudices, put downs, and sexual harassment of women are rampant and secretly approved of in men's circles—as well as being tolerated and perpetuated by women. But if God preferred the masculine as *his* own gender, who can argue with that?

Intense Feelings

A fourth parallel to today's controversy is the intense feelings generated as each group fought for their side. This was no mere intellectual pursuit. Giving up circumcision then was as emotionally charged as giving up the depiction of an exclusively masculine God is today. The Christian Pharisees and their circumcision party were adamant about keeping the past commands of God. How dare anyone say what God commanded in the past was incomplete and has now been re-

---

[2]Ibid., 52.

placed by something greater? Few things produce stronger feelings than believing you are defending God's very words. The leaders of the newly empowered Gentile Christians were equally vehement about the sufficiency of God's grace. They had come to God only through grace by faith in Jesus and could not imagine adopting the bondage of Jewish laws. Few things produce stronger feelings than issues concerning liberty and freedom.

Emotions run deep on both sides of the debate today as well. I know how strongly I feel, but I was initially very naive about how easy it would be for others to see my logic, hear my passion and become just as convinced as I was. I have been surprised at how perfectly rational people on both sides lose their composure when making their case. Feelings about gender roles may run even deeper than those about the Law because the war on women has been going on since the Fall. If redemption has any meaning for our sexuality, it's time for that war to end.

Progressive Revelation and Understanding

The debates, both then and now, highlight the progressive nature of revelation and our understanding of it. Paul wrestled with the question of the Law and why God did something temporary for so many centuries instead of something permanent. He concluded there has been a progression in the unveiling of God's revelation and that "the law was our disciplinarian until Christ came, so that we might be justified by faith. But now that faith has come, we are no longer subject to a disciplinarian" (Gal 3:24–25). The writer of Hebrews recognized that "Long ago God spoke to our ancestors in many and various ways by the prophets, but in these last days he has spoken to us by a Son" (Heb 1:1–2). God was truly speaking in the past, but the past could not contain all that God had to say for the future. Paul concluded that "now the Law has come to an end with Christ" (Rom 10:4, JB).

This progression had been so great that Paul even called the revelation of God in the law of Moses a "ministry of death, chiseled in letters on stone tablets" (2 Cor 3:7), compared to the new work of the Spirit! He said "for the letter kills, but the Spirit gives life" (2 Cor 3:6). What an incredible declaration by Paul about something which had been so clearly and directly given to God's people by God—the law of Moses. This former word from God, in light of the further revelation of Jesus, was now a "ministry of death," producing bondage and spiritual death rather than giving life. How extremely difficult this must have been for many, if not most, Jews to hear because they had been taught so conscientiously for centuries about the importance of the law. And now Paul calls the sacred, God-given law a "ministry of death"! There is a remarkable parallel here to the use of only male images for God. Clearly, God's revelation is related in primarily male and masculine images in the Bible. This was the right thing at that time. But now, to continue such an exclusive practice has become a "ministry of death," bringing both psychological death in the demeaning of the feminine and even physical death in the abuse and violence toward women which is legitimized by the idea of a male-only God.

How does the concept of the progressiveness of God's revelation apply to the incarnation, since Jesus is God's ultimate word to us? Jesus, as the preeminent and unique revelation to us of God, contains all of God that we can comprehend this side of heaven. However, there is clearly more left to learn *about* that revelation and our application of it to ever new situations. The revelation is complete but our understanding of it is not. Jesus recognized that progression when he said, "I still have many things to say to you, but you cannot bear them now. When the Spirit of truth comes, he will guide you into all the truth" (John 16:12–13). The very coming of the Spirit was an indication that we must have help in comprehending and applying what Jesus intended for future situations. Paul's teaching itself was a further example that, while in one sense God had nothing left to say after Jesus, there is a vast amount of communication *about* the incarnation and its implications that has yet to be revealed to us by the Spirit. Recognizing the feminine face of God is one of these further implications.

Not Addressed by Jesus

A sixth similarity, related to the previous one, is that Jesus never directly or decisively addressed either question. Should Judaism be the required way of life for Christians? Jesus' model at a surface level seemed to make a case for the continuation of the existing tradition. Jesus was a circumcised, practicing Jew and only occasionally tampered with the Law in order to make a point. Why wouldn't Jesus have wanted everyone to act as he did and be a good Jew? Surely someone must have argued, "If being Jewish was good enough for Jesus, it ought to be good enough for us!" In addition, Jesus himself said that he had not come to do away with the Law (Matt 5:17). How confusing! If Jesus had been direct and clear about the relationship of law to grace and Jew to Gentile, Paul wouldn't have spent most of his ministry wrestling with that very challenge. It could have been settled if Jesus had said, "The Law was good for its time but now you no longer need it. I will write my law upon your hearts. Gentiles don't need to become Jews."

Nor did Jesus directly address the relationship between God and "gender," because if he had, we wouldn't be struggling with it today. At first glance Jesus' model appears to be one which primarily affirms that, although God is likened to feminine images, he is almost always characterized by masculine ones. How many times have I heard, "If praying to God as Father was good enough for Jesus, it ought to be good enough for us." And the response is, "Of course, it is." But there are a few questions we must also ask, one of which includes: What did Jesus mean by "father," and did he mean we should never call God anything else? It could have been settled if Jesus had simply said, "Since God is Spirit, God is beyond sexuality and gender. Your languages will continue to have limitations in talking about God as personal and yet beyond gender, so you may follow my example and address God in any way my Spirit leads that is meaningful to you." Issues like new insight, progressive understanding, and Jesus' silence sometimes make those of us who are serious about the Bible feel uneasy. Red flags go up. We have seen too many Christians move into unacceptable positions about basic doctrine, morality, and social issues. In the name of progressive understanding, some would dismiss the Trinity as an outmoded relic of the past. Some would remove boundaries on sexual behavior because Jesus didn't directly address every circumstance. A few "Christian" groups dabble in the occult as another way God speaks to us. Others would add the Book of Mormon as "further revelation." There always seem to be a few charismatics who have added to the New Testament a chapter or two of "new truth" from their own personal prophecies. Sometimes the tendency of those of us who love the Bible is to want to have a simple answer to every question, usually with reference to chapter and verse. However, the straight-from-the-New Testament-clear-truth is that the Holy Spirit was really left with many things to interpret after the Bible was written! The intent of Jesus in future situations which Jesus did not directly address or face is one of those things we need the Holy Spirit to help us discern.

Circumcision: Patriarchy in the Flesh

Both circumcision and exclusively masculine language for God perpetuate the war on women. Circumcision devalues the feminine in humanity, and exclusively masculine language for God devalues the feminine in both humanity and God. The debate over circumcision was not consciously one over sexism, because the patriarchal cultural setting of the early church did not allow for the degree of awareness about sexist attitudes we have today. However, circumcision stood not only in opposition to grace but also to the new partnership between men and women in the early church. Circumcision, the exalted physical mark of Jewishness, was for males only. It was patriarchy in the flesh, so to speak. It was a badge of God's call to purity of heart and a holy life, and a sign of God's call for Israel to be a nation of priests—but only men were included in this priesthood. Uncircumcised males were even excluded from the Hebrew community. Women had to settle for being married to someone with the physical sign of the covenant which God had made with the nation of Israel.

Circumcision was performed on the eighth day after the birth of a baby boy. But the mother was still considered ritually unclean long after eight days. While her baby boy was being marked with the seal of God, she was still excluded from worship. She could not touch any religious object or attend church for forty days after the birth of a boy, and eighty days after the birth of a girl—another devaluing of the feminine (Lev 12). Circumcision, the first of many such exclusions of women from what was important, summarized the numerous abuses of the "feminine" which would follow a Jewish woman all of her life.

Today we practice a contemporary form of circumcision in the church. The Hebrews placed their patriarchal mark of circumcision physically onto their worship practices. Today we Christians place our patriarchal mark linguistically onto our worship practices when we choose to speak of God only in masculine terms. The patriarchy of the flesh has become the patriarchy of language—worship language sealed by "he" and never "she." Women are excluded from the image of God just as surely as they were excluded from circumcision.

Something Liberating Happened

Finally, something really new has liberated us in both situations (the law versus grace and the image of God) from the bondage of tradition. Once grace was encountered in Jesus Christ, there was no going back to bondage under the Law. At

Pentecost the Spirit was poured out on all flesh, both women and men. The priesthood was now opened to all who confessed faith in Christ, and circumcision became a spiritual matter of the heart, open to both men and women (Rom 2:29). On the basis of what the Spirit had done, Paul fought for grace and won.

Today, we have almost 2,000 years of the Holy Spirit's working in our understanding and application of the liberating Jesus Christ in whom there is no Jew or Gentile, slave or free, male or female. This, too, is an astounding revelation of grace, as Jesus tore down the walls in these three areas of legalism, racism, and sexism. While it has taken centuries to understand some of the implications of this liberation, a growing number of us today never want to go back to the old bondage, be it under the Law, under slavery, or under patriarchy.

I recently received a letter, from a couple who moved from our church to another city, which said, "The more we become aware of sexism, the more difficult it gets to attend church. We cannot go back to the old kind of church where men are in charge and God is masculine." I felt a mixture of sadness and excitement. I was sad about the condition of so many churches today, but excited about this couple's new consciousness of the liberation Jesus brings.

Shall we hold fast to what seems to be God's clear pattern of the past, or shall we believe the Spirit of God is leading us into a deeper application of the intent of Jesus as revealed in scripture? Just as Jesus saw in God a nurturing father, so now in the light of Jesus we look at *Abba* and recognize a strong mother. Just as Paul discovered faith and grace in the Hebrew Scriptures, so now we behold God's feminine face in our Scriptures. Just as Paul grasped a resolution of centuries of the Law in the new era of grace, so we today detect the resolution of centuries of patriarchy in expanding the masculine image of God to include the feminine. Paul searched the Old Testament and observed faith and grace as God's original intent. We have searched the same Old Testament and see the partnership of masculine and feminine in both humanity and divinity as God's original intent.

The debate today involves the nature of revelation, the image of God, the priesthood and ministry of every believer, and how we should treat half of humanity. How shall we proceed? How shall those of us in the local church and on the front lines, far removed from the lofty theological explorations of seminary classrooms and doctoral dissertations, go about resolving this issue? How will we manage the conflict that comes from challenging long-held and highly cherished ideas about God's masculinity?[3]

---

[3]The children's song on the following page, written by Jann Aldredge Clanton, is taken from *God, a Word for Girls and Boys* (Louisville: Glad River, 1993) 141–42. Used by permission.

Our God is a She and a He

Our God is a Mother and a Father too.
Our God is the Friend who will always pull us through.
Our God is a Sister who loves you and me,
And God is a Brother who sets us free.
Our God is a She and a He.
But Loving God is much more you see,
For a God who could make both you and me,
Is as great as great can be.

—Jann Aldredge Clanton

"I WONDER IF THE PEOPLE WERE A BIT UPSET WITH THE NEW LANGUAGE FOR GOD?"

Smith's Salient Sayings (For Switching Sullen Systems and Shifting Sensitive Saints)

9

Acts 15 is not only a fascinating prototype of the controversy over God language today, but it also provides a creative model for facilitating change and conflict resolution. The Jerusalem Council moved decisively against the "traditional" position and forever pointed us in the direction of liberating grace. How will churches decide on the God language debate today? Given the improbability of an all-encompassing ecumenical council such as in Acts 15, what approach can the local church take in deciding on and facilitating this significant yet controversial change? In my experience at Broadway Baptist I have discovered eight principles for managing change suggested from the patterns and clues of the Jerusalem Council. These "salient sayings" may be helpful in encouraging leaders and congregations to significant change in how they talk about God.

Saying 1

Ministry Is Messy

> This brought Paul and Barnabas into sharp dispute and debate with them (Acts 15:2, NIV).

The participants in this church fight were not bad people. They were all converted, Spirit-empowered Christians who had experienced some of the most dynamic times in the history of the church. They also fought ferociously against making changes in their established beliefs. While it may seem self-evident that congregations don't like change, for many it has yet to really sink in just how fierce that resistance is. The truth will set us free—but first it makes us damn mad!

The chapter preceding Acts 15 paints a picture of conflict, physical violence, and mob action because of the changes being introduced into the existing religious structure of Judaism. Immediately following the Jerusalem Council Paul and Barnabas have a sharp disagreement, part company, and change the makeup of their apostolic teams. In the two chapters following, proclaiming the gospel produces floggings, imprisonment and more mob violence. If the New Testament church could not be true to God's call without incurring varying degrees of conflict, neither can we.

If we believe the goal in church life is peace and harmony, then we will judge the "spirituality" of the congregation by how little conflict exists within it. But if we believe the goal is to follow Jesus, then we will accept some degree of conflict and pain as a mark of a faithful church. I do not believe it is possible for a church to be faithful to the gospel and free of tension and conflict for very long. We may ask about the degree and timing of the conflict, but we may not ask, "Is there any way to avoid all conflict?" Ministry is messy!

> Do not think that I have come to bring peace to the earth; I have not come to bring peace, but a sword. For I have come to set a man against his father, and a daughter against her mother, and a daughter-in-law against her mother-in-law; and one's foes will be members of one's own house-hold (Matt 10:34–35).

This passage makes an incredible statement, since the most stable and sacred institution of Jewish life was the family. Jesus predicted that one of the results of his coming would be division and conflict in the family, the community, and even the church. This may be especially true in our day because the church is in serious trouble. It doesn't need a mere refreshing or rejuvenation; it needs a serious overhaul. It's not just a matter of putting on a new coat of paint here and there; it's a matter of total remodeling.

Renewing the church is like remodeling your house—it takes longer than you thought, costs more than you planned, and makes a bigger mess than you ever thought possible!

One of the messes of renewal occurs when we challenge our unbalanced masculine image of God. It was particularly surprising to see the strong negative response within our own congregation when I introduced the idea of recognizing the feminine face of God. I thought we were so used to being on the cutting edge of renewal that we would take all future changes in stride. I spent weeks grieving the loss of my idealistic belief that we were beyond having serious conflict over change.

I am often asked "How is Broadway Baptist doing?" In the past, when my denial level was higher, I would say "Great!" But I was being quite unrealistic, since each of the ten major changes we have undertaken in the last twenty-five years has involved some degree of conflict and attrition. Now I have accepted the liberating truth that *all significant change will be accompanied by some degree of conflict.* So I am more honest in recent years, and when asked how our church is doing I usually respond with, "There's just enough conflict to satisfy me that we're being faithful to Jesus!"

If change is so much trouble, why do it? Even if there are biblical, theological, cultural, and practical reasons for tackling this particular change, wouldn't it be better to avoid assured turmoil? Why should we make trouble by challenging God's masculinity?

Saying 2

Good Leaders Cause Trouble

One of the most noble functions of leaders is to cause trouble. Not only must there be some measure of healthy conflict in any church attempting to be faithful to the gospel, but some of that conflict should be initiated by the leaders.

> This brought Paul and Barnabas into sharp dispute and debate with them (Acts 15:2, NIV).

It would have been easier to let the circumcision party's attack on the gospel go unchallenged because it called for such a radical change for the Jewish Christians. Why not let it ride and work itself out over the years? But Paul and Barnabas never ducked a legitimate fight. Their responsibility to be true to their understanding of the gospel and their love for the church was greater than their desire to keep the peace. George Bernard Shaw said: "Reasonable people adapt themselves to the world. Unreasonable people persist in trying to adapt the world to themselves. Therefore, all progress depends on unreasonable people."

Many pastors and church leaders are plagued with terminal niceness which keeps them from their important task of being "unreasonable" at appropriate times. A pleasant, gregarious, always smiling personality seems to be an occupational requirement to make it through the ranks of the religious hierarchy and become a pastor. I have found in myself and other pastors an annoying reluctance to lead strongly, partly because we are people who, by our psychological makeup, like to get along and take care of people. We are quite willing to make peace but usually unwilling to make trouble. I have wrestled most of my life with timidity and a lack of personal daring. A major part of my inner journey has been to overcome this inability, and only my vision and intense desire for renewal have pushed me to lead more boldly.

Phony niceness results in pseudo-community where we settle for pretend closeness and artificial *koinōnia*. But our task as leaders is not always a nice one, especially when it comes to making trouble by pushing for righteous change. We have been taught that leaders are to be servants and not troublemakers. But those two are not opposites because, while we are to serve God and not our own selfish ambitions, sometimes serving means making trouble. That is precisely how, at times, we are called to serve. We do it from a caring place, but we must do it.

There are two hazards in making trouble. First, since not all conflict is healthy, the leader needs to know what's worth causing trouble over and what's not. The conflict created by entrenched power groups in the church who resist all change is not healthy conflict. Working with these people and confronting them, if necessary, is worth the trouble, because left to their own, they will continue to hinder the work of visionary leadership.

It's not worth the trouble to struggle to change some minor organizational structure. It is worth it to create structures that get people into serious relationships. It's not worth the conflict to attempt to get worshippers to raise their hands in worship, even if we decide this is a biblical and culturally relevant expression. It is worth it to enable people to experience more of the Holy Spirit so they are liberated to worship freely in any way that fits for them.

It's not worth the bother to argue over whether the preacher (if the preacher is a man) should take off his coat and tie. It is worth it to work at fostering a friendly, informal, family feeling at corporate gatherings, however that should look in any given situation. Nor is it of any advantage to get into trouble because a leader is obnoxious or insecure, or has poor communication skills. A craving for drama, excitement and novelty is vastly different from Spirit-led trouble-making. Adventure addicts can never be good leaders because they make trouble about the wrong stuff and for the wrong reasons.

A worthwhile conflict is one which meets all three of these criteria:

(1) It fits with the over-all direction of the church's visionary leader. This leader, usually called the pastor or senior pastor, must be in favor of the change, or it should be dropped. There is room for only one vision and one over-all visionary leader in a church. The vision may be gleaned from, modified by, and enhanced by others, but it is always the basic responsibility of the visionary leader to set it forth.

(2) It has been tested with other major leaders and more are for it than against it. Many changes start with most being against, but if the change is to be pursued, the majority of the leaders (staff, elders, deacons, church council, etc.) should eventually be for it at some level.

(3) It is meaningful and relevant to people's lives. The conflict issue is important in the larger scheme of things, rather than merely being a rearrangement of structures, procedures, or pulpit furniture.

The second tricky thing about introducing conflict is to know how much change to press for at any given time. Too little change and the situation stops being redemptive. Too much change and everything blows apart. The challenge is to "maintain a mindful balance between being a caretaker of what's valuable in the status quo and risking it all to indulge in a creative destruction that brings an overall benefit."[1]

Christians must not be alarmed at the necessity of creative destruction. All change involves loss. Without loss there is no change. This is what the cross and the resurrection are all

---

[1]Gordon McKenzie, Hallmark seminar leader, quoted in the *Kansas City Star*, Feb. 5, 1991.

about. Here the Christian theology of death and resurrection is applied to the local church. This is how dying to live, losing to win, and giving to keep make corporate sense. And this is what Jesus faced as both the masses and individuals left him. He had to continually choose between diluting what the Spirit was leading him to do by making it easier and more popular, and being faithful to his vision of the reign of God.

As I write, the Soviet Union has fallen apart. Most agree there wasn't any way to get from communism to capitalism without everything falling apart. No one wants to take the journey into creative destruction, but some good things, personal and corporate, come only that way.

Of course we all know leaders who have missed the "mindful balance," and their experience makes us uneasy about pushing corporate boundaries.

> If you're one step ahead, you're called a leader.
> If you're two steps ahead, you're called a pioneer.
> If you're three steps ahead, you're called a martyr.
> And on your tombstone it will read, "Killed by friendly fire."

The great temptation for pastors and other leaders is to avoid the gender language debate because they fear causing trouble. The great need is for leaders who will take the risk to first change themselves, and then entice others to change. The great challenge is to maintain a mindful balance. How to do that best leads us to the next principle for managing change.

Saying 3

Good Leaders Work in Teams

The strongest place to stand when leading a church to make significant change is within a leadership team which supports the leader's vision.

So Paul and Barnabas were appointed, along with
some other believers (Acts 15:2, NIV).

The apostles and elders met to consider this question (Acts 15:6, NIV).

Paul and Barnabas appointed elders for them in
each church (Acts 14:23, NIV).

Are any among you sick? They should call for the
elders of the church (Jas 5:14, NRSV).

The only model of leadership in the New Testament is a
team. The words elder (*presbyteros*), pastor (*poimē*), and over-
seer (*episkopos*) are used interchangeably in the New Testament and are never seen in the singular in the context of actual
church leadership.[2] Never once does Paul appoint *an* elder or
a pastor in a church. Rather, he makes it clear that at least
several are to serve in every church as partners on a leadership
team. It would have been unheard of in that time for someone
to say: "I want to talk to *the* pastor."

Everything of any importance in the early church was always accomplished in a team setting: the Twelve, the evange-
listic healing teams commissioned by Jesus, local church
pastoring, the small group in Acts 13 which initiated the missionary journeys of Paul and Barnabas, and Paul's clear practice of having mission partners on those expeditions.

The idea of one pastor in a church is foreign to the New
Testament and promotes unhealthy spiritual dynamics. The
solo system of pastoring has contributed more to the inef-
fectiveness of churches and to pastor burnout than any other
religious structure.

In his book, *Trustees as Servants*, Robert Greenleaf writes:

We live amidst a revolution of values, some good,
some bad. . . And one of the good consequences,
in my judgement, is a greater disposition of able
people. . . to work in teams rather than to strive
to be prima donnas—not so much for idealistic

[2]William Barclay, *By What Authority* (Valley Forge: Judson, 1975)
134–40.

reasons as because the word is getting around that it makes a more serene and fulfilled life.[3]

Team leadership stands in opposition to two other models. One is the traditional model of one leader and her or his helpers. The helpers carry little authority and are seldom able to challenge the leader about anything. Special "anti-team" titles often convey the reality of this set-up, like *the* pastor, senior pastor, or other designations that would set one person apart from the rest of the team. Although I am the visionary leader in our church, I am not the only leader, and therefore I am only "one of the pastors," or "one of the leaders." The other opposing model is the democratic one where everyone is considered the same and no one is allowed to lead with authority. This system keeps the change process stalemated because the gift of leadership is not free to operate. I believe a more biblical model is a team that operates according to spiritual gifts. Each person operates with authority in the area of her or his spiritual gifts. When I explain our system the most common retort is, "The buck has to stop somewhere, so who's *really* in charge?" My response is: "It depends on which buck."

I am gifted as a visionary, not as a pastor or administrator. My job is to announce the destination. The direction buck stops with me, and there can be only one vision and one visionary leader or the church will either split or stalemate. But the time of arrival and the means of travel depend on the leadership gifts of others. For instance, the administration buck stops with the pastor who is our church administrator. When we need to start moving into whatever the current new "promised land" is, I say, "Let's go this way." Then the administrators organize and guide our journey there; those with pastoring gifts teach us to care for one another as we travel, those with wisdom and prophetic gifts give us clues about the best path, and the teachers explain what's going on.

Within a team-led local church one of the first tasks in making a change about God language is to cultivate general

---

[3]Robert K. Greenleaf, *Trustees As Servants* (Cambridge: Center for Applied Studies, 1974) 39.

agreement among the leaders that this is good or at least acceptable. Building and maintaining a team has been as difficult and frustrating as any of the changes we have made. Periodically we lose our boldness because we are stalemated by our desire to make decisions only with a rather high degree of consensus. Sometimes a team member leaves to go to other ministries or leaves because we could not work out our differences. However, I remain strongly committed to the team model. One person is never smart enough, wise enough, or spiritual enough to carry through with change, especially change as significant and fraught with difficulty as balanced God language. It takes one person to have the vision for such a change, but it takes a team to pull it off. Whatever a church calls its leadership team (elders, deacons, pastors, or other titles), the important element is that they function as cohesive, relationally-oriented partners. At the heart of every change process should be a team of covenanted leaders who are in substantial agreement.

Saying 4

Talk and Listen More Than You Want To

After there had been much debate . . . (Acts 15:7).

Notice that it was not a little debate, or some debate, but it was *much* debate. It often feels to me like frustrating, never-ending, and pointless debate. I want to get on with it, but I have teammates who keep reminding me that "much debate" is a crucial part of the process.

The Greek word in this passage means something like "a heated argument." This was not calm, cool discussion interspersed with wonderful prayer where everyone felt "spiritual." This is a picture of tension and frustration among people with strong opinions. Communication that has no place for anguished argument has little place for honesty either.

Paul Tournier said, "It is not possible for people to work together at a common task without there being differences of opinion, conflicts, jealousy and bitterness. And in a religious organization they are less willing to bring these differences out into the open. They feel quite sincerely that as Christians they ought to be showing a spirit of forgiveness, charity and mutual support. The aggressiveness is repressed, taking the form of anxiety."[4]

C. G. Jung has said that neurosis is always a substitute for legitimate suffering. There are not only neurotic individuals but neurotic churches that refuse to admit and openly talk about their suffering, fears, anger, sadness, and grief. People and organizations handle change best when they feel good about themselves and can openly talk about their pain. Making people feel badly because they are angry or resistant only makes change more difficult.

Every Christian has the right to have a place where it's safe to gripe and complain. It needs to be acceptable to a congregation for any member to say just how angry they are as they go through the change process. Remember: all change is experienced as loss at some level. The question is: will we make ourselves feel guilty about feeling mad and sad, or will we provide a safe place where feelings can be openly owned, expressed, accepted, processed and resolved in the context of respect and care?

Saying 5

Time Is on Your Side

The Jew/Gentile question was the most pressing theological question in the church in Paul's day, and he spent major parts of his letters wrestling with it. Yet it took more than ten years before the debate over whether Gentiles needed to become

---

[4]Paul Tournier, *The Meaning of Persons* (New York: Harper & Row, 1957) 38.

Jews reached the stage of convening this epoch-making council. Here is another clue to help us in the change process: If we're after true change, we must aim for the long term. It takes:

> A week to explain something.
> A month to start a program.
> A year to develop a practice.
> And ten years to change a corporate lifestyle.

When Jesus said, "I still have many things to say to you, but you cannot bear them now" (John 16:12), he understood that learning takes time. Too much teaching about something new may produce overload and extreme resistance. Many battles for change have been lost in churches, not because the changes were not good and true, but because the leaders did not put enough energy and time into staying with the implementation. Pastors often do a one-time sermonic blitz and when the change does not happen immediately, they give up. I have found we must aim for a process that may take a long time.

I often remind myself of the Rubber Band Principle by taking a rubber band and flexing it between my thumb and forefinger. It reminds me that a rubber band fulfills its function only when it's under tension; otherwise it's just a flabby piece of rubber. However, if the rubber band is stretched too far, it breaks. Wisdom is knowing how far to stretch an issue and when to pull back. So we as leaders stretch things *until they are about to break* and then take the tension off for a while. At a later time we add some tension again and repeat the cycle. We do this until the change process is complete. It takes time to move back and forth but it's better than breaking the rubber band!

If you are a church leader, your friends can be your worst enemies when it comes to timing. They will sometimes give the impression things are better than they are and "much debate" is no longer needed. Leaders should listen to God for the direction, to their friends for encouragement, and to their opponents for the pace!

In the four years since the subject of balanced God language was introduced at Broadway Baptist, the only changes in our corporate worship have been to eliminate much of the masculine gender language for God in speaking and singing. Litanies, prayers, comments by worship leaders, and sermons are usually gender-neutral when referring to God. New hymns and worship songs are adapted or written using only gender-neutral language for God. We have yet to regularly incorporate feminine images and language in Sunday morning worship although that is still my goal. I estimate another one to three years before this can begin. But there is much occurring as more of our congregation becomes accustomed to this revolutionary new idea that since God is beyond gender we may use either gender for her.

In settings other than Sunday worship services, I and others often lead in prayer by addressing God as "Our loving Mother Father God" and incorporate feminine language for God such as "she" and "her." Sometimes I mention it jokingly. Recently, when someone said, "We need to praise God and give the glory to him," I lightly responded with, "Or 'her' as the case may be." Everyone smiled, one perhaps with some tension, others because they still think it's funny. But more and more we are becoming accustomed to the idea of another way to speak about God.

I often must work at restraining myself so I do not push others beyond their toleration. As the French proverb says: We must go very slowly; we don't have much time.

Saying 6

Ask What God Is Doing

The key question to ask is: "God, what are you up to here?" The dispute in Acts 15 was not settled by quoting Old Testament proof texts, logical reasoning, majority vote, words of prophecy, or apostolic command. It was ultimately resolved by coming to see what God was doing in their midst.

And God, who knows the human heart, testified
to them by giving them the Holy Spirit, just as he
did to us (Acts 15:8).

The whole assembly kept silence, and listened to
Barnabas and Paul as they told of all the signs
and wonders that God had done through them
among the Gentiles (Acts 15:12).

It must have been tempting for the teachers in their midst
to attempt to come up with some precedent in the Old Testament. The passage quoted (v. 17) indicated the Gentiles would
come to know God but said absolutely nothing about the issue
of whether they needed to become Jewish converts first. And
surely someone must have been tempted to issue an apostolic
command or perhaps encourage the prophets to listen for a
guiding word from the Spirit. But the path taken in this mo-
mentous change was to recognize and reflect on what God was
doing in their midst among the Gentile Christians.

Most of us evangelicals were taught that the most penetrating question in the midst of any serious conflict is always,
"What does the Bible say?" That's true if the Bible has clearly
spoken, but normally when there is great conflict it's because
the Bible hasn't clearly spoken! So I reiterate that the most
penetrating question to ask in the midst of any serious conflict
is: "God, what are you up to here?" When I looked around at
the liberation others were experiencing in seeing the feminine
face of God, I asked, "God, what are you doing here?" When
some of us tried it out ourselves and observed how we were
healed and set free in wonderful ways, I again asked, "God,
what are you doing here?"

We must be clear that the foundational criteria for considering the rightness of any change is God's intent as revealed in
Scripture, and not our subjective experience. However, as I
pointed out in Chapter One in "A Hermeneutic of Renewal," it
is naive to think we can understand scripture in some objective way totally apart from our corporate experience. Consider
the years of terrible interpretations of 1 Corinthians 12 and 14
simply because most interpreters had no experience with prophetic gifts or other languages of prayer and praise. They had

difficulty understanding Paul's context because their experience was so far removed from active and appropriate expression of these manifestations of the Spirit.

A few years ago amazing things started happening when I placed my hands on people and quietly prayed for them. They would sometimes be instantly healed of physical illness, see visions, tremble, cry, feel heavy or light, shake, laugh, get hot, feel internal body parts move around, experience deep peacefulness, or often be so overcome by the Spirit that they could not stand up. I asked the key question: "God, what are you doing here?" It was then I became totally convinced that we must give up a hermeneutic which says God doesn't do those things anymore, and it was then that I found similar phenomena in the New Testament (Matt 17:6–7; 28:4; Mark 5:33; 9:26; Luke 8:47; John 18:6; Acts 2:13,15; 7:32; 9:4; 10:30; Rev. 1:17). My experience allowed me to discover new dimensions in Scripture which in turn validated my experience.

So it is with restoring the feminine face of God. Look around and pray a truly dangerous prayer: "God, show me what you are doing here." Fresh insight from God is often intuitively grasped before it is rationally comprehended. The first time I heard Christians take the motherhood of God seriously, something in me said, "Yes!" Then I searched the scriptures and reflected on what some scholars were saying and it rationally confirmed what I had intuitively sensed. When I paid attention to what God was doing in me and others I experienced a burning blaze of the Spirit in my soul: This is true! This is healing! This is God!

Saying 7

Build a Foundation of
Spiritual Power and Relational Strength

The greater the depth of the Spirit's work and the stronger the relational ties in the congregation, the more likely a church can move together in significant change.

> Then the apostles and the elders, with the con-
> sent of the whole church (Acts 15: 22).

> For it has seemed good to the Holy Spirit and to
> us (Acts 15: 28).

How did they manage to pull off such unanimous consent about a controversial issue? While we may not conclude from the account that the decision was totally uncontested, as evidenced by Paul's continuing problems with the Judaizers, they were sufficiently united that Luke could write "with the consent of the whole church." How did they come to such unanimity over a volatile issue? Why would they come to the entire church for its approval rather than have the leaders simply work out the decision behind closed doors and then announce it? I believe there were two foundational reasons which enabled them to reach community-wide agreement and which can liberate us to continual renewal and healthy change in our own congregations today.

First, the early church made changes in a spiritually charged atmosphere of wonders, healings, prophecy, and other manifestations of the Spirit. They had all experienced identifiable and often dramatic encounters with the Holy Spirit from the very beginning of their journey.

> And God, who knows the human heart, testified
> to them by giving them the Holy Spirit, just as he
> did to us (Acts 15:8).

How did they know God had given them the Spirit? Had they "come forward" in a church service? Had they prayed the Sinner's Prayer? Did someone reassure or prove to them from the scriptures that they now had the Spirit? Were their lives instantly changed? The testimony of Acts is very simple: They knew they had been given the Spirit "just as he did to us" because of the supernatural release of the Spirit, accompanied by overwhelming joy.

I am not saying manifestations of worship, prophecy, prayer languages, and praise must always be present, or you must speak in a prayer language to mark Spirit reception, because that goes further than the direct teaching of Scripture.

But, at the same time, we cannot simply ignore the criteria which convinced these Jewish leaders to make the monumental decision to not require the Gentile converts to keep the Law.

> The whole assembly kept silence, and listened to Barnabas and Paul as they told of all the signs and wonders that God had done through them among the Gentiles (Acts 15:12).

The encounter between Peter and Cornelius was initially set up for Peter by a supernatural vision (*ekstasis*, "trance") and for Cornelius by a conversation with an angel (Acts 10). Then the Jewish believers present were amazed and convinced by what they heard with their own ears that Christ came for Gentiles as well as Jews.

> The circumcised believers who had come with Peter were astounded that the gift of the Holy Spirit had been poured out even on the Gentiles, for they heard them speaking in tongues and extolling God (Acts 10:45–46).

This same story is recounted an astounding three times. In Acts 11:15 Peter says, "The Holy Spirit fell upon them just as it had upon us at the beginning," and in Acts 15:8, "God . . . testified to them by giving them the Holy Spirit, just as he did to us." How was the "beginning" described? "All of them were filled with the Holy Spirit and began to speak in other languages, as the Spirit gave them ability" (Acts. 2:4). In another account of Spirit reception, the report includes: "And they spoke in tongues and prophesied" (Acts 19:6).

The powerful and visible work of the Spirit was everywhere. Healings were common and prophetic words kept the spiritual temperature high. This is in contrast to the charismatic vacuum in many of today's churches, and it means that change often can occur there only at a rational level, rather than also at a deeply Spirit-anointed, heart level. Charisphobia (fear of spiritual gifts) limits the ability of many churches today to move with God's power and leading. It was God who created the gifts of healing, prophecy, and exalted prayer and praise in other languages—not charismatics!

The second reason the early church was able to reach community-wide agreement was that they had real relationships. The house church was the basic unit of the church, and this allowed for genuine sharing of lives and relationships that had real substance. Today we live in the world and go to church. In the New Testament they lived in the church and went to the world.

The norm of Spirit-filled *koinōnia* in the New Testament stands as a judgment against our Sunday morning isolation. Fellowship today often means coffee and cookies with superficial conversation after church, rather than the intimate sharing of our lives with one another. The only thing that changes Sunday morning crowds into community is small groups. When people ask me if we have a small groups I say, "No, we *are* small groups." These groups can enable serious, Spirit-filled, covenant relationships and provide the primary foundation on which to both inspire and cope with progressive change. The proof of the resurrection was not the empty tomb but the Spirit-filled fellowship. The creative life of Jesus operating in and through this *koinōnia* opened the way for radical change in the early church and can do the same today.

The first thing I did at Broadway Baptist thirty years ago (and would do today in a new situation) was to get people together into small groups where they could share and pray for one another about what was really happening in their lives. Next, I led the church into a new openness to the Spirit, which included fresh fillings of the Spirit, expressive worship, learning to listen to God inwardly, affirmation of a wide range of spiritual gifts, and the powerful ministry of healing prayer. This didn't mean we no longer struggled with making future changes, but making those changes from a Spirit-filled community base made an incredible difference.

The greater the spiritual power and relational strength, the greater the ability to make radical change. Committed relationships filled with the Spirit of Jesus is not just another radical idea of the church. It is the only idea of the church.

Saying 8

Compromise Allows Togetherness While Change Is at Work

> It is my judgment, therefore, that we should not
> make it difficult for the Gentiles who are turning
> to God. Instead we should write to them, telling
> them to abstain from food polluted by idols, from
> sexual immorality, from the meat of strangled
> animals and from blood. For Moses has been
> preached in every city from the earliest times and
> is read in the synagogues on every Sabbath (Acts
> 15:19-21, NIV).

These four prohibitions were distinguished from all other ritual requirements in that they were the only ones asked of Gentiles living among Jewish people since the time of Moses (Lev 17—18). They were cultic, not ethical matters; and if such practices were observed by the Gentiles, the Israelites could associate freely with them without becoming ritually unclean. The word "fornication" (*porneia*) in this context has the more specific meaning of incest as in 1 Corinthians 5:1. It forbids marriage to near relatives, and the NJB (1985) translates it as "illicit marriages." The revised NAB New Testament (1986) renders it "unlawful marriage." In Acts 15:21 James points out, beginning with the connective "For," that the Gentile Christians would have been familiar with them as customs because the law of Moses had been read in the synagogues wherever the Jewish people lived in the Gentile world.

The point of these prohibitions was to allow Jewish and Gentile Christians continued association with one another, especially at mealtimes, which at that time was the primary setting of community interaction, and the only setting of the Lord's Supper. Without them, the Jewish Christians would have considered themselves ritually unclean.

They ended up with the one eternal truth of grace and four temporary and transitional concessions. The concessions allowed them to worship together and eventually fell by the wayside. Truth can be assimilated much more quickly in a church which can continue to worship and fellowship together, than in a church filled with bitterness and tension. This guideline of temporary compromise provides a procedure for a congregation to move to balanced gender language for God by affirming its truth while placing some temporary restrictions on its implementation.

We have carried out this last principle in our church with two compromises, one on each side. On the one hand, as I have previously indicated, we have greatly reduced the use of masculine terminology for God in our speaking and singing in Sunday morning worship services. We have rewritten our hymns to eliminate all gender-exclusive references to persons and even a few referring to God. The saints are really touchy about changing the words of their familiar traditional hymns, so we tread lightly here. The result has been that we sing masculine-oriented hymns less and less and gender-neutral ones more. We learn new words to traditional hymn tunes, or a new hymn or worship song at least every month, and we learn only those which are gender-neutral in referring to God. Since we have a very contemporary worship style which uses one or two traditional hymns and five or six contemporary ones each Sunday, we have been able to make these changes fairly rapidly. Our "masculine to feminine gender ratio" for singing and speaking on Sunday morning has moved from approximately 50:0 (fifty masculine references to God compared to no feminine ones) to about 5:0 now, four years later. My goal is about 5:5, a balanced ratio. A line in the section of our Sunday morning bulletin for visitors says: "In singing, please use language for God that is meaningful to you." This is a permission for all of us to personally use other words, including feminine ones, when we are singing corporately. I usually substitute "her" for "him" and "Mother" for "Father" as we sing.

On the other hand we have asked our speakers and worship leaders to refrain from addressing or referring to God directly in feminine terms and we do not sing hymns or use litanies that do so. People are free to use whatever language fits for them in all other settings such as classes, small groups, home worship meetings, etc. But Sunday morning corporate worship is very fragile, and we have tried not to offend the sensibilities of those who feel strongly on either side. The result of our compromise is that the worship of those of us more acutely aware of gender language is not constantly upset by a barrage of exclusively masculine terms for God, and those who do not agree or who are not yet comfortable with the actual practice of feminine references to God are not disturbed by language that is offensive to them. These compromises take the culture shock out of the change while we continue to worship together and gradually become accustomed to a more theologically balanced image of God.

However, taking all the shock out of worship is a problem if it becomes the normal practice rather than the temporary compromise. The practice of gender-neutral language is inadequate for the long term not only because it depersonalizes God and does not directly refute the cultural idea of a masculine only God, but also because it is just not shocking enough! (We must use shock not for its own sake but rather for its value in helping us perceive truth in deeper ways. We need the "aha!" that comes from the fresh impact of a startling new presentation of reality.)

Jesus' calling God "Daddy" was shocking! The worship at Pentecost was so exuberant it was shocking—they were accused of being drunk! The open expressions of worship of Cornelius and his friends upon their conversion were so shocking they jarred the early church into accepting the Gentile Christians without circumcision! The worship book of the New Testament, Revelation, portrays stirring worship of loud praise, vivid body language, and shocking drama. When was the last time you were shocked in worship from something besides ineptness, bad taste, poor planning, or someone snoring?

I dream of the time when we will have Sunday morning worship which breaks through the deadening tradition of the invisible feminine. I hunger for the lofty heights of Awesome She. I yearn for the inner depths of corporate intimacy with Holy Mother. I crave to be shocked out of my little boxed-in deity and jarred into the stunning presence of Eternal Trinity. How might such a worship service look? This is the subject of our next chapter.[5]

---

[5]The poem on the next page is taken from Alla Renee Bozarth, *Womanpriest* (San Diego: Lura-Media, 1978) 166, quoted in *Exploring the Feminine Face of God*, 87. Used by permission.

Bakerwoman God

Bakerwoman God,
I am your living bread.
Strong, brown Bakerwoman God,
I am your low, soft, and being-shaped loaf.
I am your rising
bread, well-kneaded
by some divine and knotty
pair of knuckles
by your warm earth hands.
I am bread well-kneaded.
Put me in fire, Bakerwoman God,
put me in your own bright fire.
I am warm, warm as you from fire.
I am white, and gold, soft and hard,
brown and round.
I am so warm from fire
Break me, Bakerwoman God!
I am broken under your caring word.
Drop me in your special juice in pieces.
Drop me in your blood.
Drunken me in the great red flood
Self-giving chalice, swallow me.
My skin shines in the divine wine.
My face is cup covered and I drown.
I fall up
in a red pool
in a gold world
where your warm
sunskin hand is there
to catch and hold me
Bakerwoman God, remake me.

—Alla Renee Bozarth

"TRADITIONAL, NON-TRADITIONAL,
OR INFORMAL?"

How Then Shall We
Worship?

10

The language and symbols of worship should convey truth and beauty. Male-dominant worship is not truthful because it distorts the image of God, and it is not beautiful because it oppresses the people of God. How can we, in the powerful image-shaping context of worship, speak about God in a truly biblical fashion to a culture that perceives some biblical words differently?

We do not live as much by concepts as we do by images. Our words must evoke the presence of the hidden God instead of merely defining God.[1] How can we worship in such a way that we become intensely aware of God's presence, rather than engaging in an intellectual exercise of correct grammar? How then shall we worship?

William Willimon says:

> Social change is primarily symbolic change. In order for us to change, our symbols must change. Our symbols must change because they deter-

---

[1] This sentence paraphrased from Ralph N. McMichael, Jr., "God-Language and Inclusive Language Liturgy," *Anglican Theological Review* 73:4 (Fall 1991) 432.

mine our horizons, our limits, our viewpoints
and vision. . . . When women were at last given
leadership positions in the liturgy of many
churches, we soon realized how much symbolic
change needed to be made in order to adjust the
metaphors and symbols to the church's clear
vision of the role of women in the church. We
realize how limited many of our old, male-dominated, hierarchical images were—God the Father; the Heavenly King; Rise Up, O Men of God.
There could be no basic change without change
in the symbols and metaphors through which we
attempt to grasp reality and reality grasps us. . . .
The liturgy reminds us that we are more image-
making and image-using creatures than we think.
We apprehend reality only through symbols, sac-
rament, gestures, and metaphors.[2]

Are There Any Limits?

Is calling God Mother the first step to removing all boundaries from the gospel and fashioning, as C. S. Lewis predicted,
a truly different religion? Will we end up calling God something like "O Great Computer Chip" or "Almighty Pig" if we
don't stay with biblical names for God. Are there any limits?

Jürgen Moltmann, reminding us of Feuerbach's criticism,
says: "If men call God 'Father' in order to be able to find an
identity and now women call God 'Mother' in order to discover
themselves in religious terms, what would donkeys call God?
Is the Godhead just screen for all possible projections, with
the slogan, 'What's your fancy?' "[3]

We might speculate on the lengths to which God might go
if God was going to communicate with donkeys in the same

[2]William Willimon, *The Service of God* (Nashville: Abingdon, 1983)
57.

[3]Elisabeth Moltmann-Wendel and Jürgen Moltmann, *GOD—His
& Hers* (New York: Crossroad, 1991) 35.

way the incarnate Christ did with humans. So the donkey question may be more theologically profound than outlandish.

However, the point is that we certainly are not at liberty to call God anything we want. Our worship liturgy must have theological, biblical, and pastoral norms and "O Great Computer Chip" and "Almighty Pig" would go beyond my parameters for naming God.

I have found the following criteria[4] helpful in setting boundaries for naming God: Any name for God should meet all four of these requirements to be consistent with a hermeneutic of renewal and its dual focus of restoration and innovation.

- It is a naming congruent with the intent of biblical revelation. (Restoration)

- It is an expression consistent with the symbolic forms of the historic Christian community. (How restoration and innovation have been historically expressed)

- It is relevant to the meaningful questions of our existence. (Innovation)

- It is validated by its linguistic impact and ability to explain what is understood to be true. (Innovation)

- "O Great Computer Chip" and "Almighty Pig" fail all four categories. "Trinity" and "Mother" pass all four.

Can't We Just Keep Calling God Mother a Private Matter?

It is quite legitimate to ask the question of appropriateness of public worship behavior. There are some things that we do in our private devotional life we might not do publicly. At the church where I serve many of us are comfortable with the practice of other languages of prayer and praise in our own

---

[4]The last three are from Langdon Gilkey, *Naming the Whirlwind: The Renewal of God-Language* (Indianapolis: Bobbs-Merrill, 1969) 460–63.

private devotional life. But we have prohibited any such practice in Sunday morning worship because it seems unduly disturbing and difficult to explain to our many visitors. Could this be the same kind of "do it in private" matter?

I think not. Churches have been making God exclusively masculine in public for a long time, and changing in private will not reverse the damage. This is a decidedly public issue. It is the worshipping congregation which needs to affirm the feminine face of God and not just in our own private prayer. This affirmation occurs best in a balanced, open, and congregational way.

I want to remind my readers again that although I encourage you to consider female images for God and even to experiment with them, *if calling God Mother in your own personal prayer life is not helpful to you, don't do it.*

However, I am very pointedly asking all Christians to recognize the necessity of corporate worship which recognizes both male and female images of God. *Will we make room in our public worship liturgy for various expressions of addressing God so God can be affirmed in many ways?*

This means that while I may only address God as Mother privately, I am willing to sing about God as Father on Sunday morning. And while you may only address God as Father privately, you are willing to sing about God as Mother when we worship together.

The male and female-like image of God is good news, not bad. This is not something to hide or be embarrassed about. The whole world needs to know about our Mother and Father God!

Three Approaches

In her book, *In Her Own Rite*, Marjorie Proctor-Smith names three approaches for those who want to change their male-dominant language about persons and God: nonsexist, inclusive, and emancipatory.[5]

---

[5] Proctor-Smith, *In Her Own Rite*, 63.

Nonsexist

The most widely used approach to change is nonsexist language. Sometimes called gender-neutral language, it avoids using gender words, such as "he" and "him," for God or persons in general. "He who hesitates" becomes "The one who hesitates." "Mankind" becomes "humankind." God is not referred to as "he," and either the word "God" is repeated or the sentence is rephrased to eliminate the need for gender-specific pronouns. The Trinity may be referred in nonsexist terms such as Parent, Child, Spirit, or Abba, Servant, and Helper, or the widely used Creator, Redeemer, and Sustainer. In the previous chapter I proposed using some nonsexist language as a first step and transitional compromise while a congregation processes the image of God the Mother. Its strength is that it seems to have the least upsetting effect on worship-pers initially, even though it is experienced as something of a loss on all sides of the debate. Some feel the loss of Father, others the loss of Mother, and some, like me, feel the loss of both.

The weaknesses of nonsexist language reside in three areas. First, *we cannot have biblical Christianity without ever calling God Father.* This abandons the rich metaphor of the *abba* and son relationship of first-century Palestine which is a foundational metaphor in our faith.

Another serious drawback is that it is not possible to have a personal God who is neither male nor female. We have no other models of the personal but these two, and reducing our image of God to only the impersonal is totally inadequate. While such terms as Creator and Maker have their place, we must also have a way of speaking of God in personal terms. Being held in our "Maker's" arms, sitting on our "Creator's" lap, or being embraced by an amorphous glob of indeterminate gender just doesn't hold much zip for most of us, compared to getting a hug from our heavenly Mother, or sitting on our heavenly Dad's lap.

The third weakness is that by never using female images of God we continue to have a male-only image of God, conditioned by our culture's intensive and life-long cultural inclination towards God as being masculine. The feminine image of God remains unseen because many people still think, see, and feel "male" when they hear even the presumed nonsexist word "God."

Inclusive

The second approach, inclusive language, attempts to balance gender references to God and persons. Inclusive language talks about "him or her" instead of "person," and "women and men" instead of "humanity." It makes more explicit the idea that both male and female are included in the reference. In speaking of God, such terms as "Our Mother Father God" are often used. When I want to use an inclusive vocabulary and also the traditional Trinitarian name in a liturgical blessing, such as in anointing with oil or in water baptism, I often say, "In the name of the Father, Son and Holy Spirit, the One God who is Mother to us all." This both incorporates the traditional terminology and yet balances the idea of Mother and Father, as well as three and one.

Using both genders together at the same time communicates the Genesis pre-fall partnership of male and female in a striking way. It also reminds us that our metaphors are limited and we should not press any of them too far. Calling God both Mother and Father pushes us to the reality that God is truly beyond us.

A weakness may be that for some, using both male and female metaphors together at the same time (Mother/Father God) may communicate something of an androgynous God. This honors neither male nor female and removes God as person even further from our experience.

Psychological androgyny is helpful to us in a way that physical androgyny is not, and thinking of God as like a father at one point or mother at another may be more helpful than trying to think of God as both male and female at the same time.

The major weakness of inclusive or gender-balanced language, like nonsexist language, is that it is not strong enough to reach deep into our inner being and challenge our exclusively male image of God.

Emancipatory

Emancipatory language makes the issue visible. It's one thing to say that all people are of equal value. It's another to talk about sexism and call it sin. This is emancipatory language. Emancipatory language makes the feminine face of God visible by using language to confront us with our stereotyped ideas and to transform and redeem our distorted image of God. If we refuse to use corresponding feminine pronouns for God we hide behind the idea of the culture's male God and never openly challenge it. Not only is the feminine included in emancipatory language, but it is pointed out and focused upon, such as when I have referred to God as "her" or "she" in this book. If this is a new area to you, you were probably jolted every time because emancipatory language comes out and literally grabs us by the eyes, ears, and throat and says:

See what you haven't seen before!

LISTEN TO WHAT YOU HAVEN'T HEARD BEFORE!

SPEAK WHAT YOU HAVEN'T SAID BEFORE!

God may be referred to with emancipatory language not only as "Mother," but also as "sister" and "friend."[6] While I have chosen to concentrate on God as Mother, I do not want to perpetuate the stereotype that womanhood is summed up in birthing and caring for children just as we would not sum up manhood in impregnating and working. Women are also sisters, lovers, bosses, workers, and friends who are competent, assertive, and gifted in every area of human endeavor.

A drawback to this approach is that it may initially appear to some that we are not being faithful to the Bible because emancipatory language is so counter-cultural. This can result in offending those who do not understand or do not hold to

---

[6]Sallie McFague, *Models of God* (Philadelphia: Fortress, 1987) 78.

the position being articulated here. It is their worship which then becomes disturbed and broken.

Another drawback is the awkwardness of change and the confusion of being initially misunderstood as theologically liberal, radically feminist, or New Age.

As one can see, there are weaknesses in all of these solutions because all metaphors for God have limitations, and this may be especially true with today's new gender awareness. Making peace with anthropomorphism (using human characteristics to describe God) is the price we must pay for the Christian truth that God is a personal rather than a nonpersonal Ultimate.[7]

God in Two Voices

The 1991 movie *Switch* makes a creative attempt to tackle the challenge of making God personal yet not exclusively male or female. Perry King plays a true male chauvinist, demeaning all the women in his life. He dies and is refused admittance to heaven unless he can find one woman who likes him. As a further complication, he is sent back to earth as a beautiful woman, which sets him up to be on the receiving end of the sexism he has been dishing out to women for years. The play on male and female roles and stereotypes continues throughout the movie. The male hero in a woman's body has several conversations with God, and with the obvious theme of sexism God could not be portrayed as male, but yet God needed some kind of voice. The writers chose to have God speak in two voices simultaneously, one male and one female. The female and male authoritative caring voices speaking at the same time created a fascinating effect of a God who was personal and one, yet encompassed both male and female in a way that did not

---

[7]This sentence paraphrased from Eleanor Rae and Bernice Marie-Daly, *Created in Her Image* (New York: Crossroad, 1990) 21.

seem strange. Why is the secular movie community more creative than the Christian community? How then shall we worship?

A Call to Decision and Action

Nothing will change business as usual in our churches unless those of us who are convicted by the Holy Spirit first change our own behavior and then work towards change in the church. There is a natural sequence of decisions which can be taken by individuals and/or a local church.

Personally decide to stop using gender-exclusive words for people.

I did not even think about my gender-exclusive language for God until I began changing my language about persons. As we added women to our staff of pastors I noticed in our team meetings that it was no longer appropriate for me to talk about "us and our wives," "Man has sinned," "we guys," or "the love of mankind." So I changed the way I talked to include both genders.

Only then did I begin to notice how I talked about God in exclusively masculine terms. Calling God "he" but never "she" became a glaring omission in my world of symbols. I believe one reason so many Christians do not consider gender-inclusive God language important is because they, both men and women, have yet to take the first step toward relating to women as equals with men, and changing their language about persons accordingly.

Buy a New Revised Standard Version of the Bible and use it! It is the only translation available at this time which uses nonsexist language for persons.

Stop using masculine pronouns for God.

Pronouns have a power of calling forth images that is all out of proportion to their tiny, almost inconspicuous use in our language. We cannot stop every time we use masculine names and pronouns for God in worship, teaching, or conversation and explain the original context with its current change in meaning. We can teach about these issues as I am doing in this book and in the classroom setting. However, this does not handle the immediacy and fragility of the worship setting, nor the constant imprinting of our minds by the repetitious use of masculine pronouns for God which constantly sends image shaping messages to our hearts and minds.

You can make this change in your speech and writing without calling attention to it. Not calling God "he" and "him" may seem difficult at first, but keep working on it. It took me several months to get the hang of it.

Start calling God Mother in your personal prayer life.

I preface these next two steps with the reminder to do this only if it is meaningful to you, or you sense God's call for you to experiment. Passing on these two steps will not keep you from any of the others.

If it seems right to you, experiment. Call God Mother out loud right now! Nobody's listening but you and God, and only one of you will be embarrassed! Give yourself time to acclimate to something that may feel very strange. It took me two years to really get comfortable and sense God's maternal presence, but then I drive with my emotional brakes on and you may not need to take that long.

See if calling God Mother does not eventually communicate an increased sense of God's majesty, care, and closeness.

Experiment with using feminine pronouns and metaphors for God with others.

This is a bold and brave step. You may be scorned, ridiculed, and hated. You will almost certainly be nervously laughed at, given startled looks, and questioned about such non-traditional behavior. Depending on your ease with verbal communication, you may find yourself anxious and tense at first. It took me three years to be at ease, and I'm a professional talker!

Because of people's reactions, it is always best to start in a small setting where it will most likely be okay with all those present. When you feel safe, work up to the places where using emancipatory feminine images for God is riskier. I started very cautiously one day when I was asked to lead the prayer at our local Baptist pastors' meeting and prayed "God you are like a mother and a father to us all." I think it probably passed over everyone except for my personal friends, who were aware of my concerns.

The key to using female metaphors for God publicly is our own personal comfort level. One person said to me, "Personally, I am okay with calling God 'Mother,' but how could I invite my friends to a church where God was referred to in feminine terms? They might be uncomfortable or not understand."

My response was to ask: "Are *you* really comfortable with talking about God in feminine terms?" Often we project our feelings on others, believing these others to be the ones who are uncomfortable and not us. Getting our own feelings settled means we really can be more inner directed and truly at ease about what others think.

Ask others to study this issue.

Pass this book around. Form a study group. Ask your church leadership team to read about the subject, pro and con. Offer a class. But don't become a part of the annoying "language police," going on a campaign which might alienate some. Rather, offer information with grace and good timing. Christians are better enticed by gracefulness, than clobbered by self-righteousness.

Encourage your pastors, worship committee, elders, deacons, or leadership team to change worship language about persons.

Call their attention to all the BOMFOG in your church services. (That's Brotherhood Of Man and Fatherhood Of God talk.) Ask your church worship leaders to stop singing songs that use gender-exclusive language for persons. Or to not sing those verses which contain such language. Or rewrite any phrases or lines in hymns that use gender exclusive language such as those that refer to humanity as man. This says we are willing to take a public stand against sexist language.

Every time the congregation sings a hymn which contains a sexist word or phrase about persons, point it out in a kind but clear way to the pastor or worship leader immediately after the service. Most pastors and worship leaders have never even thought about it. You will raise their awareness in an acceptable fashion in this way. There is no excuse for using sexist language about persons in the church of a holy and righteous God who desires justice and mercy for all people. This issue is not debatable.

Some of the changes can be easily made:

> "Rise up O men of God" can be changed to "Rise up O church of God" or "Rise up O saints of God."

> "Good Christian men rejoice" can become "Good Christians all rejoice."

> In the third verse of Holy, Holy, Holy, "Tho' the eye of sinful man" can become "Tho' the eye of sinfulness."

Rewriting hymn lyrics can be a technical challenge if the congregation uses hymnals. If words are printed on an overhead or in the worship service handout, it becomes much easier. I have found most people do not mind changing a few words to become more inclusive of persons. The real tension is over God language, and that is the next natural step.

Promote the adoption of a church service policy of nonsexist (gender-neutral) language for God.

This is more difficult, but you can begin by calling the attention of the pastors, music leader, or worship committee to the excessive and exclusive use of male imagery for God. Share how it affects you, not how stupid and sexist you think it is. I have reported to our worship committee with words like,

"I moved in and out of discomfort, even suffering, last Sunday morning with all the male imagery for God." Or "I found it difficult to worship with all the 'Father' language this morning." Sometimes I would count the number of times God was referred to with male words in the songs, prayers, Scripture, and spoken words. "Did you know that we referred to God as 'he' or 'Father' fifty-seven times this morning?" Many are amazed at how high the masculine word count is and begin to think more about it themselves.

Sometimes a church can make a first step by agreeing to reduce the number of masculine references to God. Sing songs about God as male less and ask your worship leaders and speakers and those who pray to be aware of the increasing number of persons whose worship is disturbed by constant male references to God.

Rewriting hymns can be more difficult because churchgoers are often very resistant to changing the words to extremely familiar hymns, even when they are open to feminine language for God. It sometimes feels like too much of a loss to give up the old familiar hymns, so this can be a sensitive area. Those open to changing existing hymns may consider such changes as: From "Joyful, Joyful We Adore Thee" the words of the second line of last verse, "Father love is reigning o'er us, Brother love binds man to man" can become "God, Creator reigning o'er us, God's one family hand in hand."

A congregation might decide to learn only those new songs which do not include gender references to God. Contemporary worship songs can be made nonsexist by either changing some words, rewriting verses, or singing them to God rather than about God. "I will enter his gates with thanksgiving in my heart" can become "I will enter your gates." "In his time" can become "In your time."

Ask those with a poetic bent to write a different set of verses to the tune of a familiar hymn. Sometimes this is much better than changing existing hymns because the "upset" factor is lower. The goal is to reduce as much as possible the massive amount of male God language. And it does take time, energy, and diligence.

*Encourage your church to begin incorporating
emancipatory feminine metaphors into its liturgy.*

This is the last bold brave step in calling God Mother in addition to Father. Celebrating the feminine side of God should
not be relegated to the fringes of our church life. If we want to
hear the feminine voice of God, we must be willing to call her
by name. If we want to see the maternal face of God, we must
be willing to image her as Mother. If we want to sense her
presence, we must be willing to have our damaged receptors
healed of years of patriarchal conditioning.

Sometimes I am disappointed about the upset caused over
doing away with wonderful traditional hymns about God as
exclusively masculine, because none of it had to happen. *We
really don't need to discard or rewrite our traditional hymns
about Father God if we will also use hymns to Mother God.* It is
amazing what only a few references to God as feminine can do
in a church service amidst other references to God as masculine. The enforced silence about the feminine of God can be
broken with only a few words.

I believe the day will come in many, if not most, of our
church gatherings when it will be just as natural to sing and
speak of the maternal side of God as it is to pass the offering
plate, read from the Bible, and call God Father. And arguments
for segregating God into exclusively masculine categories will
be as embarrassingly out of place as segregating the races!

Pray

This is a spiritual journey, a godly battle, and a righteous
goal. Saturate all your longings, hopes, and actions with
prayer.

Pray that the words of your mouth and the images of your
heart will be acceptable in God's sight.

Pray that God will energize spiritual gifts in your church,
especially ones of faith, leadership, wisdom, prophecy, administration, mercy, healing, and creative ability, so that your con-

gregation can be renewed in its heart and mind, in its images and words about God.

Pray your church will regain the power that Jesus experienced in naming God "*Abba*, Father" in his day, by the addition of naming God "*Imma*, Mother" in our day.

Pray for a new generation of worship leaders, song writers, liturgists, poets, writers, pastors, and teachers who can lead us in the elegance, art, and beauty of gender-sensitive worship.

Pray that God will raise up gifted Christians with a heart for God and a love for Jesus Christ who will write wonderful new music, worship litanies, and prayers that affirm the feminine face of God and enable us to express our praise in fresh and inspiring ways.

When we look into the face of God, what kind of face do we see?
The shape of that face and the look of those eyes will determine
whether we shall be healed or wounded once more.

—Lynda Shillito, Co-pastor, Broadway Baptist

Blessing Song

May the blessing of God go before you.
May Her grace and peace abound.
May Her spirit live within you
May Her love wrap you 'round
May Her blessing remain with you always.
May you walk on holy ground.

—Sister Miriam Therese Winter[8]

---

[8]Words and music by Sister Miriam Therese Winter. Copyright: Medical Mission Sisters, 1987. Reproduced with permission of copyright owner.

Dear Heavenly Father... well of course, you're not actually a male, but like a caring parent.
The Bible says He is like a mother, too...but we can't say that here.
Now by saying "He" I didn't mean that God is male, but rather I was using "He" in an inclusive way--that is, not gender-specific, as they say.
This is hard work. There must be a better way.
Yeah!
R. Hatem '93

© R. Hatem 1992. Used by permission.

Postlude: A New Vision

Remember at the beginning of this book the story of Doris and Sam and their visit to church? Let's imagine what it could be like after a number of years and after the church has experienced revival and renewal. The Holy Spirit has energized the lives of many members in a new way, making Jesus more real to them. There is a new intimacy with God, resulting in confidence to give witness to Jesus Christ and to have compassion for the disenfranchised. A ministry of healing prayer has begun in the church, and there is physical and emotional healing. The new wine of the Spirit has even cracked the old wineskins of traditional worship. Words can't describe the glorious singing, thundering praise and joyous sense of God's presence, but I can report some of the new symbols of the partnership of male and female in leadership and language in their church services. The male and female spoken metaphors for God are completely balanced in this service, eight male images and eight female. Let yourself flow with the pictures and words.

Coming into the church building, you are met by a team of greeters and ushers which includes both women and men. You notice the visible partnership in almost every area as the worship leaders, a man and a woman, step forward and begin the service. They follow the order of service decided upon the previous week by the Worship Committee, a team of women and men who are responsible for each Sunday morning service.

The service begins with the words: "May the God who mothers us all, bear us on the breath of dawn, and make us to shine like the Son, and hold us in the palm of her hand."[1]

The congregation prays the Lord's Prayer as it is traditionally spoken, beginning: "Our Father who art in heaven, hallowed be thy name."

One hymn of the four sung this morning uses gender images for God. The words are:

1. Bring many names, beautiful and good,
    celebrate, in parable and story,
      holiness in glory,
      living, loving God:
  Hail and Hosanna!
  bring many names!

2. Strong mother God, working night and day,
    planning all the wonders of creation,
      setting each equation,
      genius at play:
  Hail and Hosanna,
  strong mother God!

3. Warm father God, hugging every child,
    feeling all the strains of human living,
      caring and forgiving
      till we're reconciled:
  Hail and Hosanna,
  warm father God!

4. Old, aching God, grey with endless care,
    calmly piercing evil's new disguises,

---

[1] From Mary Kilsby as reported in *The Wall Street Journal*, April 27, 1992.

    glad of good surprises,
    wiser than despair:
    Hail and Hosanna,
    old, aching God!

5. Young, growing God, eager, on the move,
    seeing all, and fretting at our blindness,
      crying out for justice,
      giving all you have:
    Hail and Hosanna,
    young, growing God!

6. Great, living God, never fully known,
    joyful darkness far beyond our seeing,
      closer yet than breathing,
      everlasting home:
    Hail and Hosanna,
    great, living God![2]

At one point the congregation enthusiastically joins in a responsive reading:

To the Holy One who is our eternal Mother and never-failing
    Father,
    We offer all that we have and all that we are.

To the Word whose mercy shatters every illusion,
    We offer all that we have and all that we are.

To the Sustainer who transforms degradation into glory,
    We offer all that we have and all that we are.

To the one God from whose womb emerged the infinite
    universe of terror and beauty,
    We offer all that we have and all that we are.

To the Creator who wove galaxies and started them on their
    numinous journeys,
    We offer all that we have and all that we are.

To the Lord of history, who works through imperfect actions of
    imperfect creatures,
We offer all that we have and all that we are.[3]

The scripture is read from the New Revised Standard Version and paraphrased lectionaries which, aware of recent
changes in the English language, are careful to use inclusive
language where permitted by the Greek and Hebrew. One passage refers to God as "Father" once and "him" once. This is not
changed.

Several persons are baptized during the service. Since the
New Testament gives no specific directions about who should
baptize, this church has authorized all its members to baptize.
One member, a woman, has been instrumental in leading her
husband to the Lord and she baptizes him. A teenager baptizes another teenage member, her best friend. The language
and symbols of ministry are available to all the believers in this
church.

As each is baptized, the words used are: "We, your sisters
and brothers in Christ, now baptize you in the name of the
Father, Son, and Holy Spirit, the One God who is Mother to us
all." This form maintains the classical language for Trinity, yet
recognizes the need for a gender-balanced metaphor.

Both men and women collect the offering, and the offering
prayer begins with: "Abba, mother, our God! You are our mother,
caressing and kissing the pain away. You are our father, holding us and never turning from our side."

A gifted woman pastor/teacher gives the sermon this
morning. She is one of a team of four pastors, two women and
two men, who lead the church. Only one of these pastors is
supported full time by the church, while one has an outside
half time job, one works as homemaker, and the other works
full time outside the home. During the sermon, pronouns like
"he" or "she" are usually avoided in referring to God, and once
the pastor says "Our Father God in heaven calls us to listen!"

---

[3]From Bell, *Street Singing & Preaching,* 107–8. Copyright © by
Martin Bell. Excerpted by permission of Abingdon Press.

The Lord's Supper is served by several singles and married couples from the fellowship, both women and men. All know they are ministers and priests representing Jesus to the congregation.

The benediction is:

May the blessing of the God of Abraham and Sarah, and of Jesus Christ, born of our sister Mary, and of the Holy Spirit, who broods over the world as a mother over her children, be upon you and remain with you always. Amen.[4]

✠

"Faith has need of the whole truth," says Teilhard de Chardin. Now is the moment in history for the church to see more of this truth in the awesome light of God's revelation of herself as recorded in Scripture. Only when we are buttressed with biblical truth and compelled by the Spirit of Jesus will we be able to venture into the painful and energy-consuming process of change.

Is it okay to call God Mother? It is not only okay but it is just and holy, righteous and necessary. Now is the time to break the conspiracy of silence about the feminine face of God. God's Word is rousing itself again, wrestling itself free from the grip of patriarchy and sexism. The Bible is true, and truth is always about the work of breaking bonds and setting us free. Bless the arousing and rejoice at the coming of the Living Word!

---

[4]*Supplemental Liturgical Texts*, 41, The Standing Liturgical Commission of the Episcopal Church (New York: The Church Hymnal Corp.).

Scripture Index